THE WORLD'S MOST
INCREDIBLE
STORIES

THE BEST OF FORTEAN TIMES

THE WORLD'S MOST
INCREDIBLE STORIES

THE BEST OF FORTEAN TIMES

Foreword by Lyall Watson

Selected and edited by Adam Sisman
Line illustrations by Hunt Emerson

AVON BOOKS ◆ NEW YORK

AVON BOOKS
A division of
The Hearst Corporation
1350 Avenue of the Americas
New York, New York 10019

Copyright © 1992 by
Eddison Sadd Editions
Line illustrations copyright © 1992
by Hunt Emerson

Published by arrangement with
Eddison Sadd Editions Limited

ISBN: 0-380-76754-6

AN EDDISON · SADD EDITION
Edited, designed and produced by
Eddison Sadd Editions Limited
St Chad's Court,
146B King's Cross Road,
London WC1X 9DH.

Phototypeset in Century ITC Book and Frutiger 77 by Wyvern Typesetting, Bristol, England.
Printed and bound by Bath Press, Bath, England.

First Avon Books Trade Printing:
May 1992

AVON TRADEMARK REG. U.S. PAT. OFF. AND IN OTHER COUNTRIES, MARCA REGISTRADA.

10 9 8 7 6 5 4 3 2 1

Contents

Foreword by Lyall Watson 6

Editor's Preface 8

Introduction by the editors of
Fortean Times 10

Heaven's Above! 14

Life Imitating Art 16

Coincidences 18

Twins 20

What's in a Name? 22

Mutilations 24

Medical Curiosities 26

Inside Stories 28

Frozen 30

Hermits and Recluses 32

Fugues 34

Missing Persons 36

Swamp Cat Fever 38

Felicity, the Scottish Puma 40

Lizard Man 42

Monsters of the Deep 44

Strange Deaths 46

Mysterious Deaths 48

Resurrections 50

Dooms 52

Fires 54

Spontaneous Human Combustion 56

Plants 58

Embeddings 60

Miracles 62

Bleeding Statues 64

Frog Falls 66

Ice Falls 68

Falls	70	Marine Mysteries	136
Fish Falls	72	Lightning	138
Pennies from Heaven	74	Meteorological Curiosities	140
Poltergeists	76	Snipers	142
Ghosts and Visions	78	Sleep	144
Inept Crime	80	Phantom Hitch-Hikers	146
Not Their Day	82	Mass Hysteria	148
Strange Lights	84	Astonishing Recoveries	150
Does Grey Matter?	86	Nowt so Queer	152
Headbangers	88	Weird Science	154
Hard to Swallow	90	Antiquities	156
Haunted Houses	92	Vampires	158
Occult Crime	94	Hairy Children	160
Homing Rings	96	In the Post	162
The Crying Boy	98	Bird Abductions	164
Explosions	100	Levitation	166
Feral Children	102	Subsidences	168
Mommy Dearest	104	Psychic Powers	170
Surprise! Surprise!	106	Electric People	172
Over-reactions	108	Rat Kings	174
Crop Circles	110	Mississauga Blob	176
The Hole Story	112	Alien Abductions	178
Swarms and Migrations	114	Minds of Their Own	180
Freak Animals	116	The River Boy	182
Animal Sabotage	118	Religious Curiosities	184
Animal Attacks	120	Clonehenge	186
Fair Game	122	Foafs	188
Not so Dumb?	124	Hoaxes	190
Fishy Stories	126	Acknowledgements	192
Elephants	128		
Kangaroos	130		
Out of Place	132		
Under Their Noses	134		

Foreword

Science is a very peculiar process ...

It claims to be objective, interested only in finding explanations for the phenomena of the natural world. It fosters the image of dedicated men and women labouring selflessly in the service of global understanding. In reality, such paragons are hard to find, because the system is loaded against them. It is basically unscientific.

Take a simple and personal example. I choose to believe in the electron. It *is* a matter of choice and I decide in its favour because it is a construct that makes sense and has proved useful. But I have never seen an electron—and I never will. Even if I had access to the equipment necessary to demonstrate an electron's existence, I wouldn't know where to begin. So I have to take someone else's word for it. Which makes the electron, for me at least, not so much a scientific fact as an article of faith.

I am not alone in this dilemma. There is just too much going on, even in one's chosen field, for anyone to keep up with it all. So each of us is obliged to accept much of what we are told, and encouraged in this acceptance by a system which involves review of the evidence by our peers. The major journals insist on approval by no less than seven such referees before they will publish anything new and controversial.

Most workers accept that these procedures are cumbersome and make science inherently conservative and resistant to change. But what is not generally acknowledged is that this is a political process rather than a scientific one. It depends upon personal preference, upon the votes of a scientific jury—every member of which would be disqualified from any normal inquiry on the basis of blatant conflict of interest. And yet it is on the verdict handed down by such courts that we are expected to exercise our preferences and construct our beliefs about the world. And that just isn't good enough.

What we need is a truly impartial investigator—a sort of scientific ombudsman—to provide the voice of reason, to speak out for curious individuals against the vested interests of those in authority. And, happily, there has been such a man. His name was Charles Fort and he set up an ongoing inquiry into everything out of the ordinary, calling attention to all those inconvenient events that elude easy explanation and exceed the limits of what established science deems prudent and possible.

I have spent the last twenty years of my life exploring the soft edges of science, pursuing shadows just beneath the surface of current understanding. And I know that there is a vast field of unusual experience, from all over the world, just waiting to be examined. The problem is that reports of it are, by their very nature, anecdotal, and therefore dismissed as unacceptable to science. I happen to think that this is not just a pity, but a terrible waste, and I am deeply grateful to the army of Forteans who continue, with energy and humour, to add to our collection of wild talents and make anthologies of this sort possible—and useful.

Let's put a little more 'Lo!' back into logic—and let the real world back into the study of science, where it belongs.

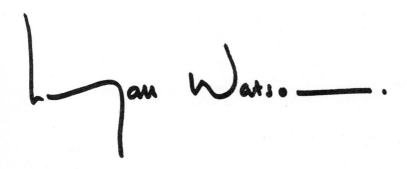

Dr Lyall Watson

Editor's Preface

Fortean Times began publication as *The News* in September 1973, and at the time of writing is in its fifty-seventh issue. What follows is a personal selection of some of the best of the last eighteen years.

I emphasize 'personal' and say 'some of' advisedly. First, because any selection inevitably reflects the taste of the person doing the selecting, and no two people would be likely to agree as to what constitutes the 'best' from over 2700 printed pages. Second, because what is right for a serious (sometimes), relatively-small circulation (so far) journal is not necessarily suitable for inclusion in a book like this one, aimed at the widest possible readership.

For this reason the bias of the book has been towards including material from what is now the magazine section at the front of *Fortean Times*, leaving out both the longer, in-depth pieces which tend to be of more specialist interest and the more idiosyncratic columns which need to be read regularly to be appreciated fully (apologies in particular to Doc Shiels).

One advantage, however, has been in helping to narrow the horribly difficult task of selection. This has been a job where deciding what to leave out has been much more difficult than what to put in. I hope that the success of this volume will necessitate a follow-up, enabling me to fill some of the gaps.

Another editorial decision requires explanation. *Fortean Times* has worked like a team, with members contributing both columns and clippings on a regular basis. It seemed to me that it would be confusing to credit some contributors in an otherwise anonymous book; and that any list of credits would be invidious, because some members of the team would be left out.

My thanks to Marjorie Misiewicz and Tim Wells-Cole, for helping at the most difficult stage; to the staff of Eddison Sadd, and particularly Ian Jackson, for their forbearance; and most of all, to Paul Sieveking and Bob Rickard for help and advice throughout.

Adam Sisman

The owner of this house – a vicar in Murten, Switzerland – returned home to find one of his chimneys twisted a full 180 degrees. A builder who secured it could find no cause for this mystery movement. The vicar checked with the local weather office and was told that there were no other similar reports. Besides, he added, 'The other two chimneys are normal. It's amazing.' The Province (Vancouver) 19 September 1980.

Introduction

BY THE EDITORS OF *Fortean Times*

Showers of beans and fishes; kangaroos on the loose in Chicago; fires in the sky; spontaneous human combustion; houses that drip blood; toads encased in solid stone; weird archæological discoveries ... this is the type of material which has been gathered in the quarterly magazine *Fortean Times* since it began publishing in 1973. Anomalies can be fun and yet at the same time deeply disturbing, because they undermine the notion that everything is under control. Everything is *not* under control; we don't know everything; the unexpected does happen.

When anomalies are experienced, they are frequently edited out by the witness himself. If they are recounted, however, they are usually not recorded; if recorded, usually not transmitted; and if transmitted, often not believed.

Two opposite responses to the threat posed by anomalies come from debunkers and from cranks, those who explain away and those who mythologize. In the case of UFOs, for example, debunkers regard sightings as misperceptions or hoaxes, while cultists tend to form religious associations around a doctrine of salvation or instruction by celestial visitors. Other believers insist on forcing all the evidence to conform to a single explanation, for instance that UFOs are extraterrestrial craft.

Hard-nosed rejection and gullibility are not the only possible responses to anomalies. A third alternative is offered by the approach of the American journalist and philosopher Charles Fort (1874-1932), after whom *Fortean Times* is named. Fort didn't believe. His method was to suspend belief or disbelief in favour of temporary acceptance until such time as further evidence comes along; to substitute observation for explanation; and to tolerate uncertainty indefinitely. The aim is an inclusive cosmology, one that accepts, without moral judgments and without rationalist censorship, the entire range of repeated human experience. As Fort put it: 'When I come upon the unconventional repeating, in times and places far apart, I feel—even though I have no absolute standards to judge by—that I am outside the field of the ordinary liar.'

Charles Fort's *The Book of the Damned* was published in New York in 1919. John Cowper Powys said it was 'a book that set a person's intellect with a wholesome jerk upon its own feet.'

A six-legged lamb, born on a West Wales farm in 1985. While not exactly common, such freak animals are reported fairly consistently; for example, another six-legged lamb was photographed in Nebraska in 1980. Amateur Photographer *31 August 1985.*

Fort was a cynic about science. He observed how scientists argued for and against various theories, facts and types of phenomena according to their own beliefs rather than to the rules of evidence. He was appalled by the way that any datum which did not fit 'the collective paradigm' was ignored, suppressed, discredited or explained away (which is quite a different thing from explaining a thing). He called such rejected data 'The Damned' because they were 'excommunicated' by science, which acted like a religion. 'The monks of science,' he wrote, 'dwell in smuggeries that are walled away from event-jungles. . . . Science has done its utmost to prevent whatever science has done.'

Like the Chinese, Greek and other ancient schools of philosophy, Fort had notions of the universe-as-organism and the transient nature of all apparent phenomena. Fort's 'doctrine of the hyphen', in which everything is in an intermediate state between extremes, is summed up by Martin Gardner in his *Fads and Fallacies in the Name of Science*: 'Because everything is continuous with everything else, it is impossible to draw a line between truth and fiction. If science tries to accept red things and exclude yellow, then where will it put orange? Similarly, nothing is 'included' by science which does not contain error, nor is there anything 'damned' by science which does not contain some truth.'

'I cannot say that truth is stranger than fiction,' wrote Fort, 'because I have never had acquaintance with either . . . there is continuity between what is called the *real* and what is called the *unreal*, so that a passage from one state to the other is across no real gap, or is no absolute jump.'

Modern science is catching up with Fort. James Gleick, author of the best-seller *Chaos*, characterizes the new field of chaos physics by the 'Butterfly Effect': 'the notion that a butterfly stirring the air today in Peking can transform storm systems next month in New York.' Fifty-six years earlier, Fort had written: 'Not a bottle of catsup can fall from a tenement-house fire-escape in Harlem without . . . affecting . . . the demand in China for rhinoceros horns.'

Fort criticized modern science for its reductionism, its attempts to define, divide and separate. 'Every science is a mutilated octopus,' he wrote. 'If its tentacles were not clipped to stumps, it would feel its way into disturbing contacts.' Labels and hypotheses

A Canada goose leading a flock crashed to the ground, apparently hit by a meteor. 'It looked like a laser beam had struck it. The bird just stopped dead in its tracks,' said farmer Duncan Tesloss of Northamptonshire. It was found with a hole in its back and two further holes in its breast. Daily Express *19 March 1987.*

are of course limited by language: 'What we observe is not nature itself,' wrote the physicist Heisenberg, 'but nature exposed to our method of questioning.' Or, as the Duck said in *Alice in Wonderland*: 'When I find a thing it's usually a frog or a worm.'

Fort wanted to show that every established faith and theory is based on 'exclusions'; 'nothing can attempt to be, except by attempting to exclude something else.' Fort cut at the very roots of credulity. 'I go on with my yarns,' he wrote. 'I no more believe them than I believe that twice two are four.' Again: 'I cannot accept that the products of minds are subject-matter for beliefs.'

Strange objects in the sky, monsters by land and sea, humanoids and unearthly men—these are the archetypal stuff of dreams, creatures of universal myths and fairy stories, yet spilling over at times into phenomenal reality, a region that lies somewhere between the 'hard' reality of nuts and bolts and the 'psychological' reality of dreams.

Collections of oddities have abounded since ancient times. Philosophers, essayists, travellers and natural historians have all contributed to the rich literature on anomalies. Traditional societies had a framework in which to study such 'freaks of nature', usually as omens or portents of social change.

The reporting of strange events became increasingly marginalized in western culture after the triumph of scientific rationalism. Today, most coverage of anomalies is confined to filler paragraphs in the newspapers, written inaccurately and for laughs. It is left to publications such as *Fortean Times* to fulfil the ancient task of dispassionate weird-watching.

'Witchcraft always has a hard time,' wrote Fort, 'until it becomes established and changes its name.' Collecting Fortean material, though hugely entertaining in itself, serves the wider purpose of loosening the straitjackets of dogma and fostering a more tolerant attitude to the wide range of human belief. The world is far stranger and more fascinating than any '-ism' can encompass.

Paul Sieveking and Bob Rickard

THE WORLD'S MOST
INCREDIBLE
STORIES

THE BEST OF FORTEAN TIMES

Heavens Above!

Space is the province of scientists – so far. Somehow they've made it seem a bit dull. But space is a strange place, maybe even stranger than anybody thinks . . .

STAR WARS?

In the last decade there have been around 80 unexplained explosions in deep space. A bang on 5 March 1979, 50 times more intense than any previously recorded, occurred 180,000 light years away in the large Magellanic Cloud outside our galaxy. A vast quantity of lethal gamma rays were produced in a fraction of a second and scorched across space, and were picked up by eight widely scattered space probes. It differed from typical gamma ray bursts in that its emissions were at unusually long wavelengths.

Ray Klebesadel, a leading scientist at Los Alamos, said this event was definitely not a supernova explosion. 'The odd thing is that its source was an area only about 187 miles in diameter with a whole lot of energy erupting in a fairly small sector. It resembled a high-energy bomb blast,' he said. Nuclear physicist Stanton T. Friedman declared: 'Tremendous activity of this sort could well be life out there involved in a war.' Said James Oberg at Houston: 'It is a legitimate theory that "star wars" may be taking place.'
Herald Tribune 25 May; *National Enquirer* 25 September 1979.

TENTH PLANET

The Institute of Theoretical Astronomy in Leningrad has calculated that there should be a tenth planet to our system, out beyond Pluto at about 54 times the radius of Earth's orbit. The calculations were based on an analysis of the perturbations in the orbit of a comet known as '1862–3' which appears to be drawn towards 'a planetary body' which has so far remained 'invisible'. There may also be an *eleventh* planet, 100 times Earth-radius out from the sun and twice as big as Earth. The theory cannot be tested until 1992, when '1862–3' is due for a reappearance.

Astronomers of the Livermore Radiation Laboratory, California, believed *they* had evidence of the existence of the tenth planet. A team led by Joseph L. Brady worked on perturbations in the orbits of Halley's Comet and two other (unspecified) 'celestial bodies' with a computer. It suggested a body three times the size of Saturn against the constellation of Cassiopeia – this is near the centre of the Milky Way which is quite bright, making it almost impossible to locate 'Planet X' visibly or by radio-telescopes.
Novosti Bulletin no. 16287; *Daily Mail* 1 May 1972.

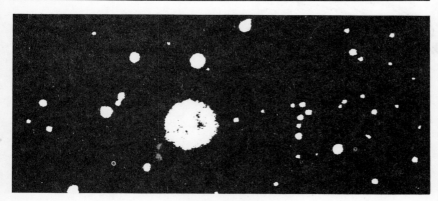

COSMIC QUERY
To the right of this large, bright object – nebula PK 274 + 3 – a constellation of stars appears to form a question mark.

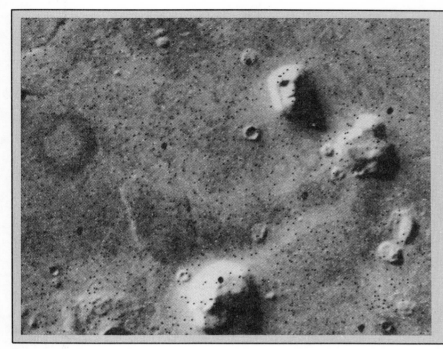

FACING UP TO MARS

This picture is one of many taken by the US Orbiter spacecraft Viking 1 as it circled Mars in search of a landing site for Viking 2. The huge rock formation in the centre, apparently showing a humanoid face, was taken from 1162 miles above the planet's surface. The speckled appearance of the photograph is due to bit errors, emphasized by the enlargement. The face is over a mile wide. Are we looking at an alien Sphinx?

HEAVENLY HUNT FOR A 20,000-YEAR OSTRICH

For thousands of years, a remote colony of Bolivian Indians have gathered once a year to dance and drink for days. Why? They have forgotten, they told archaeologist George Michanowsky. But astronomers of the American space programme now think that those celebrations may pinpoint a cataclysm far out in space, 10,000 to 20,000 years ago.

The Indians, they believe, are commemorating the violent death of a star – a super H-bomb explosion that blazed up in the sky and for a few months would have been as bright as the moon. John Brandt, one of the N.A.S.A. astronomers who did the detective work, commented: 'If this is right – and there is no obvious argument against it – it would be the closest explosion to earth that we have identified.'

The astronomers started the hunt when they found a giant wisp of gas, the so-called Gum Nebula, surrounding one of the mysterious pulsars that flash like a lighthouse many times a second. It was in the constellation Vela, in the southern sky, and it was very like the débris left when a star comes to a violent end, part of it exploding out into space, the rest collapsing into an unimaginably dense and tiny 'crushed' star – the pulsar.

The Vela space catastrophe should have been nearer, and more spectacular, than any of the four such explosions historically recorded, the astronomers argued. But there was no record of it until the astronomers called in the archaeologists and advertised for anything that could conceivably be a primitive record of an explosion in the sky. Their advertisement stirred the memory of Michanowsky. He had first recorded this unexplained Indian rite nearly 20 years before. And it had seemed to be associated with ancient carvings on a rock, of which he could make no sense.

For there were four small circles which fitted a rough cross of stars in the sky – and a larger circle, in the place where the bright star Canopus can be seen. There was a still larger circle nearby – at a point where nowadays we see no star at all, but very close to the mysterious Gum Nebular and its pulsar. Could this be a primitive record that once a very bright star had blazed up at this point? This unremarkable bit of sky still has special meaning for the Indians who call it the Gateway to Hell. According to another legend, one of their sacred symbols, the Heavenly Ostrich, was hunted across the sky by savage dogs and killed at this point. Michanowsky hopes by radiocarbon dating the rock with the carving to put a date within a few hundred years to this closest-ever explosion. *Daily Mirror* 27 October 1973.

Life Imitating Art

Sometimes things seem to happen which bear an eerie resemblance to stories or sayings. Could there be a cosmic joker up there directing events?

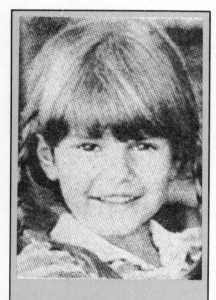

NATURE FOLLOWS ART

Actress Judith Barsi, 11, who portayed a girl slain by her father in the film Fatal Vision, was killed by her father. Jozsef Barsi, 55, a self-employed plumber, shot his wife Maria, 48, and daughter, soaked their bodies with petrol and set them on fire in his house in West Hills, California. He later fatally shot himself.

Neighbours said Barsi had previously threatened to kill his wife and daughter and burn down his house. *USA Today* September 1988.

BULL WRECKS CHINA SHOP

● The 18-month-old bull escaped from a cattle market in Otley, Yorkshire, and headed for Peter Jordan's shop, coming in through the door like a normal customer but then knocking over cabinets of china, crushing coffee tables and destroying lamps and ornaments. It was finally lured away with a young heifer. *Daily Telegraph + Daily Star* 25 September 1980.

WILD GOOSE STORY

● As a Republic Airlines plane landed in South Dakota a large goose smashed through the cockpit window. The pilot was injured, but the co-pilot managed to land the plane safely. The pay-off of this synchronistic gag is that the company symbol, with which the plane is emblazoned, is a flying goose! *New York Post* 8 November 1983.

IS IT ART?

● The London version of *Dracula* had to move out of its rehearsal hall because it had been pre-booked by the National Blood Transfusion Service.

● Fire broke out during the witch-burning scene in Arthur Miller's *The Crucible* and gutted an arts centre in Istanbul. The Astral 2 Cinema in Soho caught fire after showing *Erotic Inferno* and *Hot Acts of Love*. Hours after the premiere of Cheech and Chong movie *Up In Smoke* at the Plaza 2 Cinema in Lower Regent Street, the adjoining Plaza 3 caught fire. *Sunday Times* 29 November 1970; *Daily Mail* 29 July 1976; *Evening Standard* 19 October 1979.

● An open-air reading of Shakespeare's *The Tempest* in Manchester was stopped by a cloudburst as was an open-air rehearsal of Handel's *Water Music* at Redland in California. The conductor brought back the sun with *Hymn to the Sun*. The St Matthew's Parish Players had to cancel their open-air performance of the mystery play *Noah's Flood* in a Tolworth pub car park when they were washed out by torrential rain. *Reveille* 3 September 1976 & 10 June 1977; *Daily Star* 16 June 1980.

● During filming of a robbery for *Straight Time* outside a jewellers in Hollywood, thieves held up the staff and got away with £250,000 worth of gems. Everyone – staff, film crew, actors and spectators – thought the thieves and the manager shouting for help were part of the film. *Weekend* 5–11 April 1978.

● The baby son of a couple staying in Julie Christie's farmhouse in Wales was drowned in a shallow pond. Six years before, in the film *Don't Look Now*, Julie Christie played the mother of a child drowned in a pond. Constable Frank Podmore, who gave evidence at the inquest, bore the same name as one of the pioneers of The Society for Psychical Research, who was also found drowned in a pond. *Shropshire Star + Daily Mail* 2 April; *Eastern Daily Press* 3 April 1979.

● A thousand-pound antique throne was smashed to bits by heavy waves after it had been set up on a beach for a King Canute cigar advertisement. *Daily Mirror* 25 April 1978.

● In the film *The China Syndrome*, made before the Three Mile Island nuclear accident, a character remarks that a cloud of waste would wreak death and destruction over 'an area the size of Pennsylvania'. Earlier in the year, a local magazine had a fictional story called *Meltdown at Three Mile Island*, and even got the date right – 28 March. *Daily Mail* 30 March & 2 April 1979.

● Novelist Bill Granger's first thriller concerns an IRA plot to blow up the yacht of a British lord and cousin of the Queen while he is sailing in the Irish Sea. *The November Man* was published as a paperback less than three weeks before IRA bombers assassinated Lord Mountbatten on his yacht off the northwest coast of Ireland. In the thriller, the American hero foils the plot at the last moment. *Toronto Star* 29 August; *Herald Tribune* 30 August; *Evening News* 24 August 1979.

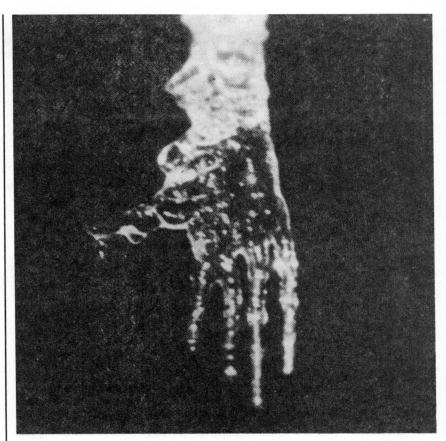

These icy fingers on her kitchen window appeared on the day that Carol Alspaugh took her sister to hospital for a hand operation, only to find it cancelled because of an injury the previous day – caused by a falling icicle.

TWICE UPON A TIME

● In Palma, Majorca, a young lady, Maria Bisbal, sawn-off shotgun hold-up *artiste extraordinaire*, pulled 14 heists; until one day she left behind a dainty high-heeled shoe, stuck in an iron grille while she fled. Enter the handsome detective: the shoe fits, Maria confesses all ... off to court they go (judicial, that is, not royal ...) *Daily Express* 3 September 1979.

● To Mary and Joseph, a carpenter, a son, born on Christmas Day. Sorry, folks, it's Mary and Joseph Austen of Swindon. They're calling him Joseph Charles (JC?). *The Spectator* (Canada) + *Daily Mail* 26 and 27 December 1979.

● Storks bring babies in Israel? Migrating storks caused long blackouts by touching electricity cables with their wings. No light, no television. Doctors expect a rise in the birth rate. *News of the World* 2 December 1979.

● Narcissus: 23-month-old Leila Ahmed is believed to have drowned in a pond after becoming fascinated by her own reflection. *Daily Express* 4 September 1979.

Coincidences

Some coincidences seem so perfect that one can't help feeling that there is some logic behind them.

NAMESAKES

● John Corfield from Manchester wrote to the *Sunday Express* (29 July 1984) about his Ibiza holiday the previous week. He and his wife Mildred were given the wrong hotel room, which had in fact been booked for a Jack and Mildred Corfield who had travelled out on the same flight.

● On 11 August 1984, Karen Dawn Southwick, 22, was married at St Michael's and All Angels, Tettenhall, near Wolverhampton. She was given away by her father, Alfred G. Southwick. Three hours later another Karen Dawn Southwick, aged 22, was married in the same church, given away by her father, Alfred G. Southwick.

The two brides had not met before the preparatory get-together with the vicar. There was a slight flaw in the congruity, however; the fathers' middle names were George and Gordon. Alfred George had never met Alfred Gordon, but believed they might be distant cousins. *Shropshire Star* + Wolverhampton *Express & Star* 8 August; *Sun* 9 August 1984.

● Victor John Foti, 64, of Fairbanks, New York State, checked into a hospital in Rochester for a quadruple heart bypass operation. He was understandably surprised to find, in the adjoining bed, another Victor John Foti. If this was not coincidental enough, it turned out that his namesake was also from Fairbanks, but aged 59, had been admitted for the same operation. To avoid confusion the hospital decided to distinguish the two patients by their weight. Victor the lesser, the first one to be admitted, said they had been getting each other's mail for 20 years, and actually met seven years before, but 'we have never had anything like this before.' *Die Rheinpfalz* + *Daily Express* 11 February 1986.

ACCIDENTAL COINCIDENCE?

● Mrs Sue Alton was riding with some friends along Pilgrim's Way, a footpath near Dorking when her horse bolted. She was thrown headfirst against a five-foot-tall stone monument, and was killed almost instantly. The monument had been erected in 1873 to mark the spot where the Bishop of Winchester, Samuel Wilberforce, had fallen on his head and died when his horse put a hoof in a hole. *Western Morning News* + *Daily Telegraph* + *Daily Mail* 30 March 1987.

CHANCE ENCOUNTERS?

There can be few stories as enigmatic as the following. Erskine Lawrence Ebbin was knocked off his moped by a taxi and killed in Hamilton, Bermuda. It was the same taxi with the same driver, carrying the same passenger, that killed his brother Neville in July the previous year. Both brothers were 17 when they died, and had been riding the same moped in the same street. Ah! but history never quite repeats itself – the time of both accidents differed by (only) 50 minutes. *Liverpool Echo* + *Scunthorpe Evening Telegraph* 21 July 1975; *Buenos Aires Herald* 22 July 1975.

● But perhaps the most remarkable tale of a chance encounter is that of young Roger Lausier. When he was four years old he strayed away from his mother along the beach at Salem, Massachusetts. He paddled for a while and then got caught by a powerful undercurrent, and would have drowned but for a woman who brought him ashore and revived him. The rescuer refused all rewards, and left wishing the infant luck. Nine years later, Roger was a strong swimmer and was tracking a shoal of bluefish when he heard a woman scream: 'My husband is drowning! My husband is drowning!' Roger saw that a heavily-built man had fallen from his power-boat and was floundering helplessly. He paddled his inflated raft over in time to clutch the drowning man's hand, and kept him afloat until another boat got to them, and they went safely ashore. In the hospital the grateful woman kissed the boy: 'I'm Alice Blaise, and I can't thank you enough for saving my Bob.' Roger had no idea who Mrs Blaise was until the story came out during a presentation to him by the Massachusetts Humane Society. He had saved the husband of the woman who had saved him on the same beach nine years previously. *Sunday Express* 21 April 1974.

● **Peter Bacon of Eyam, Derbyshire, crashed into a car driven by Peter Bacon of North Anston, Sheffield.** *Daily Mirror* **9 February 1985.**

● **A couple of months later, John Stott, whose car crash was witnessed by Bernard Stott (no relation), and investigated by WPC Tina Stott, was taken back to a police station where the trio was met by desk sergeant Walter Stott.** *Weekend* **8–14 May 1985.**

● **'Is this a million-to-one chance? I received two Christmas cards, one from a son in Britain, and one from a son in Los Angeles. There are both exactly the same.' Letter from Mrs Freda Hurst in** *Daily Express* **14 December 1973.**

● **Veronica Mullens and Anthony Pitt were married at Dowlais, Glamorgan. The names were recorded next to each other on the Merthyr Tydfil birth register 22 years ago.** *Sunday Mirror* **3 March 1974.**

SAME NAMES

● **Patricia Ann Tranter, 30, of Ketley in Shropshire, went into hospital to have a baby. In the next bed was a stranger, called Patricia Ann Tranter, 24, of Ketley in Shropshire (they lived a mile apart). They gave birth on the same day, and met in the same church when the babies John and Julie, were being christened.** *Daily Mirror* **23 April 1973.**

● **An error by the American Inland Revenue gave John Seeman of Tampa, Florida, an identity crisis. John Seemann of Cairo, New York, had the same social security number, was born on the same day in the same city, and both had fathers called John. The only difference was Cairo John's extra 'n' on his name.** *Globe* **30 September 1980.**

● Confusion reigned in Bulawayo Magistrates' Court. Smart Ngwenya, 25, faced a charge of tampering with a car several weeks earlier. But another Smart Ngwenya, waiting to give evidence in a different case, was brought into the court room. The mistake was realized after the charge had been read and denied. Embarrassed court officials hustled him out and led in another Smart Ngwenya (ngwenya means crocodile) who also turned out to be the wrong man. The 'correct' Smart Ngwenya was brought in at the third attempt. *Rand Daily Mail* 6 October 1979.

● Patricia Kern of Colorado was sent a tax demand for $3000 from a job she had held in Oregon, a state in which she had never set foot. Inquiries showed that Patricia DiBiasi of Oregon owed the taxes. Both were born Patricia Ann Campbell, on 13 March 1941, and shared a social security number. Both had fathers called Robert, both married military men within 11 days of each other, both worked as bookkeepers and had children of 21 and 19. *Philadelphia Enquirer* 2 May; *National Enquirer* 3 May 1983.

POORLY PUSSIES
These two closely-related kittens broke legs within hours of each other. Ahhhh!

Twins

Stories like these tend to be dismissed individually as just one of those things – but taken together, they suggest a strange and sometimes sinister pattern . . .

IDENTICAL TWINS

● **Pauline and Pat Collister, 26 years old, are believed to be Britain's only identical twins married to identical twins, Peter and John, aged 27. On 11 August, Pauline and Pat gave birth within an hour of each other at Scarsdale Hospital, Chesterfield, Derbyshire.** *Aberdeen Press and Journal* **13 August 1984.**

● **Identical twins Lynn and Kay, 33, gave birth to their first babies on the same day at Southmead Hospital in Bristol. Lynn had an 8 lb 12 oz daughter, and six hours later Kay had a son weighing 7 lb 15 oz.** *Telegraph* **28 September 1984.**

● **Twins Roberto and Marco made a 3000-foot parachute jump near Milan airport, and Marco broke his right leg. Driving home later, Roberto crashed, and broke his right leg.** *Sunday Express* **25 November 1984.**

TWIN TALES

Jacqueline and Sheila Lewis were adopted at birth by different families, and neither knew the other existed. Twenty-seven years later, they were admitted to Southmead Hospital, Bristol, on the same day with the same hereditary skin disorder, and put in the same room. They soon discovered they were identical twins and that Sheila's husband had died on the same day, two years earlier, that Jackie had divorced her husband. *Daily Mail* 2 July; *Daily Telegraph* 3 July; *National Enquirer* 31 August 1976.

● Sometime in August 1939, in Piqua, Ohio, identical boy twins were adopted by two families who were told that the other baby had died. The Springers lived in Dayton, the Lewises in Lima 80 miles away. Six years later, while completing adoption papers, Mrs Lewis learned by accident that the other twin was alive. When she said that she had called the child James Edward, the court official said: 'You can't do that. They named the other little boy James.' James Springer grew up thinking his twin was dead, while James Lewis didn't know where his twin was, and hesitated for many years before tracing him through the red-tape jungle of adoption courts. In February 1979, at the age of 39, they met. In their lives apart, the two James married and divorced Lindas and remarried Betties; and had taken holidays on the same beach in St Petersburg, Florida. Both were into carpentry and mechanical drawing, both had had police training and occasional 'law enforcement' work. One is now a security guard, the other a records clerk. They called their eldest son James Alan and James Allen. When they met, their families noted similar speech patterns, mannerisms and posture. But Lewis had short hair combed back and Springer long hair combed forward . . .

● On 27 July 1939, a few days before the birth of the Ohio twins, an unmarried Finnish student, Helena Jacobsson, gave birth to twin girls in Hammersmith Hospital in London. They were christened Dagmar Daphne Margaret (Daphne, the elder by twelve minutes) and Gerda Barbara. Both were adopted, Barbara growing up in London and Daphne in Luton. In 1979, at the age of 39, they met. Barbara Herbert and her family lived in Dover, while Daphne Goodship and her family lived in Wakefield. Both their adoptive mothers died when they were children; both had worked in local government offices; both miscarried their first babies, then each had two boys followed by a girl – though Daphne had two more children later; and both had met their husbands at town hall dances when they were 16. They both liked carving, though Barbara uses wood and Daphne soap; and they were wearing identical white petticoats at their reunion. This time the difference was one of weight: Daphne had been dieting. *Boston Globe* 20 February; *South Middlesex News* 22 February; *Daily Mirror* 24 February; South Africa *Sunday Times* 4 March; *Midnight Globe* 27 March; *Sunday People* 10 June 1979.

● In July 1979 twins Ruth Johnson of Lowell, Massachusetts and Allison Mitchell Erb of Mount Vernon, Maine, met for the first time since they were adopted 26 years ago. Each is a hairdresser with a daughter called Kristen, and each has one other child. The previous June they had both watched a television discussion on the right of adopted persons to discover their origins, and both started to search for the other. *The Spectator* (Canada) 24 July; *Herald Tribune + Daily Mail* 25 July 1979.

BLACK AND WHITE

These twins, one black and one white, were the subject of an unprecedented legal wrangle in 1978. The mother, a West German woman, launched a double paternity suit on the grounds that she had ovulated twice in one day, having made love to a white German and a black American soldier within hours. In 1939 a black woman in North Carolina also had different-coloured twins, in this case a white son and a black daughter, but the father of both seems to have been 'coal-black Herbert Strong'. Other cases are on record, from the USA, Liverpool, Denmark and Berlin.

SIMULTANEOUS DEATHS OF TWINS

The so-called 'Cot Death Syndrome' is still one of today's persistent medical mysteries, and the spectre of it must loom in the minds of all parents of new-born children. The only good to come out of such tragedies are the sparse clues about the condition, leading to its eventual detection and treatment, but that is little comfort to Arthur and Linda Connolly, whose twins Samantha and Gabrielle died on 8 October 1983.

The identical twins were just four months old, and had been put to sleep in different rooms of their parents' guesthouse in Rhyl, North Wales. Mrs Connolly found Gabrielle dead first, in her cot on the first floor. Horrified, she and her husband dashed up to the second floor where Samantha was sleeping. Mr Connolly said: 'It was hard to describe the horror. When we found one child dead we thought, "Oh, God. No – the other can't be dead too." But she was.' What compounds the mystery is that the twins had died at exactly the same time.

The Connolly twins are not the first such case. Twin boys, aged seven months, also died in separate cots, in Bacup, Lancashire, earlier that same year, 1983. *Sunday Express + Sunday Times + Sunday People + Observer + News of the World* 9 October; *Daily Express + Daily Star + Daily Telegraph + Daily Mail* 10 October; *Guardian + Scottish Daily Express* 11 October; *Scottish Daily Express* 13 October 1983.

Tragically, it happened again recently. Three-month-old twins, Kevin and Louise Croucher died together in the cot they shared in Denton, Manchester, in the night of 9/10 May. *Sun* 11 May 1984.

What's in a Name?

Some names seem peculiarly suited to their owner's behaviour: or is it the other way round? Is there a relationship between what we're called and what we do?

A WRIGHT NUTTER

Bride-to-be Ann Wright is resigned to becoming A. Nutter when she weds. But she has vetoed fiance Jeremy Nutter's plan to combine their surnames by deed-poll – and make her A. Wright-Nutter. Ann, a receptionist from Marple Bridge near Stockport, met Jeremy at an April Fool's Day party in 1983 ... and she thought his name was a leg-pull. He is proud of the Nutter name, however, which means scribe. *Daily Mirror + Sun + Daily Express* 19 June 1987.

FISH CLUMPINGS

● In Haddenham, Cambs., Mr and Mrs Pike live next to the vet, Colin Fish. The Haddocks are up the road, and their neighbour is Mrs Salmon. Mr Guppy and Mr and Mrs Fish live at the other end of the village. *News of the World* 27 June; *Daily Mail* 28 June 1982.

● Three men were fined for stealing rainbow trout from Mr Herring's fish farm in Hampshire. The police who caught them were led by Chief Superintendant Pike. *Daily Star + Daily Mail + Sun* 16 November 1982.

BIRD GATHERINGS

● In 1969, John Bird moved into Old Gardens Close, Tunbridge Wells, Kent. Over the next decade, several other birds became his immediate neighbours: David Nightingale, Roger Wren, Tim Sparrow and Bill and Pat Duck. Their local pub was the Swan. *Sun + Daily Express* 21 June 1980.

● A duck farmer in Lincolnshire employs two people called Crow, four Robbins, a Sparrow, a Gosling and a Dickie Bird. The latest recruit at Newport police station, Gwent, joining two policemen called Pidgeon, a Partridge, a Nightingale and a Bush, is PC Talbot Thrush. *Daily Telegraph* 3 June + 2 September 1982.

● Burglar Kenneth Pigeon of Cleveland (U.K.) was caught by Reginald Peacock and arrested by Detective Constable George Bird. *Daily Telegraph + Daily Express* 31 December 1982.

● Gorzo the performing parrot was stolen from a theatre in Morecambe, Lancs. The police had a clue – the thief's registration spelt PEK. Eventually they traced it – to Stanley Parrott, 31. *Daily Mirror* 5 September 1978.

A delightfully-named printers and stationers in Londonderry.

NAME GAMES

● **Three fortunate people who managed to scoop nearly £50,000 each on Littlewoods pools are John Gamble, Mr Riches and Janet Luck.** *Evening Standard* 14 March; *Sun* 15 March 1984.

● **A man who stole three Jack Russell puppies from a farm near Truro, Cornwall, is being hunted by Police Constable Jack Russell.** *Sun* 19 April 1984.

● **The Examining Attorney in the extradition hearing in New York of Joseph Doherty, who escaped from prison in Belfast, is Ms Ira H. Bloch.** *Guardian* 6 April 1984.

WORD PLAY

A performance of Snow White at the Bristol Hippodrome ran with only six dwarves when Dozy was taken to hospital because of drowsiness. Barry Gnome, 74, from Yorkshire, came out of retirement for the part. *Daily Telegraph* February 1988.

● Notes for teachers, issued to accompany a one-hour play about young homosexuals by the BBC's education broadcasting department, suggested that homosexual activity should be seen as part of the normal development of teenagers. The notes were written by Dr Martin Gay, a consultant child psychiatrist in Avon. *Daily Telegraph* 24 March 1988.

● In June, a lecture on 'Depression and anxiety disorders' was given at the Royal Edinburgh Hospital by Professor Jules Angst. *Guardian* 3 June 1988.

● James Careless, 32, of Wolverhampton, was crushed and killed on 20 September when his vehicle overturned during a drive along a Lanzarote beach in the Canary Islands. *Daily Telegraph* 21 September 1988.

● Congressman Pat Swindall of Georgia faced corruption charges. Thomas Gilbert Swindells, a Liverpool shipping office manager, was done for fraud in 1980. *Daily Telegraph* 11 November 1988.

● Clifford Tidy was taken to court for allegedly failing to clear rubbish from his garden. Ian Tidey was fined for littering after a solicitor called Philip Circus had seen a cigarette packet thrown out of his car. *Sun* 16 January 1989.

James Bond, 15, a pupil at Argoed High School, North Wales, and a candidate for examinations in 1990, was given the examination number 007 by a computer quirk. For those who don't appreciate the point of this story, it should be explained that the code number of the famous fictional secret agent James Bond was also 007.

FORLETTA WORDS

● 'A Torquay man has been fined £200 for swearing at police. Nicholas Forletta, 24, pleaded guilty to using abusive language on April 19.' *Daily Telegraph* 7 June 1986.

● James Bond was slashed in the face with a beer glass by Terry McCann. McCann, 20, of Kingshurst, Birmingham, was given two and a half years' youth custody. *Sun* 28 June 1986.

● A coach owned by Swansdown Coaches of Inkpen, near Newbury, Berks, was travelling on the M4 near Reading in heavy rain when a swan crashed through the window injuring two passengers. The swan was killed. *Daily Telegraph* 4 August 1986.

● The man with the job of selling lifejackets at a Bedford marina is 27-year-old Will Drown. His hobby is swimming. *Sun* 5 May 1986.

Mutilations

If it's painful to read the stories that follow, think how much more painful it must have been for the victims. Yet most of them have mutilated themselves.

HANDS OFF

During a murder trial at the Old Bailey, Robert Draper told how a man paid him £50 to cut off the man's right hand. Leslie Tainton, 32, wanted to punish himself for being unfaithful to his homosexual lover, Peter Faiers. The two met Draper in a pub, where he agreed to do the job, and after drinking to get up courage, they went to Faiers' home in Leeds. Tainton drank wine and sniffed glue as the others tied his arm to a bannister rail, and Draper severed the wrist with two blows of an axe. Draper fled to London where, it was alleged, he killed another homosexual with the same axe in a row over a television programme. *Daily Telegraph* + *Western Mail* 7 May 1982.

'DO IT YOURSELF'

Even more painful was the bizarre case of Kallie Fortuin, a 19-year-old South African, who was forced to castrate himself at gunpoint. Fortuin had raped an old lady, and was caught riding her bike the next day by the lady's son and friend. At gunpoint they took him to a remote river bank, gave him a knife used to castrate pigs, and told him it was either snip it or snuff it. Without the aid of books, training or anaesthetics, the youth set to work, and after, the men took him to a police station. When he was brought to trial for the rape, Fortuin told the court he had seen how pigs were castrated, so he 'knew what to do'; and a doctor confirmed that he had made a very neat job of it too. In view of this unusual retribution Fortuin escaped both hanging and a life sentence – he got ten years – and the lady's relatives were simply warned not to take the law into their own hands again. *Daily Telegraph* 3 September 1981.

Dr Surendra Nath Jain, of the West Park Nursing Home in Wolverhampton, who had performed more than 400 vasectomies, vasectomised himself. He said he did it to demonstrate to patients that the operation is simple, and quick, in an effort to calm their fears. He normally allows 20 minutes for the operation, but performed it on himself in 30 minutes with an anaesthetist standing by. The British Medical Association were 'surprised', adding that Dr Surendra had done nothing unethical. A spokeswoman said: 'As far as we know this is the first time its been done.' *News of the World* 27 December 1981.

SAW LOSER

A man from Pontiac, near Detroit, astonished doctors by cutting off his left hand with a power saw twice in one year. The first self-mutilation occurred in February 1989 and was said to be an attempted suicide. Surgeons reattached the severed member using microsurgical techniques and kept the man under observation in a mental hospital for seven months before discharging him with a month's medication.

Less than a month later the poor chap walked out of the hostel where he had been staying, bought a 7-inch circular saw at a local hardware store, and checked into a motel where he repeated the assault. This time the cut was so jagged that doctors were unable to sew the hand back on. An ambulance was rushed to the scene, and the man told police officer John McLain that he thought the hand was useless and he didn't want it anymore.

'In 25 years of medicine, I've never seen a case where someone has deliberately cut off their hand twice,' confessed emergency department medic Dr Robert Aranosian. Hostel director Anthony Drabik commented: 'We feel very badly about this.' *Detroit News* 27 September 1980.

NO ARM DONE

When James Bradley, 25, strolled into St Charles' Hospital, Ladbroke Grove, London, and asked the nice people behind the counter to cut off his arm, he was turned away. Later he returned, but with a tourniquet tied around the remains of his arm, which was missing from above the elbow. 'I had a message from God,' he explained. He says he was ordered to lose his arm, and after the Hospital's refusal to help he wandered onto the tube line in North Kensington, put his right arm on the track and waited for a train. The deed done, he applied a tourniquet and walked the half mile back to the Hospital. *Daily Express* 8 July 1974.

LEGLESS

Michael Downing, 40, jobless and living alone in London, took a hacksaw and sawed off his left leg below the knee. Doctors said the amputation was so neat they would have no trouble sewing it back on again. Michael appeared not to be in shock and chatted throughout his travel – but he refused to have the leg back, saying 'it would be against God's orders.' One doctor said: 'Mr Downing's condition is outside our normal experience.' Michael suffered little loss of blood, no pain and no traumatic shock. After the main report came a second item saying that Michael had been in hospital before after cutting off several fingers 'for practice'. An ambulanceman said: 'He seems to have an obsession about cutting parts off his body.' Michael was being referred for psychiatric treatment after his recovery. *Sun* 19 + 20 November 1981.

FINGER THIS

Artist Henry Benvenuti stormed magnificently out of the office of the *Soho Weekly News*, New York, leaving behind, on the reception counter, his briefcase, a rat trap with a dollar bill in it, and two fingers. Henry had come to see Gerald Marzonati, the paper's art writer. 'He said he wanted to rap about the art world,' says Gerald. 'I told him, "Look man, I'm on a deadline, finishing a column. Leave your number and I'll call you back."' Henry, who had been calling from the reception desk phone, was annoyed at being fobbed off, and left his 'message' on the desk. He calmly took a small axe out of his briefcase and lopped off two fingers. Receptionist Donna Frost, said: 'Nobody screamed. He didn't make a sound. There wasn't much blood, just a few drops. He walked out of here so calmly I thought it was a piece of theatre – until I saw the fingers. You can still see where the blade cut into the counter!' Police found Henry in a taxi and took him to Bellevue Hospital, but the fingers could not be reconnected. *St Catherine's Standard* 27 November; *Herald Tribune* 1 December 1979.

...BUT IS IT ART?

COX LOSS

Roger Cox, a 35-year-old father of eight children, cut off his penis, and as his wife joined him in prayer, cast it into a fire at his home at Saron, near Denbigh, Wales. He says he did it so that he can devote himself 100% to preaching. His wife said that her husband's justification was in *Matthew* 19:12, which goes: '... and there are eunuchs who have made themselves eunuchs for the sake of the Kingdom of Heaven.' *Daily Telegraph + Sun + Western Mail + Shropshire Star* 18 March 1982.

Medical Curiosities

Medical literature is full of strange, grotesque and bizarre stories. Here are a few of each . . .

HIS BROTHER'S KEEPER

In a bizarre reprieve from the spectre of a tumour in his chest, Andrew Donker learned that for 21 years he had been carrying his unborn twin in his own chest cavity. The discovery was made during a medical examination for Army enlistment, and X-rays showed a huge shadow beside Andrew's heart and lungs. His application was rejected, but further tests at Liverpool's Broad Green Hospital, showed the tumour, which was nearly as big as a lung, contained human hair and embryonic characteristics. It was removed in a three-hour operation, but there was no obvious clue to its sex. A doctor said it was caused when one twin fails to develop and is absorbed by the other. *Sunday People* 11 December 1983.

GROW YOUR OWN

● **Mark Bowker, 9, of Chalgrove in Oxfordshire, grew a new fingertip after the original was severed in a door at school. Doctors at Oxford's John Radcliffe Hospital said that such regeneration is well documented in children of up to about three years old, but never before in a nine year old. *Sunday Telegraph* + *Sunday Mirror* 8 April; *Daily Record* 9 April 1990.**

WONDERS OF VALIUM

● In 1980, an airline pilot was involved in a car accident and was in a coma for three months. He had a temporary improvement, but lapsed into a vegetative state in 1982. His eyes were open and he occasionally uttered words. On 12 March 1990, the 45-year-old man was given a shot of Valium during routine dental work in the University of Wisconsin Hospital. He fell asleep for about five minutes, then woke up and started talking. He was able to answer questions, say his name, feed himself and walk. Hours later he lapsed back into the vegetative state, and was given a second dose that brought him out of it for about 90 minutes.

The man subsequently received different barbiturates that allowed him to remain lucid for 10 to 12 hours. His neurologist, Dr Andres Kanner, said the problem was to find a combination of drugs the man could take orally that would prevent a relapse. This was a case unique in medical records, and some medical experts claimed that the patient had been misdiagnosed, while others said the case deserved further research. *Evening Standard* 28 March; *Atlanta Constitution* + New Jersey *Record* 29 March; *New York Daily News* 30 March 1990.

● A drug that might become popular for its sexual side-effects is Anafranil (clomipramine, Ciba-Geigy), the first tricyclic antidepressant authorized specifically for the treatment of severe obsessive-compulsive disorder. *Drug Topics* 5 February 1990. Three incidents have been recorded in the anecdotal literature in which patients on Anafranil experienced orgasms every time they yawned. However, Anafranil doesn't usually produce the hypersexuality sometimes associated with such antidepressants as Tradozone (Desyrel, Mead Johnson).

FALSE PREGNANCIES IN MALES

The latest report of a male 'pregnancy' concerns a 40-year-old married man who wished to have another child but his wife didn't. Subsequently, the man's abdomen began to protrude and his weight increased by 20 pounds. Symptoms similar to those of morning sickness also developed. The conditions eventually subsided as he and his wife 'talked out' their disagreement. (Evans, Dwight Landis: 'Pseudocyesis in the Male', *Journal of Nervous and Mental Disease*, 172: 37, 1984.)

CANNIBAL DOCTORS ROW

Nurses at a neonatal unit at Leeds Infirmary have accused two doctors, Alexia Soulioti and Heather Durward, of cannibalism. They were devising a new treatment for babies with hydrocephaly, which involved giving the child a drink of its own brain fluids, drawn off by lumbar puncture. However, the horrified nurses allege that the doctors each had a sip first.

Normally, the accumulation of cerebrospinal fluids is diverted by an implanted 'shunt', which drains it into the oesophagus. Unfortunately, the shunt frequently inflamed its environs, sometimes resulting in dangerous infection. The doctors hit on the idea of returning the cerebrospinal fluid to the baby direct. During a staff medical discussion, someone half-jokingly suggested the doctors should have to taste their own medicine first. So they did. The resulting outrage among the nurses caused the experiment to be discontinued after the first attempt.

Writing in the *Lancet* under the headline 'Trial Abandoned in Disgust', Drs Soulioti and Durward describe the event: 'Following initial incredulity, a pilot study was grudgingly allowed in one baby provided that a significant number of doctors were observed to imbibe a significant volume of the offending fluid. We are proud to report that the Haldane spirit still beats in the breasts of young scientists. We can assure you that cerebrospinal fluid tastes just like sea water, and the baby found that it greatly improved the taste of his artificial milk feed.' *Daily Telegraph* 19 August 1989.

WRINKLED RETAINER SACKED

A French doctor is literally a self-made woman. At the age of 52, Dr Daniel Kretzschmar was fed up being a divorced father of two. He had always felt himself to be more feminine than masculine, and had been taking a course of hormone treatments. Sex-change operations are illegal in France, so Daniel went to Belgium – but an accidental death during a similar operation while he was at the clinic made Daniel decide to look elsewhere. He became convinced that he could castrate himself. 'I chose a Sunday, a day I was least likely to be disturbed at home. I began at 9am. I took it one step at a time. It was just like cutting my fingernails, or taking off a wart. I had no pain thanks to a local anaesthetic. My anatomy book was my instruction manual. I just kept cutting. I was totally absorbed in the technical aspects of the surgery. I did the operation in two stages, the left and the right sides.' In between, Daniel broke off for lunch and rest, fixing himself steak and vegetables. 'During the operation, I got up to answer the 'phone three times. I knew I always had the 'phone nearby and if anything started to go wrong I could ask someone to help me. In fact, in the middle of the second half of the operation I phoned my secretary. I had three patients to see that Sunday. After the surgery I just had time to clean my room. I put all the waste in the trash can, then I saw my patients. Afterward, I went out for a meal in a restaurant.' Later, Danielle as s/he now prefers to be called, acquired female genitals through surgery in Amsterdam. Although his professional and family life have been rebuilt, Dr Kretzschmar has found that there are still some patients and members of his family who cannot bring themselves to accept what he has done.

Dr Kretzschmar as Daniel and Danielle.

Inside Stories

Pork chops, baked beans, bullets, thread, coins, bus tickets, snakes . . . it's amazing what some people carry around inside them . . .

SLEEPING GIRL SWALLOWS SNAKE

An 11-year-old girl from the Sabirabad region of the Caspian Sea Soviet republic of Azerbaijan, identified by her first name Matanet, fell asleep in a field after picking tomatoes in the sun and woke up choking. She was rushed to a childrens' clinic in Baku and made to drink $3\frac{1}{2}$ pints of salt solution. She then vomited up a semi-poisonous 25-in Caucasian cat snake, said *Pravda* on 19 August 1987. An hour later she left the clinic with her parents and went home feeling fine, according to the *Kent County Daily Times* and the *Houston Chronicle* (20 August). *The Scotsman* of the same date said she was being treated for a swelling in her stomach, caused by the snake's bite.

HAZARDS OF XMAS PUDDING

Marie Hefferman was 13 when, eating Christmas pudding, she swallowed a coin. Twelve years later, Marie had a coughing fit and brought up the coin. *USA Today* + *Daily Telegraph* + *Guardian* + *Daily Express* + *Scotsman* 21 December; *Daily Mail* 22 December 1984.

HARD TO SWALLOW

We've all felt that 'butterflies in my tummy' sensation, and felt the odd 'frog in the throat', but God preserve us from the following revolting fate . . .

Yeter Yildirim, a 15-year-old Turkish girl, had suffered mysterious stomach pains for five years. In that time she changed from being a happy-go-lucky farm girl into a moody, withdrawn outcast. Her pains and vivid headaches alienated her friends and caused the family to be shunned by suspicious villagers after she failed to respond to local folk-healers and their magic charms. So Yetter's family moved 80 miles to Ankara, where they eventually took her to a hospital. Picture the scene: the doctors come to her parents clutching the X-rays and say matter-of-factly: 'Don't worry, we can easily remove the snakes.' 'Snakes? What snakes?' shout her parents, staring alternately at the doctor and the girl in horror. Yes, there were three of them – water snakes – 'slightly thicker than string and nearly a foot long.' The doctors can only surmise that the girl must have swallowed them as eggs while drinking from a stream when she was ten years old, since when they grew inside her. *Daily Star* 28 June 1979.

BULLET AND BUS TICKET

● Major Richard Bingley, 68, of Newton Abbot in Devon, went to a London hospital in December 1988 suffering from a pain behind his left eye. Surgeons recovered a bullet. In 1952, during the Korean War, he had been shot four times in the thigh, but medics found only three exit holes. It was thought that the remaining bullet travelled in his bloodstream to his heart, where it crossed the central wall, presumably through a convenient hole that the Major must have had since birth. From the left ventricle it passed through his aorta, and so up to his head. The journey took 36 years. The hospital kept the bullet for their museum. *Daily Telegraph* 30 December 1988; *Daily Mail* 3 January 1989.

● 'All my life my husband [aged 75] has been troubled by deafness' wrote Mrs Jack Crackers in a letter to the *Bradford Argus* (18 February 1987). 'Then, when we were in Sweden, he got a sweet stuck in his throat and after I gave him a good thump on the back a bus ticket issued in Buxton, Derbyshire on 2 May 1927, shot out of his ear. "I must have stuck it in my ear when I was on my way home from school," he said.'

A BEAN IN HER EYE

It was just before the schools broke up for the summer holidays. Sarah Jayne Tait, aged six, from Edinburgh, came home one day upset and crying. Her left eye was painful and badly swollen. Her teachers and her family could see nothing in Sarah's eye, and neither could the doctors in the Sick Children's Hospital. Finally, a specialist at the Eye Pavilion put a probe round behind her eye – and out popped a baked bean! Sarah Jayne had no idea how the bean got there. She doesn't even like baked beans! *Scottish Sunday Post* 23 July 1989.

PULLING THE WOOL . . .

In three weeks, schoolboy K. Sivalingham from the Malaysian village of Sungai Siput, produced over 80 pieces of red, green, yellow, blue and white thread from his right eye. His mother, Vijayeletchumy Ganeson, 30, said it began one morning when he complained of pain in his right eye and started pulling threads from under the eyelid. 'He would wash his face and then the process would start all over again.' Satisfied that he was not tricking her, she took him to hospital, where staff maintained a round-the-clock vigil to ensure against fraud. They watched closely as the right eye swelled slightly about every two hours and a small ball of thread dropped out of the lid. The threads were always the same colour as the shirt he was wearing at the time. The medical profession was baffled. Tests established only one thing – the threads were genuine cotton.

As the boy's fame spread, hundreds arrived daily to camp outside his house, and his mother was obliged to take him on a circuit of doctors and *bomohs* (medicine men) in search of a cure. After several days of treatment with holy water from a Hindu temple, the threads stopped. *New Straits Times* 10+19 May; Vancouver (BV) *Sun* 27 May; *Sunday Express* 2 June 1985.

CHOP CHOP

Julia Schumansky, a 63-year-old grandmother from Hartsville, Tennessee, noticed 'a little knot on my backside' in July 1989, but didn't worry about it until it shifted and was jutting out of her left buttock. She had it checked out, and urgent exploratory surgery was carried out to see if it was a malignant tumour. 'When she awoke from surgery on 2 October, she was told that a pointed 4-inch chop bone had been removed. She couldn't remember the last time she had eaten pork chops.

Dr Roger Duke, Julia's physician, estimated from the amount of tissue which had grown up around the bone that it had been there from five to ten years. He speculated that the 5 foot 1 inch and 217 pounds of Julia's layers of fat had prevented her from feeling the original penetration. The nature of this penetration is not explained.

Frozen

Whether or not animals can be successfully revived after being frozen for indefinite periods, the fascinating thing about ice is that it preserves bodies intact ...

FROZEN ALIVE

On the morning of 19 January 1985, and while his parents slept, two-year-old Michael Troche wandered out of their Milwaukee, Wisconsin, house wearing only light pyjamas. The temperature outside had plummeted to 60 degrees below zero during a cold spell, breaking records from Michigan to Texas. He soon collapsed in the snow. When his anguished father found him several hours later, he was literally frozen stiff. His limbs were hardened, ice crystals had formed on and beneath his skin, and he had stopped breathing for an unknown time. He was rushed to the city's Children's Hospital where 18 doctors and 20 nurses worked on him for six hours. Dr Kevin Kelly, a specialist in hypothermia, described Michael as 'dead, extremely dead'. One report says that doctors actually heard the ice crystals in his body cracking as they lifted him onto the operating table. As his blood was warmed in a heart-lung machine, and his body thawed, drugs were used to prevent his brain swelling. His arms and legs began swelling as fluid leaked from ice-damaged cells, and incisions had to be made to allow the tissue to expand. Dr Thomas Rice said that they knew of no one who had survived when the core of their body had dropped below −16°C, as Michael's had done. He remained semi-conscious for over three days and then made rapid recovery. There is minor muscle damage to his left hand, and he has had some skin grafting on his limbs to cover the deep incisions, but he avoided critical brain damage. This is attributed to the wind-chill which froze him so rapidly that his metabolism had very little demand for oxygen. Our last report shows him leaving hospital after a good recovery. Detroit *News*, AP + major English dailies of 4 February; *Daily Mail* 1 March; *Daily Telegraph* 30 March 1985.

A WONDER FROM THE TUNDRA

Contemporary reports of entombed animals seem to be all but non-existent, so it seems all the more significant when a report appears in one of the more sober British newspapers, *The Times*, which describes the case as 'one of the geological oddities of the century'.

According to the Soviet news agency Tass, goldminers excavating at a depth of 30 ft below the surface of the Siberian tundra region of Yakutia discovered a torpid newt which they were astonished to see revive and begin to move when put down in the sun. 'It crawled slowly ... on its five-fingered limbs, turning its head, with round bulging eyes, from side to side.'

The miners took the newt to the geological department of their local mine, where it was kept for several days in a glass vessel before it died. The body was preserved and exhibited at the geological museum at Yakutsk, which also displays woolly mammoth remains found preserved in permafrost.

The fact that the newt is reported to have come from the same depth in the permafrost in which such remains have been found not unnaturally fuelled speculation as to the length of time the newt may have survived entombed in torpor. A Professor Nikita Solomonov, the director of the Institute of Biology at the Siberian department of the Soviet

Academy of Sciences, is quoted as saying 'Many species of salamander can remain in anabiosis (a state of reduced animation) in permafrost for tens, hundreds and even thousands of years and revive under favourable conditions.' He also stated there had been several very similar cases in Yakutia before.

If this startling claim of extended vitality in amphibians is substantiated, it would be of great significance to the study of entombed animals as a whole. However, scientists in the West have not yet been persuaded of the truth of such interpretations.

A more orthodox explanation for such cases was offered by an unnamed 'scientist' in the Natural History Museum in London, who recalled a similar case 15 years ago: 'An animal was thought to have revived after thousands of years, but it was decided eventually that it had slipped down a crack in recent times into the permafrost layer and hibernated until it was recovered.' *The Times* 26 June 1987.

● In July 1985, the body of a woman was discovered entombed in a glacier near Verbier, in the Swiss Alps. She was identified as Regina Spring, from England, who was reported to have disappeared on 2 August 1981, aged 34. *Standard* 30 July 1985.

● A glacier on Mont Blanc in France gave up the bodies of four Americans, entombed after their B-17 crashed in 1946. *Daily Record* 21 September 1988.

AN ICY HANGAR

In June 1988 six American P-38 fighters and two B-17 bombers were located under 260 feet of ice in Greenland. The saga began on 15 July 1942 when these planes, forming 'Bolero' squadron, were flying to a refueling stop in Iceland on the way to Britain. They ran into bad weather and a German submarine jammed their radio communications. Low on fuel and unable to find their destination they turned back to Greenland where they belly-landed on the ice about 10 miles inland. After 10 days all 25 crew were rescued, but a secret Norden bomb-sight was left aboard one of the planes. This was recovered afterwards by Major Norman Vaughan using a dog-sled. He was the last man to see the eight planes of the so-called 'Lost Squadron', and now is an eager member of the team which successfully located the planes. The picture dates from 1942 and shows one of the P-38s after it was forced into an emergency landing on the ice.

Hermits and Recluses

Here are some modern cases of those who, for one reason or another, have turned their back on their fellow-men.

RUNNING FROM THE WARS

D. B. Benson lived wild in the Kiamichi mountains of Oklahoma for 34 years. As an 18-year-old he was drafted into the Army Air Corps in September 1942 and was stationed in Texas. He was bullied mercilessly as an illiterate hick, and within a year he went AWOL. Back home in Heavener, Oklahoma, a friend told him the military police were after him and that he faced execution. Believing this to be true, he fled to the mountains with a bundle of clothes, a pistol, some ammo and a knife.

When the ammo ran out, he killed rabbits, squirrels and birds with stones. His throwing arm was deadly. When his Army clothes had become rags he found a coffee-can key and sharpened it on a rock to make a needle. An old sock provided thread to mend his clothes. These finally fell away, and he fashioned a loin-cloth out of an old piece of denim he found.

'I completely lost touch with humanity,' he said. 'I talked to the animals – even sang to the squirrels. Living in the outdoors I rarely got sick. When I did I'd take to a cave for a few days until the illness cleared up. Fresh streams were my bathtub, and fine sand became my soap. Soon I learned how to catch fish bare-handed for food.'

After some years, Benson found a dog. He named it 'Dog'. 'We became inseparable. He slept at my feet and hunted for both of us.' More years passed and Dog died of old age. Benson felt even more lonely. Middle age was creeping up on him. He could not move around as easily as before, and even a minor injury could keep him down for days.

Finally, in 1977, at the age of 53, he walked up to his parents' home and knocked on the door. His mother and father, aged 90 and 83 respectively, were no doubt suitably astonished. Eighteen months later he obtained an 'other-than-honourable' discharge from the Army, and became a free man ... or had he lost his freedom? *National Enquirer* 14 July 1981; *Daily Mail* 1 August 1979.

AWAY FROM IT ALL

Matteo Grillo, 15, was having supper at his home in Palermo, Sicily, in 1943, when a raid by British bombers began. He fled with his brothers and sisters seconds before their home was flattened. He ran to the forest and was still there 45 years later. In 1988, a picture of Matteo appeared in a newspaper and was recognized by his sister Rosalia who thought he was dead. He was shown the wonders of modern civilization, but decided to continue his hermit's life in his forest hut where he lives with 12 dogs, re-reading his Bible from cover to cover, and existing on a diet of fruit, berries, roots, herbs and spring water, varied with occasional picnic leftovers. *Daily Mail* 25 August 1988.

ALL A MISTAKE

December 1986 saw the death of Cesar Yakoub Doweik at the age of 82. He first came to Egypt early in the century and taught French for 15 years. Convinced (erroneously) that he would be forced to leave Egypt after the Suez war in 1956, because he was Jewish, he got his sister to hide him in her cellar – where he remained for the next 22 years, until Egyptian–Israeli relations improved in 1978. 'He was like a hermit who rarely talked and was too afraid to burn a light at night,' said his sister. All he had was a tiny radio and the Cairo newspaper *Al Akhbar*. When finally he left the cellar he had no desire to leave the house. *Weekly World News* 3 February 1987.

OVERSLEEPING

● Presley Bishop came home from work depressed on 1 October 1978 in Littleton, Colorado, and went to bed. He stayed there for three years, during which time he wore a hole in the bed, lost 9 stone, grew a beard down to his stomach and fingernails six inches long. In August 1981 his widowed sister Bernice, in desperation, called in the cops and he was moved to a nursing home bed in Denver. Asked by police how he felt he replied: 'Fine.' It was the first word he had uttered since he had taken to his bed. *Daily Star* 27 August 1981.

● In 1932 a young Russian woman in England came down with flu and was instructed by her doctor to stay in bed and rest until he saw her again. Unfortunately, he forgot to come back and the woman was still in bed 40 years later.

Her mother looked after her until she died, and then a brother-in-law took over. She was eventually seen by another GP and referred to gerontologist Dr Peter Rowe at Taunton in Somerset. It took seven months to persuade the by-now 74-year-old 'flu' victim to get back on her feet. Dr Rowe described the case in a 1978 issue of *The Lancet*.

● However, this lady doesn't hold the record for staying in bed. In the winter of 1917, an old woman of 94 died in Scarborough, Yorkshire, after two days' illness. She had taken to her bed 72 years before, when her father had forbidden her to marry her fiancé. She got up only once, to leave Cambridge for Scarborough.

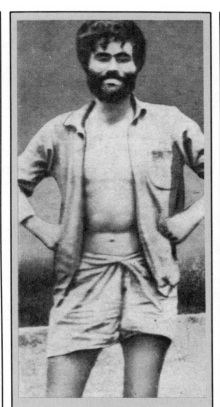

REAL-LIFE TARZAN

In 1956, a well-educated Australian of 27 called Michael Fomenko, sickened by the world of humans, retreated into the steamy snake-and-crocodile infested jungles of north-eastern Australia. He hunted wild boar with a knife, and birds with a bow and arrow which he had made himself. Now – because he has slowed with age and a leg that was ripped open by an attacking pig – he shoots game with a rifle which he bought with his bi-weekly disability cheque of a hundred dollars. He occasionally appears at Smith's Store in the settlement of Ayton on the edge of the jungle, where he spends his allowance on food and sweets for the neighbouring aborigines. *National Enquirer* 6 October 1981.

DARK SECRET

Ukrainian Dmitri Kozlovsky spent 36 years on rotting mattresses in two fetid tomb-like structures in fear of his past. At the beginning of the war he fought in the Soviet Army but was taken prisoner by the Germans, under whom he worked as a bricklayer. He eventually managed to successfully escape, but did not join the pro-Soviet Ukrainian resistance, fearing retribution because he had been given extra rations for good work performance. His family hid him in 1944.

The Soviet newspaper *Socialist Industry* said 'his eyes grew accustomed to the dark and his hearing became as sharp as a beast.' In December 1980, when he was found by police after all his relatives and close friends had died, he had forgotten how to speak and was filthy, unshaven and evil-smelling. He had lost all sense of time. 'He stood and trembled as if from fever and cried in a pitiful child's voice and tears poured from his colourless eyes eaten up by the darkness,' the newspaper said. It added that he had not been punished and was about to start work, aged 62, at a boiler plant. *AP* 12 June 1981.

Bungkas, a widowed father of three, climbed up a 40-foot palm tree on the Indonesian island of Madura in 1970 'for no other reason but to obtain safety', according to the newspaper *Kompas*. He stayed up there for the next 17 years. He never washed himself and lived on food and drink brought by relatives and visitors which he hoisted up in a plastic bag on the end of a string. *Canberra Times* 13 August 1987.

Fugues

The word means 'loss of awareness of one's identity, often coupled with disappearance from one's usual environment.' Concise Oxford Dictionary.

THE BIG SLEEP

On Christmas Day 1985, James McDonell rang the doorbell of his house in New York, to be greeted by his wife Anne. He had been missing for 15 years, and had been declared legally dead after 7 years.

His fugue began in 1971 with two car accidents in which he suffered concussion and other head injuries. One day he complained to a friend of a headache, went for a walk and never returned. He 'came to' on a Philadelphia street, with no identification, knowing only that his first name was James. He took the surname 'Peters' from a nearby store sign. The former postal supervisor said his memory returned when he bumped his head on Christmas Eve. *New York Daily News* 27 December 1985.

JOHN DOE HAS IDENTITY PROBLEM

In October 1989, police in Topeka, Kansas, found a man wandering without any identification. He said he didn't remember who he was or how he got there. He was known as John Doe until 10 February 1990, when relatives who saw him on television identified him as Melvin Wolf, 53, a small appliance repairman who had disappeared from his sister's home in Angleton, Texas, the previous August.

Then, a Topeka television station reported that Wolf was also Jim J. King, a successful insurance salesman from Burbank, California, who had gone missing on 31 March 1978 under 'suspicious circumstances'. Employees of a Prudential Life Insurance Company office in Los Angeles said they recognised the man as Mr King, their lost colleague, whom they thought had been abducted and killed. On 6 March, a third identity surfaced – that of Robert J. Hart, a Denny's restaurant employee in Washington D.C.

Mr Wolf/King/Hart went to stay with his Wolf relatives in Angleton at the end of February. His sister, Donna Caskey, said the family lost track of him for many years before he turned up in Angleton in 1986. During much of that time they heard stories that he was living in California. Rick Selig, a therapist at the Topeka Psychiatric Clinic, said the man suffered from psychogenic amnesia – total memory loss usually brought on by an extremely stressful event. He was trying to find out what this event was by hypnotherapy.

The Pentagon said that Mr Wolf joined the Army in 1953 and was stationed in West Germany from 1957 to 1960. He left the service in 1961. Although Wolf, King and Hart had different social security numbers, they listed the same birthplace, West Allis, Wisconsin, and the same high school in Johnson Creek, Wisconsin. However, the school says its records show that none of the three men studied there. Did they look up John Doe? Augusta (Georgia) *Herald* 13 March 1990.

WHITE SLAVERY

There was a legend in Ethiopia about the 'white natives': some white children up in the hills who had fair hair and blue eyes. No one seemed to know where they were. Then in the summer of 1989, Haile Mariam Gadessa, 25, and his sister Tegest, about 20, walked into the American consular office in Addis Ababa, claiming to be Americans abandoned 20 years earlier. 'I have a memory', said the girl. 'It is of my mother. She is very tall and white. And we lived in a house made of bricks.' Their skin was deeply tanned and cracked, and their features disfigured by years of exposure to the sun. They had light brown eyes and curly light brown hair.

All they knew of their past was what they were told by the native couple who raised them. The story went that their father had fallen ill, and together with their mother was flown out of Ethiopia for treatment. The children were left in the care of a housekeeper, an Oromo tribesman, who took them to live with his relatives in a mud hut. The boy was trained to tend cattle, sheep and goats, while the girl was given to another family as a maid. Mrs Carol Rose, the U.S. Consul, said: 'The mystery is that we have no record of the parents asking the embassy for help in finding the children, and neither does anyone else.' *Daily Express* 3 August 1989.

In the report in the *Sunday Mirror* (27 August 1989), Haile Mariam Gadessa had *two* sisters, Tegest and Lesa (all three are shown in a photograph), and it was Lesa who was given to another family as a maid. They claim they were tormented and beaten because of their skin colour.

The story gets transformed when reports by the Florida journalist Ron Laytner appear (*Sunday Mirror* 15 October; *Sunday Mail* (Scotland) 28 October 1989; *Take a Break* 31 March 1990). The second sister is not mentioned in these reports. Haile resembled a bent, arthritic old man. Tegest was thin and malnourished, with twisted hands. Both had broken noses and many missing teeth. They had been brought up in the Omo Valley by a family called Gadessa. The Gadessa woman said she was given them by a brother who said something terrible had happened to a white family where he worked as a guard. He handed them over with a photo album which the woman destroyed. She gave them

Haile Mariam Gadessa and his sister Tegest, who were abandoned by their white parents in Ethiopia twenty years ago.

Ethiopian names.

Research by Layter and others suggests that the parents were a white U.S. soldier and his wife. The father walked out on the family, and the mother was murdered in 1969 on her way to Nairobi with the children. Haile remembered the long drive, the breakdown, being a frightened toddler with his mummy suddenly not there, and him and his baby sister alone in a native village. The tribe numbered about 200, and they were seven hours' ride from the nearest road.

The children were overworked, beaten and starved. After Tegest reached puberty, she was constantly raped, sometimes by 20 men at a time. Once she complained to some passing policemen, but instead of protecting her they beat and raped her. She gave birth to a black baby in 1986 which she cared for devotedly. Two women befriended her: Gadessa's old mother and a woman in Sabeta, near Addis

Ababa, to whom she was hired out as a maid, and who paid for her schooling.

In Sabeta, Tegest saw her first white person. 'People said: "There is your family – why don't you go with her?" But I was afraid,' Tegest told Laytner through an interpreter. 'Another time, when I'd been beaten, I was taken to a clinic with white nurses. They felt my hair and examined my body. They were surprised that I spoke Oromigna, but they didn't say anything.' Heile saw a car in Sabeta when he was 17, the first one he had seen since he was kidnapped. He hoped to find his parents in it, but it held black people. Another time he ran after a car carrying whites, shouting that he was their kidnapped boy, but they ignored him. Eventually, Tegest's employer took pity on the lost children and arranged for them to be taken to the American consular office. 'My dream', said Tegest, 'is to live in America among my own tribe.'

Missing Persons

No one knows why people go missing – unless, of course, they're found.

VANISHING CHILDREN

● At 2.06pm, on 8 April 1969, April Fabb, 13, cycled out of Metton village, Norfolk. At 2.15 her bike was found half a mile down the narrow lane to Roughton. She had disappeared in broad daylight, within earshot of picknickers and workers in the fields.

● At about 3.00pm, on 5 March 1970, David McCaig, 13, began to bicycle the half-mile to school in the Wallasey area of Liverpool, for his favourite lesson in French. The next day his bike and cloak were found, and that's all.

● At noon 22 June 1974, Alison Chadwick, aged 10, left her home in Old Manor Drive, Isleworth, Middlesex. It was a normal Saturday lunchtime, her favourite bangers and mash was imminent – but she nipped out to fetch her swimming costume from a friend's house in the next street. That was the last time she was seen. Police took 15,000 statements, and no clue was too insignificant to follow up – but nothing could be discovered at all. *News of the World* 11 August 1974.

● At 7.30am, on 6 June 1964, Keith Bennet, 12, waved goodbye to his mother to walk the last few hundred yards to his Granny's house in Longsight, Manchester ... and has not been seen or heard of since.

● On 1 September, Pamela Exall, 21, went for a walk along the beach at Snettisham, Norfolk, never to be seen again. Late at night on 28 October, 15-year-old Kim Baille was dropped just outside her home in Red Cross Way, Southwark, South London, by the taxi she shared with three friends after a dance. Somehow she never made the 50 yards to her front door. *Daily Mirror* 6 September; *Sun* 6 November 1974.

These and other cases, unsolved to this day, were re-opened by Paulette Pratt in 1972 in a big feature called 'The Children who Vanish without a Trace' *Observer Magazine* 29 October 1972, only to find that in all cases the authorities were *still* baffled. Occasionally papers get this bee in their bonnets and do a feature on missing persons (MIs). For example, the *Sunday Mirror* for 18 + 25 August 1974 also chronicled the lack of progress in these, and the cases of Stephen Paul (vanished from outside his home in Fakenham, Norfolk, at 5.00–5.20pm, 2 September 1969); Christine Markham, last seen at 11.09, 21 May 1973 less than 200 yards from her Scunthorpe home; and Lucy Partington, 21, who left a friend's house at 10.15pm to catch the last bus to Cheltenham, on 27 December, and somehow didn't, though the stop was a short walk away.

Speaking of such cases, Paulette Pratt, wrote: 'Not the least baffling aspect of all this is the realization that no one knows how many children vanish in this way. A reasonable estimate is that several thousand children are reported missing each year in one circumstance or another, and a significant proportion are never found.' And of her efforts to determine just what that 'significant proportion' was, she adds: 'Scotland Yard was approached several times during the course of this research, but refused to give even a brief interview, on the grounds that missing persons procedure is being reorganized.' But even in the police network, 'There is as yet no attempt at the sort of national index for missing persons that there is for example, for stolen cars ... in the absence of research the national pattern is not known. And on a purely practical level, there is no central source to which detectives from any part of the country can refer, when a child vanishes without a trace.' But whatever the administrative hangups, cases continue to mount on a staggering pile.

MORE MISSING PERSONS

● Mrs Florence Newitt disappeared leaving behind a new £2000 car, a handsome income from rented property, and her washing-up half done in her home at Christchurch, Dorset. *Daily Express* 5 May 1974.

● Anna Saint, 26, drove a taxi, and on the morning of 9 December 1974, she was on duty as usual outside Newcastle station. Later that day, her blue cab was found abandoned in a quiet street three miles from the station. Her handbag, containing £28, was on the seat, her coat still in the boot. After extensive investigations, police confessed their mystification. *Daily Mirror* 11 December 1974.

● Graham Marden, 45, an unmarried businessman from Egmont Road, Poole, Dorset, filled up his red Volkswagen Polo at the Rownhams Service Station on the M27 motorway near Southampton at 5am. After paying his bill, he asked the cashier the way to the gent's lavatory, and was last seen walking towards it. After an hour, the cashier went to look for him, and then called the police, who searched the surrounding woods in vain with tracker dogs. Marden appeared to have no personal or financial worries. 'If he planned to disappear,' mused a police spokesman, 'why did he fill his car with petrol first and leave it at the pumps? And why choose a service station miles from anywhere? We are mystified.' *Portsmouth News* 25 January 1989.

CADAVER CONFUSIONS

In the 'Great Blow' of 1913 on the Great Lakes, 12 lake vessels vanished and 250 to 400 sailors perished. Many bodies, some from the Canadian steamer *J. J. Caruthers*, washed up along the eastern shore of Lake Huron. Thomas Thompson of Hamilton, Ontario, received a telegram from his daughter, Mrs Edward Ward: 'John has been drowned. Come at once.' Mrs Ward believed that her brother, a 27-year-old marine fireman, was among the dead from the *Carruthers* which listed a 'J. Thompson' on the payroll.

Thomas Thompson travelled to Goderich and viewed the body. Like his son, it bore the tattooed initials 'J. T.' on the forearm. Distinctive scars on John's nose and leg corresponded with scars on the dead man. Also matching were two deformed toes and some dental peculiarities. Mr Thompson and his wife and daughters all agreed it was John, and the body was sent to the undertaker. One daughter was not convinced, however. She knew that her brother's 'J. T.' tattoo was topped by an anchor, which was missing on the corpse – but she was overruled by her father.

Scanning a newspaper in Toronto, John Thompson read of his own death, and returned home to Hamilton to find his family in black, and a flower-bedecked coffin in the parlour. His mother was overjoyed, but his father, who had bought a graveyard plot and incurred other expenses, was able to contain his elation. The dead man was never positively identified, and was interred in Hamilton's Holy Sepulchre cemetery. Dwight Whalen: *What's Up Niagara* (1983).

Swamp Cat Fever

The best-known is probably the 'Surrey Puma', but out-of-place animals, particularly alien big cats (ABCs), are popping up everywhere, all the time.

The sighting of a strange animal at Bedhampton, just north of Portsmouth, on 21 May 1985, initiated the long-running saga of Hayling Island's Mystery Cat. Telecom worker Andrew Clarke had just boarded the 6:00 am train for Portsmouth when he caught sight of a four-foot long, lynx-like cat lying in an adjacent field. The police were alerted, via Andrew's mother, whom he phoned on reaching Portsmouth. Much to Mrs Clarke's annoyance, her son's sighting wasn't taken very seriously, with the police calling out 'Here, kitty, kitty' as they searched the field. Not the sort of treatment you would get in Godalming! *Portsmouth News* 21 May 1985.

In the event, however, Andrew Clarke had the last laugh. On 26 July 1988, a female North African swamp cat (*Felis chaus*) was knocked down and killed by a car on Hayling Island, a few miles south of Bedhampton. Late in the evening, Ron Ware observed the animal standing in West Lane and called out to it as he drew alongside in his station wagon. But as the cat stood motionless, another vehicle passed and collided with it. The driver didn't stop and 60-year-old Mr Ware took the animal's body to his home nearby. *News* 28 July 1988.

Some days later, when the cat was identified by Marwell Zoo Director John Knowles, the usual debate ensued on how the rare animal came to be on the island, and despite the fact that this animal is not resident in any English zoo, the ubiquitous travelling circus was blamed for its appearance. A circus *was* in the area at the time but the owners denied keeping wild animals.

Thoroughly perplexed by the affair, John Knowles said: 'One cannot think that a free-ranging animal is going to go over the causeway [half-mile-long road bridge] to Hayling. I would say somebody took it there by sea or by car.' *News* 9 May 1989.

Despite John Knowles's doubts, the cat may have gone over the causeway. Shortly before the swamp cat was killed, an identical animal was seen twice in the garden of Mrs J. Such at Farlington, five miles north-west of Hayling and if Andrew Clarke's 1985 sighting involved the same beast, it would appear to have lived perfectly happily in the area for at least three years. *News* 30 July 1984 + 18 May 1989.

Because of the fears that it had been illegally imported, the swamp cat was tested for rabies by the Ministry of Agriculture. No trace of the disease was found and

the body was returned to the Wares, who have recently had the animal stuffed as a charity fund-raising attraction.

Well, as far as the Ministry of Agriculture officials were concerned, the story ends here; as they rather smugly announced: 'We think it is very likely to be a one-off. We have a fair idea of where it [the swamp cat] came from, but the evidence is circumstantial and we cannot say any more about that.' *News* 30 July 1988.

Nevertheless, at 10:00 pm on 4 August 1988, this one-off suddenly became a two-off, when Raymond Oliver, cycling home from work, was on an industrial estate access road at Hilsea, some four miles west of Hayling. A two foot-tall, darkish, slate-grey, cheetah-like animal walked rapidly across the road, eight feet in front of him. This brief sighting in Quartermaine Road (a name redolent of darkest Africa!) ended with the animal vanishing into long grass bordering a railway embankment. *News* 18 May 1989.

Two weeks later, on 11 September, the three-off occurred, when schoolteacher Brian Swanson and his wife Brenda disturbed a totally black, cheetah-like cat while exercising their dogs on Portsdown Hill. Flushed out of hiding in a cereal field by the Swanson's alsatian-cross doberman, the animal bounded towards them through the approximately 18-inch-high crop, like a 'miniature cheetah'. On seeing the couple, however, it rapidly diverted its course and disappeared into nearby bushes. The observation had only lasted about three seconds, but the Swansons were able to note the cat's 'beautiful shiny coat', long tail and legs and pear-shaped ears. *News* 9 September 1989.

The next report takes us back to Hayling, where, at 11:00 am on 6 October, Bruce Eacott braked and skidded his car on Ferry Road to avoid hitting a 4-foot-long, grey, puma-like cat that bounded in front of him. Identical in every respect except colour to the Portsmouth 'cheetah', the animal turned its head to look at the startled driver before disappearing into roadside shrubbery. *News* 6 October 1988.

Following a rather daft item in the Portsmouth *News* on 7 October, in which Alexander McKee (discoverer of the *Mary Rose*) was pictured attempting to entice the animal with a plate of 'Whiskas', the cat refused to appear for a whole month. Then around 16 December, PCs Stewart Paton and Pat Curran (a name to Spoonerize!) were driving near the mainland side of Hayling Bridge at 3:30 am, when they encountered a strange animal in the road.

PC Paton described the event as follows: 'There were two foxes and this very distinctive other animal, which had no tail, playing together in the road. It was about the same height as the foxes, but it had very long legs and its body wasn't as long as theirs. It was a very strange animal, definitely not a fox.' As the pair drove towards

The swamp cat killed by a car on Hayling Island in 1988.

the group, the animals scattered and disappeared into roadside bushes. *News* 16 December 1988.

This rather weird report was to be the last known sighting of the Hayling ABC until things started hotting up again in the Summer of 1989, with the Portsmouth *News* mentioning two undetailed reports from Emsworth and Purbrook. The paper also reported that Hayling Animal Sanctuary owner John Walker intended to trap the creature, and even the Ministry of Agriculture were back on the scene, coyly suggesting that a two-off may, after all, have been possible. Hayling police, meanwhile, said that they were investigating the situation.

Felicity, the Scottish Puma

The story that follows shows how hard it is to establish the truth about ABCs through a fog of poor reporting, even when, as in this case, the cat was captured!

In October 1979 Farmer Ted Noble saw a large cat-like creature stalking the ponies at Kerrow Farm, Cannick. He was 'in no doubt it was a lioness'. Six policemen and two gamekeepers searched the area nearby without success. Scottish *Sunday Express + Sunday Mail* 28 October 1979.

Over the next few months at least a dozen witnesses in the Cannick area reported seeing some form of big cat, and Forestry Commission rangers were warned not to go out alone, and to carry rifles. 'We do not believe there is a lioness, but we are taking precautions just in case.' In February the police announced their searches to be a failure. Aberdeen *Evening Express* 14 November 1979; *Observer* 10 February 1980.

The following summer, Marcus Pacitti, of Aberdeen and a friend were walking in Achnashellach Forest, when they were confronted with what they first took to be a stag but which 'must have been a puma'. Scottish *Daily Record* 26 July 1980. On 30 July 1980, the *Daily Express* reported that there had been two sightings in the 'past few days'.

Since his first sighting Ted Noble continued to catch glimpses of a huge cat, and to find sheep with their throats ripped and bones crunched. Near the beginning of August 1980 he saw it again. The police, having searched the area before and found nothing, did not respond. Noble and a neighbour decided to set their own traps. Scottish *Sunday Mail* 17 August 1980.

On 6 September 1980 an Australian tourist and his wife, returning to Inverness after visiting the Highland Gathering at Braemar, saw what appeared to be 'a heavily built black lioness ... with a long tail'. This was at 6:45pm, near Corgarff, Inverness-shire, on the Ballater to Tomintoul road, not far from the infamous 'Devil's Elbow'. Aberdeen *Press & Journal* 9 September 1980.

Back in neighbouring Rossshire: shock! ... the 'puma' is shot! Double shock! ... it's a dog! Two workers on the Crannich Estate, Ardross, near Alness, tracked for two miles a black beast they believed to be a panther, responsible for attacking sheep, lambs and even deer. When shot, they discovered it was a feral cross-bred Alsatian/Collie. The 'Great Highland Puma Mystery' was pronounced 'solved'. *The Scotsman* of 27 October 1980 included a photo of the unfortunate dog looking suitably villainous.

Several days later, at Rancho Noble, another mystery cat is in the bag. Using a sheep's head as bait, Ted Noble finally captured his puma. It was a vindication: 'People were beginning to think I was nuts the way I was obsessed with capturing this animal.' The authorities had never taken seriously the idea of a puma on the loose, nor the claims of many witnesses – now here, in a cage, was a real live puma, a genuine *felis concolor*. Ted, and his son Julian, were carrying out their daily check of the trap when they heard growling and knew they were successful. The trap was near the cottage of pensioner Janet Chisholm, who had seen the beastie a number of times, and had encouraged Ted to trap it.

Naturally many papers claimed the end of another 'Mystery of the Glens', while a few others – notably *The Scotsman* – reported that Ted 'and others who have seen the tracks ... think the puma may be one of two. Farmer Arthur Cadman, Ted's neighbour, said the second puma was lighter in colouring. Mrs Chisholm even claimed she had seen *three puma cubs* in the area.

Eddie Orbell, director of the Highland Wildlife Park, near Aviemore, was one of those dismissive 'experts' who had pooh-poohed the idea of a puma on the loose, preferring to believe that witnesses were misinterpreting carelessly or inadequately observed more common animals. Orbell was asked by police to give this one a home. 'I will obviously have to eat my words,' he said sheepishly to reporters. He turned up with a stun-gun, but contrary to stories of the beast 'snarling and spitting' to the contrary, he didn't need it. The puma went quietly. No one smelled a rat, just yet . . .

Biggest coverage was in the Scottish *Daily Record*; other sources include *The Times, Guardian, Daily Telegraph, Daily Mail, Daily Star, Daily Express, The Scotsman, Shropshire Star*; all of 30 October 1980.

More questions were raised than answered by the capture of the puma at Noble's farm. Far from eating his words, he huffed: 'I've never believed there was such a thing as this legendary "Highland Puma". I can't believe this animal has been roaming wild

since 1973 . . .'

What alerted him? The puma, it seems, far from being a terror-of-the-glens for seven (other reports say four) years, was elderly, rheumatoid in one leg, lame, well-groomed, overweight, so tame it purred for visitors to the Wildlife Park the next day, and generally too domesticated to have survived in a wild environment. 'I fear somebody may have played a hoax on Mr Noble', said Orbell, suggesting that some rash owner had released his unwanted pet only days, or even hours, before the capture. Police, worried by the growing muttering of 'Hoax!', called off their search for the remaining one or more pumas that only hours before they had been so ready to believe existed in the area. *Daily Mail + Daily Record + Daily Star + Daily Express + Daily Telegraph + Guardian + Aberdeen Evening Express* 31

October 1980.

The easy way out would be to believe that someone planted the puma in Ted Noble's trap. Any suggestions of feral pumas gives the authorities a headache. But Ted wouldn't keep quiet, bristling with indignation at suggestions that he might even have been party to the 'hoax'. He received timely support from Bob High, secretary of the local Farmers' Union, who saw the developing media circus as diverting attention from the *real* issue – the continuing depredation of livestock. He said many farmers, particularly in the Eastern Highlands, had seen the puma and would not speak out for fear of being laughed at. *Daily Record* 1+3 November 1980.

On 16 November 1980 two sheep were found savaged near Garve, in Ross-shire. According to Dr Hans Kruuk of the Institute of Terrestrial Ecology, they were killed in a way 'very typical' of puma. Garve is about 20 miles north of Cannick and well within a puma's hunting range. Farmer Eddie Smith, who lost one of the sheep, says: 'I feel that a second puma is on the loose'. *Daily Record* 17 November; *The Scotsman* 18+20 November 1980.

CAT STUFFED

Felicity was a main attraction at the Highland Wildlife Park near Kingussie before dying in February 1985, at the ripe old age of 16. She has been stuffed by an Edinburgh taxidermist, and is now on permanent display at Inverness museum. *Scotsman* 23 September 1985.

Felicity, the puma found wild in the Highlands, reclines (stiffly) on an Edinburgh park bench.

Lizard Man

In the last hundred years at least sixteen 'abominable swamp slobs' (ASS) have been reported on mainland U.S.A., including the South Carolina Lizard Man.

The 'Lizard Man' episode began when Christopher Davis, a shy black youth of 17 from Brownstown near Bishopsville in South Carolina, drove his father's brown 1976 Toyota Celica down a deserted road across Scrape Ore Swamp on his way home. A short distance past the swamp, near an open field and a cotton crop, he had a flat tyre and pulled over to fix it. As he was putting the tools away, he saw something running across the field towards him. It was about 25 yards away and had red glowing eyes.

Davis jumped into the car. Jerking the door shut, he found himself in a tug-of-war with the creature, which grabbed a partially rolled-down car window. 'I could see him from the neck down – the three big fingers, long black nails (one report says 14 inches long!) and green rough skin. He was strong.' He got the door shut and took off. 'I looked in my mirror and saw a blur of green running. I could see his toes, and then he jumped on to the roof of my car. I thought I heard a grunt and then I could see his fingers through the front windshield, where they curled round the roof.' One report said the creature grabbed the windshield wipers. Davis accelerated and swerved, and the creature tumbled off into the darkness. Other versions of his testimony add that the creature was at least seven feet tall, had long arms, skin like a lizard, snake-like scales and mossy arms. Also that the creature clung to his door handle as he drove away, only letting go when he reached 35 to 40 m.p.h. Another variant has the creature jumping on the roof after Davis had driven only two yards. It then fell off and chased

A similar frog-like creature witnessed by police officers in Loveland, Idaho, in 1972.

on foot up to 40 m.p.h. According to one account, the Lizard Man 'reeks of rot, and has a disturbing orthodontia problem'.

When Chris Davis reached home, he honked until his parents came to the door and then he ran inside. His father, Tommy, an electrician, investigated but found nothing except the wing mirror was 'twisted round funny'. A few days later he found scratches on the roof. 'All I can tell you is that my son was terrified that night,' he said. 'He was hysterical, crying and trembling. It took a while before he was calmed down enough to tell us what happened.'

Chris Davis told his family and friends about the creature, but didn't call the police, figuring they wouldn't believe him. Two weeks later, on 14 July, Tom and Mary Waye found their Ford 'chewed up' near the swamp. Besides scratches, trim had been pulled off and bite marks were visible in the fender well. Some reports said a hood ornament was missing and wires were pulled out of the engine. Police investigated, and a friend of Davis told them what the latter said he had seen. Davis was called in to tell his tale. The creature was dubbed Lizard Man and the story hit the papers. Sheriff's deputies and neighbours spoke highly of Davis, the youngest of seven children. 'We checked out his reputation and he's a pretty clean-cut kid, no drinking or drugs,' said Lee County Sheriff Liston Truesdale. 'He's also agreed to take a polygraph test or go under hypnosis. We may do that when I get a chance.'

After Lizard Man had hit the headlines, a construction worker called George Hollomon came forward to say that in late June he was filling a jug with artesian water near the swamp when a 'big healthy creature with big eyes' jumped at him from the woods, and chased him down a desolate road that runs along the swamp's south side. By the end of August, Sheriff Truesdale was maintaining that the Holloman sighting was 8 or 9 months earlier. He saw 'a large object that at first he thought was a tree,' said Truesdale. 'Then he looked round and saw it moving. It was huge and black, and when a car passed and light reflected from its eyes, they looked sorta reddish. Then he stated that it ran back into the swamp.'

State trooper Mike Hodge began spending his midnight shifts patrolling the swamp with Lee County Deputy Wayne Atkinson. They both came to believe that here was definitely something out there. On the night of 24 July, teenagers Rodney Nolf and Shane Stokes from nearby Turkey Creek were cruising near the swamp with two girlfriends about 3:00 am when 'something dark' darted 20 feet in front of their car. 'It was too big to be a deer. It stood on its hind legs, but was too muscular to be a man. It seemed to be about seven feet tall,' said Stokes, 15. 'It turned its head once and its eyes glowed, don't know exactly what colour. But it ran across the road past the bridge and into the

The original 'Creature from the Black Lagoon', from the classic 1950s B-movie.

swamp where Interstate 20 meets Highway 15.' The boys wanted to investigate, but their girlfriends refused. Instead they drove to the sheriff's department.

'I don't doubt they saw something,' said Anderson. 'They were visibly upset.' After checking the site, Atkinson and Hodge drove down tree-shrouded and unmetalled Bramlett Road leading into the swamp, and saw three 40-gallon cardboard drums that had been dragged from a dump, crushed and scattered on the road. A few saplings had their tops ripped off about 8 feet up. Then they noticed enormous three-toed footprints 14 inches long, 7 inches across and an inch deep in the hard ground. The prints were 40 inches apart and the officers followed them for 400 yards. They drove to the end of the road, returning five minutes later, when they found fresh tracks across their tyre marks, leading into the

woods. They both felt as if they were being watched. A heavy shower washed the tracks away the following afternoon, but three plaster casts had been taken which Sheriff Truesdale intended sending, along with some photographs of other footprints, to the FBI for identification. The sheriff was convinced there was *something* in the swamp. *Houston Chronicle* 31 July + Fort Wayne (IN) *News Sentinel* 30 July + *Boston Globe* 30 August 1988.

● **The Lizard Man excitement died away after August 1988, but in the following summer six residents, all credible witnesses like Davis, swear that they saw a large oblong object in the sky that looked like a turtle on its back with lights on it, the brightest lights, other than the sun, they had ever seen. Charlotte (NC)** *Observer* **23 July 1989.**

Monsters of the Deep

We all know about 'Nessie'. But once you start looking you find that almost every deep lake contains its own monster, and the oceans are full of them . . .

LAKE MONSTERS: SWEDEN

● Anton Stockel, of Kiruna, had taken his son's family to their summer cottage in Salmi, near Lake Tornea. They had just begun boating when his grandson, Per, cried: 'Grandpa, what is that moving on the lake?' Stockel said: 'We saw, about 400 metres away, a creature which slowly moved towards the deeper waters. Its colour was coal black, and its length about 15–20 metres.' Stockel said his father had seen a monster in the lake 'well over 60 years ago'.

● Sweden's most famous monster – the *Storsjoodjuret* (=the monster of Lake Storsjon) – has been seen again, wriggling in the water with serpentine movements. A family of three, from the town of Gavle, spotted its humps just above the surface at about 23:30 one evening. They estimated its length at 10–20 metres. It left a huge wash when it finally disappeared. *Arbetet* 17 July 1985.

At this time of year the sun is above the horizon most of the night, so it is reasonable to suppose there was enough light, at half past eleven, for a good sighting. 'Storsjon' means 'The Great Lake', so the monster might also be called 'The Great Lake Monster'.

TWO LAKE MONSTERS

It seems that two motorists, George Locke and Robert Cooke, decided to camp for the night on the shore of Echo Lake near Hay City, Nebraska, when their car became stuck in mud. 'They were awakened in the middle of the night by a tremendous splashing in the lake, and looked up just in time to see a huge animal, the like of which they had never seen, disappearing in the darkness. They describe the animal as having a neck as long as a giraffe's and a horn in the middle of its forehead.' It was also said that local farmers blamed the mysterious disappearances of their livestock on the monster. *Daily Express* 16 July 1923.

STORSJON HUNT

A new investigation of Lake Storsjön, in central Sweden, was announced in April by Sten Rentzhog, director of the local Ostersund museum and director of the newly-founded Society for the Investigation of the Great Lake. He said a 12-man team would probe the 243-feet-deep lake this summer, possibly using submarines.

Lake Storsjön has a long 'monster' tradition, and sighting reports go back 350 years. Rentzhog's group has collected 400 accounts dating 'between 1635 and last month'. Lars Thofeldt, a botanist and teacher, said sightings had described 'large worm-like creatures . . . [and creatures] with a long undulating neck with a horse's mane.' An interesting feature is that one of the earliest accounts says the beast is large enough to coil itself around one of Storsjön's many islands. *Sydsvenska Dagbladet Snällposten* 5 April; *Saginaw News* (MI) 10 April; Nairobi *S. Nation* 24 May 1987.

On 25 April 1977, a Japanese fishing-vessel, the Zuiyo-maru, *found a strange carcass in its nets as it trawled in waters east of Christchurch, New Zealand right. Forensic opinion was that the animal had been dead about a month. It smelt so bad that the crew had to throw it back, but not before Michihiko Yano had taken photographs and made the inset sketch. Subsequent scientific examination failed to reach any definite conclusion about what appears to be a plesiosaur which had somehow survived for millenia.*

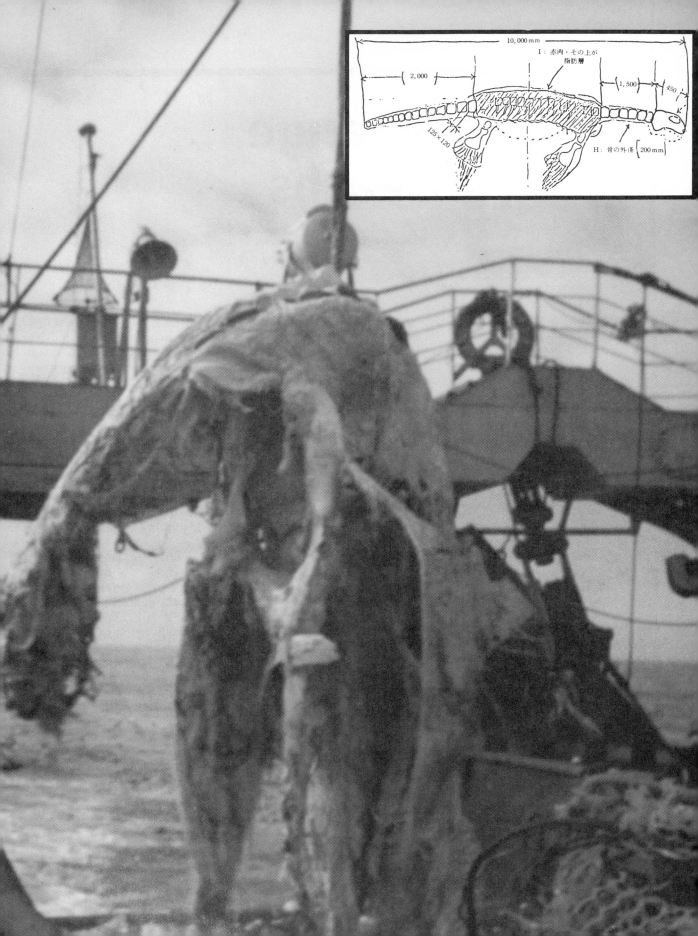

I：赤肉・その上が脂肪層

10,000mm

2,000

1,500

450

125×120

H：骨の外径 200mm

Strange Deaths

Dying is a strange business at the best of times, but some deaths have a particularly strange quality to them . . .

MARSEILLES MURDER?

Monsieur Emile Herve, 47, was taken ill at home, and police inspector Jean Darian drove Dr Joseph Cambassedes to his house in the rue Camille Flammarion. As a power failure plunged the Herve house into darkness, they were taken upstairs to the sickroom by a member of the family with candles. They left the door open for more light as the doctor bent over his patient. The doctor said: 'We are too late, he has just died!' Immediately the door slammed shut, blowing out the candles, and a gunshot rang out. Then the door was opened as the family rushed in to find out what had happened, their candles revealing an astonishing scene. The doctor was face-down over his dead patient, dead with blood oozing from a gunshot wound in his back – and on the floor by the inspector was a .22 rifle. Detectives were called, and an examining magistrate ordered an immediate reconstruction of the scene. The two dead men were left on the bed, the same candles were lit, the door was opened, the rifle (which had been fingerprinted) was stood back against the wall. After a search failed to find an intruder, and the windows were found closed from the inside, all the circumstantial evidence pointed to the inspector. They went through the reconstruction several times, the inspector still protesting his innocence – but it was only near dawn that he was cleared – as he was implicated – by an accident. A gust of wind slammed the door shut, knocking the rifle down, with its muzzle pointing to the bed.

THE FATAL KISS

The *Lanzhou Evening News* said that a bridegroom killed his new wife at a wedding reception in north-east China with a kiss on the neck which was too passionate and long. Guests heard a scream and rushed in to find bride and groom unconscious on a sofa. Doctors decided that the kiss had caused heart palpitations. *Shropshire Star* 1 October 1986.

NOVEL DEATHS

● A 70-year-old Long Island woman, Eleanor Barry, was suffocated in her bedroom, on 18 December 1977, when one of the many 'towers' of books, old newspapers and press-clippings fell, knocking others, pinning her to the floor and muffling her cries. *Minneapolis Star* 21 December 1977.

HOLE IN THE HEAD

In the movie *Network* the late Peter Finch gave an Oscar-winning performance as a batty newscaster called Howard Beale, who threatens to commit suicide on television before millions of viewers. The suicide which may have given the writers the idea happened back in 1974 when 30-year-old Chris Chubbock shot herself in the head while reading a news item. She was the presenter of a local news programme, reading the news and interviewing local personalities. Soon after the live programme began, technical trouble ruined a film clip of a shooting in a Sarasota bar. Ms Chubbock continued saying: 'In keeping with Channel 40's policy of bringing the latest news in living colour, you are going to see another first – attempted suicide.' Then, pulling a .38 revolver from her lap beneath the desk, she held it to the back of her head and fired. As she slumped forward thousands of viewers saw the screen blacked out. A spokesman for the television company later said she must have planned the attempt because they found on her desk an 'unscheduled script' outlining a special news bulletin on her own suicide. *The Sun* 16 July 1974.

The killer telephone, after the pre-Raphaelite painting The Death of Chatterton.

KILLER PHONES

● Jason F. Findley, 17, of Piscataway, New Jersey, passed a stringent all-day physical examination for acceptance into the U.S. Military Academy at West Point on 16 May 1985. On 21 May he was at his grandmother's house after a day's work at Muhlenberg Hospital, Plainfield, New Jersey, waiting for his mother to pick him up. He was talking to his girlfriend, Marsha Stevens, on the phone when she heard an odd click on the line. This was followed by a gasp and the sound of the television in the background. Jason's grandmother found him unconscious, still holding the phone in his left hand. He was pronounced dead shortly afterwards at Muhlenberg hospital.

A preliminary autopsy failed to determine the cause of death. The New Jersey Bell Telephone Company found the telephone properly grounded and working normally. 'There was no indication of any extraordinary charge of elec-

tricity,' said a spokesman. 'If there had been a large electrical charge, the phone would have been damaged and the lines burned – and there is no evidence of that having happened.' Findley was lying on a wooden bed which couldn't conduct electricity.

The case was referred to Marius Lombardi, special forensic investigator with the New Jersey Medical Examiner's Office, who told AP wire services on 31 May that about six people had died in the United States in similar circumstances. A New Jersey woman contacted his office to say she was knocked unconscious for two hours in 1984 by a high-voltage shock from her telephone. Several weeks before the Findley death, a man from Whitehouse Station, New Jersey, was found unconscious with a telephone in his hand. He said later that he had experienced an electric jolt.

In 1984, nearly 12,000 people in the U.S.A. were taken to emergency rooms because of

injuries related to telephones, according to the Consumer Product Safety Commission in Washington. Of those cases, 100 people died, although the Commission didn't know (or reveal) the exact details.

Lombardi said that Findley had a haemorrhage of the inner ear, leading him to suspect that he had died either from an acoustic shock, an inaudible high-pitched sound capable of stopping the heart; or from an electric surge. Lombardi disagreed with the telephone spokesman, saying it *was* possible that a lightning bolt had travelled along the phone wires without leaving visible damage. There had been an electric storm over Scotch Plains New Jersey the night Findley died. Huntsville *Times* 30 May; AP newswire 2 June; *The New York Times* 11 September 1985.

● Two people were killed in Toulouse, France, by lightning travelling along telephone wires, according to police reports. One was a fireman being alerted by a colleague to deal with storm damage, and the other was a young girl telephoning her boyfriend, who was thrown to the ground. *Neue Zurcher Zeitung* (Zurich) 18 August 1984.

● Telephones can kill in more indirect ways. A 28-year-old Brooklyn woman speaking on a public telephone was killed when lightning struck a flower-pot on a ledge eight storeys above her, causing it to fall about 115 feet on to her head. A passer-by had to tell the victim's mother, left hanging on the phone. *Daily Express* 17 July; *Canberra Times* 18 July 1985.

Mysterious Deaths

'Cause of death unknown' is always a more disturbing verdict than any other. Here are some unsolved deaths that remain mysterious . . .

HEADS IN THE SAND

In April 1982 the body of a man, wearing only underpants, was found on a beach at Woolacombe, North Devon. He was kneeling, with his head buried in the sand. Police established his identity as Michael Townsend, an apparently fit 60 year old from Bath. A police officer told the coroner's inquest that at 3:15pm on the day of the death, he was on the cliff at Marine Drive and watched through binoculars as a man slowly walked out to sea. The officer, John Iddes, thought it was odd that the man appeared to make no effort to swim, but losing sight of him, assumed he had returned to shore. At 3:40pm the body was discovered in the strange position on the beach. With some understatement the coroner concluded: 'This was a most unusual death.' *North Devon Journal + Herald* 22 April 1982.

THE SCREAMING DEATH

A coroner at Pangbourne, Berkshire said there was no physical explanation of the sudden death of Mrs Sheila Shearer, a healthy mother aged 30 – it seemed likely, he added, that a bad dream caused her to die of fright. Her husband, Hugh, said that on the morning of Monday, 20 October, his wife did not get up when the alarm-clock went off, but began breathing heavily and shouting. 'Her eyes were wide open and fixed. She was shouting loudly, so I gave her a good shaking but this had no effect whatever.' Then suddenly she was dead. *The Times* 23 October 1969.

At about 6:00am, Sergeant Robert Rush, of Santa Maria, California, who had just returned from Vietnam three days previously, was roused from sleep. His wife Patricia was shaking him. Then she gave a short scream and collapsed dead. Resuscitation attempts by Rush and a policeman failed to revive her; and there were no clues to her death. Patricia was 23 years old. It's not quite true that there were no clues – there was one which was both tantalizing and useless. The girl's parents revealed that Patricia's sister, Beverley, died in a similar manner in 1963, aged 17. She had been swimming, in Porterville, California, when she emerged from the pool, looked around wildly with a horrified expression on her face, gave a ten-second scream, stopped breathing and fell dead. An autopsy then failed to identify any cause of death. The parents, who have two surviving daughters, say they are worried in case the same happens to them, and felt that in Patricia's case too, the cause of death would remain a mystery. This was so – Dr John P. Blanchard, Santa Barbara County's autopsy surgeon, could only find that the girl died of 'natural but undetermined causes'. Newport *News*, Virginia + *Times-Herald* Reno, Nevada + *Evening Gazette* 18 January 1968.

CAUSE OF DEATH . . . UNKNOWN!

Three boys, aged between 16 and 20, were found dead in the living-room of a house in Nottinghamshire in early February 1972. They had been playing guitars – which were acoustic – no electrical equipment around. One was the son of the woman who owned the house, the other two had been put up for the night. When the woman came back from shopping she found one boy slumped in a chair, guitar on lap, the others on the floor. A detective inspector said: 'The cause of death at this moment is a complete mystery.' One wisp of a clue: the lady said the house was noticeably warm. *Sun* 9 February 1972.

MANHOLE COVERS TURN NASTY

Odis R. Sitton met his end at the hands of an apparently enraged 110-lb manhole cover as he drove to work through the streets of Rochester, New York, reports the *Victoria* (British Columbia) *Times-Colonist* of 31 August 1989.

Sitton, 57, was travelling down one of the town's main roads at 6:00am on 30 August when – as our picture shows – the cover leapt from the road and smashed through the windscreen of his car.

Police and gas board officials ruled out the possibility that a gas explosion had sent the cover flying. They were reduced to suggesting it had been dislodged by another vehicle, perhaps a truck, driving over it.

Officer Thomas Nagel said the solid steel cover had been fitted only the day before, in place of one that had been cracked. UPI/West Warwick (Rhode Island) *Kent County Daily Times* 31 August, and

the *Weekly World News* 17 October, which also has the story, reports that the unfortunate Mr Sitton was 'on his way to work on the construction of a sewer tunnel when the sewer lid killed him.'

Another manhole cover killed a pet bull-terrier in Harlem on 15 December 1989, reported UPI on the 16th. The cover had mysteriously become electrified, causing the pooch to leap head-high after stepping on it.

HIGHLAND MYSTERY

On 19 September 1938 a highlander came across the body of a man by a stream on the south face of Ben Avon, near Braemar in Scotland. The next day a police party of six set out to find the spot. They found a man in a dark suit with a light check pattern face-down at the edge of the stream. Nearby was a plain walking-stick, a bowler hat, and a brown attaché case containing pyjama trousers, two collars, a toilet roll, scissors and matches. On a rock ledge was set out some shaving gear, and it seemed to the party that the man had been about to shave when whatever happened happened. He'd been dead for two months – there had been no reports of missing persons, and had nothing on him to help identify him. The Grampian police were baffled by the man's dress, completely out of place for camping out halfway up a Cairngorm mountain.

DEATH BY YOGA

● Robert Antosczyk, 29, a yoga instructor and university student, of Ann Arbor, Michigan, apparently died while meditating in a yoga posture. He was found, two days dead, still in the position. Doctors are mentioned as thinking that his heart slowed down sufficiently to starve his brain of oxygen, finally stopping it forever. So much for yoga. *Daily Express + Daily Mirror* 30 June 1975.

Resurrections

Nobody comes back from the dead, of course.
Or do they . . . ?

DEATH IS A BAD HABIT

Musyoka Mututa, 60, had been lying for a day in his coffin in the village of Kitui, 100 miles from Nairobi, when pall-bearers came to his home, sprayed the supposed cholera victim with insecticide to ward off flies – and he sat up asking for a drink of water.

Musyoka had come back from the dead before, according to reports in Kenyan newspapers the *Daily Nation* and the *Standard.* When he was three, his body, wrapped in sheets and blankets, was being lowered into a grave when he let out a cry.

After another kiss-of-death, he told reporters: 'There appeared to be a row over why I was picked. Some angels decided to return me. I sat thinking under their wings, then they escorted me back to earth. Death shall finally come. This I am certain about.' And he was right. Four months later he 'died' again, was left unburied for two days in case of revival, but this time the angels let him in. *Daily Express* 27 May; *Daily Mail* + *Sun* 1 June; *Philadelphia Enquirer* 2 June; *Daily Mail* 23 September 1985.

GRAVE MISGIVINGS

The funeral service of an 81-year-old Berlin man was interrupted when mourners heard him clearing his throat in the coffin. He was rescued and revived successfully. The incident drew a lot of public discussion in which the public could hardly have been reassured by the statement from Professor H. J. Mallach that in West Germany alone at least 20 persons a year are buried alive. Following on the statement by Dr Peron-Autret that about 200 people a year suffer the same fate in the U.S.A., the lack of attention to this horrifying phenomenon seems surprising. Helsinki *Helsingen Sanomat* 27 October 1983.

ON THE WAY OUT

● For seven hours, relatives of Kabilo Kiptoo, a woman from Kararia, 150 miles north of Nairobi, believed she was dead, according to the Kenya News Agency (26 June 1987). She was reputedly 130 years old. Her burial was arranged the same day. As her coffin was about to be lowered into the ground, she sat up, talking incoherently, and stepped out of her coffin. When they realized their mistake, villagers slaughtered a white lamb and scattered its intestines around the grave to prevent evil spirits haunting the district. People who come back to life signify good fortune for the tribe. *Standard* 26 June; Houston *Chronicle* + *Bild* (Germany) + *Daily Mirror* 27 June 1987.

● On the 9 August 1987, Munir Mahidun, 65, had been ill for a week with asthma at his house in Pontian, about 180 miles south of Kuala Lumpur in Malaysia. His wife, his eight children, and neighbours believed he was dead when his constant coughing stopped, along with his pulse, and his body became cold and motionless. About four hours later, when the last rites were being administered at the house before burial, he sat up and asked why everyone was crying. *New Straits Times* + *Express* + *Star* 12 August; *Victoria Times-Colonist* 13 August 1987.

● In June 1986, Henry Lodge, 63, had a heart attack while fixing fuses. As he was about to be dissected by Dr Phillip Campbell in the Los Angeles mortuary, he opened his eyes and yelled for help. Lodge was back home at the time of the report, but Dr Campbell was on leave suffering from nervous exhaustion. *Sunday Express* 8 June 1986.

● When a tyre burst in 1977, the hearse carrying Gerry Allison to his funeral on the outskirts of Los Angeles overturned and crashed tail-first into the front window of a rival undertaker's parlour. The hearse doors burst open and flung the coffin through the window. Bystanders were astonished to see Allison, dressed in white burial robes, stepping out of the shattered glass. The crash had brought out of a coma which doctors had mistaken for death. *Weekend* 14–20 September 1977.

● On 21 May 1980, police in Martinsburg, West Virginia, found a former commercial pilot, Charles K. Herrell, 56, unconscious in his car. They took him to the county jail, where coroner Walter Fix declared him dead. Just before he was placed in a cooler at the Brown Funeral Home, an attendant unzipped the plastic bag for a final check and found him breathing. He was rushed to hospital and revived. He suffered from hypoglycaemia, characterized by blackouts when his blood sugar dropped too low. *Middlesex News* 23 May; *New Straits Times* 24 May 1980.

● On 8 December 1985, Kishan Buwaji Katore and his wife were found lying in a pool of blood in their house in what appeared to be a double murder. The wife's head had been severed and Katore's throat was slit. Both were pronounced dead. A few hours later, a frightened policeman heard knocking from inside the refrigerated hospital morgue. He found the blood-stained Katore shivering inside. He recovered after emergency surgery. *Houston Chronicle + Duluth (Maryland) News-Tribune + Guardian + Sun* 12 December 1985.

● In 1969, Mrs Kim Nevitt was found on a beach at Southport, Lancashire, apparently dead from hypothermia following a drug overdose. Dr John Benstead had a knife poised to begin the post-mortem in a nearby hut when he noticed a tear. She was rushed to hospital and made a complete recovery. **Daily Telegraph 16 January 1987.**

GRAVE DISTURBANCE

Togbui Siza Aziza, a Togolese jujuman, was placed in a coffin; the lid was nailed down; the

Covered with earth and mortar, Aziza climbs from the grave, watched by an astonished crowd.

● On 18 March 1983, Karla Wood, a cocktail waitress of 22, from Champaign, Illinois, was found in a death-like state from a drink and drugs overdose. Placed on a morgue table ready for autopsy, she was noticed swallowing. Her condition later said to be 'satisfactory'. **St Louis Globe Democrat 18 April; Daily Express 19 April 1983.**

coffin was lowered into an ordinary grave, piled with concrete slabs, a layer of mortar, then more concrete slabs. Aziza is a member of 'Afrika Adzeu', a group which promotes African mysticism, and says he can spend seven days underground; but in this case he settled for three hours. His wife sat at the head of the grave with a bowl of herbal mixture, which she could be seen to stir several times, while Aziza's voice could be heard clearly from below ground. After two hours and twenty minutes, as the crowd began panicking, he agreed to come out. The ground shook, and suddenly Aziza burst through the mortar, shoving concrete slabs aside. Not only that, but the lid of the coffin was still nailed down, a cloth and some 'mystic equipment' were still inside. He also achieved something else remarkable: emptying an entire football stadium while the match was still in play, when rumour got round that a dead man had risen from the grave. Aziza says he has had supernatural powers since childhood, vanishing when he was one year old and returning when he was seven, emerging from the village dumping pit. He claims to understand the language of animals, and to be able to cure a wide variety of diseases, usually after meditating underground. *Pretoria News c.1974.*

Dooms

Some people seem not just unlucky, but doomed . . .

FLYING DOG
● A woman of 79 was killed when an Airedale terrier fell on her head from a tower block window in Essen, Germany. The dog was unhurt. *Daily Mirror* 19 April 1990.

KILLED BY KINDNESS
● Mario Morby, 12, a cancer patient who had received two million post-cards of get-well support from around the world, was discovered dead underneath a stack of about 500,000 postcards that had toppled over and suffocated him. *Winchendon Observer* 19 December 1988.

GIANT BUDDHA KILLER
● Ten people were killed as a 350-ton stone Buddha slid off a barge as it was being taken to a rock in the Hyderabad Lake in India. Some drowned and others were trapped under it. *Sunday Express* 11 March 1990.

PROVING HER POINT
● Narian Wlodarski, who cam-paigned against drunk driving, was killed when a jeep driven by a drunk slammed through her house in Chicago and crushed her as she slept on a couch. The driver had a record of drink-driving arrests. *Manchester Evening News* 12 June 1990.

CRASH KILLS 'SAFEST TEENAGE DRIVER'
In July 1989, Michael Doucette, 16, from Concord, New Hampshire, was honoured as America's safest teenage driver in a contest called 'Operation Driver Excellence' held in Detroit. He won a $5000 scholarship, a trophy and the use of a 1989 Dodge for a year. Ironically and tragically, he was driving the Dodge on 23 February 1990 when he crashed head-on with a car driven by Sharon Ann Link, 19, on her side of the road. Both were killed. Police said that Doucette appeared to have fallen asleep at the wheel. Augusta (Georgia) *Chronicle*, Rockland (New York) *Journal-News* 25 February 1990.

DROWNED IN DRAIN
● Ex-publican William Arthur Holmes, 38, dropped his keys down a drain in Rhodes Street, near his home in Castleford, West Yorkshire, on 10 May 1990. He removed the cover, the weight of his body carried him forward and he got stuck. He drowned in 15 inches of water. The next morning a neighbour spotted his legs sticking up out of the drain. A blood sample showed he had drunk the equivalent of about eight pints of beer. *Pontefract Express* (Yorkshire) 19 July 1990.

BELT DRIVE
A Los Angeles motorist who strapped his teddy bear into the passenger seat but failed to do up his own seat belt was killed when his car spun off the road and fell 35 feet. The bear was undamaged. *Independent* 4 March 1988.

HARD LUCK STORIES
● Nitaro Ito, a Japanese restaurant owner from Osaka, planned a bizarre campaign to be elected to Japan's house of representatives. He asked friends to beat him up, and then stabbed himself in the thigh, hoping to draw sympathy from voters and the publicity of running his campaign from his hospital bed. Unfortunately for him he had stabbed too deep and died from loss of blood in the 20-yard walk from his car to his house. Vancouver *Sunday News* 23 September 1979.

● Student David Reynolds de-scribed in an essay how he was shot dead at a Hartford motel where he worked as a night clerk. A few nights later he was shot by a mystery intruder. He had even got the time of death right. *Weekly News* 23 June 1979.

● A man who went fishing on the banks of the Amazon's Rio Negro was attacked by infuriated bees after he struck their nests while trying to free his line from a tree. To escape, he leapt into the river, where he was devoured by piranha fish. *Daily Telegraph* 12 August 1077.

● During the British firemen's strike, one of the army's Green Goddesses rescued an old lady's cat from a tree. After tea and biscuits, the army left and ran over the cat in their fire engine. *Sun* 14 January 1978.

● A man was knocked down by a car in New York, got up uninjured, but lay down in front of a car again when a bystander told him to pretend he was hurt and collect the insurance money. The car rolled forward and crushed him to death. Mark Harrison was killed as he worked in a field by bouncing wreckage from a plane that crashed nearby. The same fate befell his father a few years before. Malaysia *New Sunday Times* 10 July 1977.

● Twelve men in a village near Rawalpindi died in succession as they went down a well which contained gas leaking from a kerosene-powered water pump. And seven died of suffocation near Ahmedabad after a man fell into a cow-dung pit and six others jumped in to rescue him. Delhi *Statesman* 12 April 1979; *Guardian* 30 July 1979.

● Fifty-three Hindus returning from a religious dip in the Ganges were killed and 12 injured when their bus plunged into a river, 65 miles from Allahabad. Unsympathetic magic? *Leicester Mercury* 9 February 1978.

● Thankamma Mathai, 20, wore an artificial bun at her wedding in Trivandrum, near New Delhi. She collapsed and died as she walked down the aisle. A doctor found a snake bite on the nape of her neck. It was supposed that a small snake had coiled up in her bun overnight. Recent research at Melbourne University has shown that every year after mating, the entire male population of the marsupial Stuart shrew keels over and dies. Immediately after his marriage in Council Bluffs, Iowa, Greg Cundiff, 23, stricken by nerves and heat, hit his head on the altar steps and, tragically, never regained consciousness. *Sunday Express* 10 July 1977; Madras *Sunday Standard* 8 April 1979; *Daily Mail* 26 June 1979.

● A South Korean fisherman, preparing his catch landed in New Zealand, thought the tuna he was about to gut was dead. It flicked its tail, sending the knife he was holding into the man's chest. *Shropshire Star* 4 June 1979.

● Villagers cut off the heads of a religious leader and his wife in the Philippines after challenging them to prove there was a life after death. *Reveille* 11 May 1979.

● A woman in Boise, Idaho, had a cornea graft and died from rabies transmitted by the donor, seven weeks after the operation in Atlanta, Georgia. *Rising Nepal* 18 March 1979.

Fires

Why do fires start for no apparent reason, and why do some people seem to cause fires wherever they go?

THE BERICI HILLS MYSTERY

The trouble started in San Gottardo, a mountain village of 500 people above Vicenza in northern Italy, on 14 February 1990. Aldo Calgaretto saw the fuse box outside his house start to burn. Electricians found no faults, but even before they left, the new fuse box was in flames. Within two days, other bizarre events struck nearby houses on the narrow winding lane called Via Calora. Televisions switched themselves on and off, indicator lights flashed on a locked car, an armchair caught fire, as did a pair of ski boots and a plastic canopy. The electricity men returned with a sophisticated machine but the plastic switches melted.

When the fires started, Lucio Donatello, one of the joint mayors of San Gottardo, thought the village was affected by mass hysteria, but he soon changed his mind. 'One day I discovered my car engine running with all the doors locked. Then the right front door burst into flames in front of my eyes. Another time, I was given a jolt when the electric razor I was using caught fire in my hands!'

Mr Donatello and the other mayor, Giancario Zuin, visited Via Calora to restore confidence. As they stood talking, the parked car they had arrived in caught fire. 'We watched the rear plastic light slowly melt in front of our eyes,' said Mr Zuin. 'There was more and more smoke and then it burst into flames. I couldn't believe it.'

The next event was Bertilla Moran's house filling with acrid smoke. The wheelchair used by his disabled father and kept under the stairs had caught fire and was destroyed. Dozens of people began to complain of headaches, sickness, stomach pains, and skin inflammations that seemed to be resistant to medication. Pets went off their food, while sheep, goats and chickens became restless.

Police, firemen and electricity men were unable to explain the events. Reaction in the village ranged from bafflement to terror. There was talk of the devil, UFOs, Martians, the supernatural. Some experts suspected 'excess electricity produced by high-power generators at a nearby U.S. communications base'. The only reason many refused to leave was the fear that their homes would burn down in their absence and they would lose everything. Many families took turns to sleep so there was always someone to watch for fires. *Sunday Express* 11 March; *Guardian* 22 March; *National Enquirer* 9 April 1990.

FIERY FAMILY

The van Reenan family (with eight children) have had to move from their second home in Plettenberg Bay, South Africa, because of fiery persecutions. The family claims that an estimated hundred fires had broken out in about three months from 5 May. Carpets, toys, curtains, chairs and beds would suddenly burst into flame, putting them in 'continual terror'. 'Our two family Bibles began showing scorch marks,' says Mrs van Reenan. 'They got worse day by day, until one day both Bibles caught fire at the same time.' This convinced them that they were under attack by something 'evil', a view supported by Reverend Jacobus van Zyl of the African Methodist Church, who himself has seen at least a dozen fires spring out of nowhere in their home. Apparently local housing officials and policemen have also seen things suddenly smoulder and blaze, and a forensic examination of various items, concluded that no chemicals were causing the phenomena. The truth remains a mystery. *National Enquirer* 4 November 1975.

THE HUMAN FLAME-THROWER

Benedetto Supino, a 10-year-old boy, can set objects ablaze by gazing at them.

Benedetto is the son of a carpenter, and lives in the resort of Formia, not far from Rome. A fairly shy and studious boy, he is slightly embarrassed at all the attention he is getting for purely involuntary incidents. It began in 1982, when a comic he was reading in a dentist's waiting-room caught fire. One morning he awoke to find his bedclothes on fire – he was painfully burned. He does not smoke and the incident mystified and frightened him and his family. 'I don't want things to catch fire. But what can I do?' he shrugs.

A plastic object held by his Uncle Erasmo burst into flames as Benedetto stared at it. Everywhere he went furniture, fittings and objects smouldered. Pages of books were scorched where he touched them. Along with the fiery phenomena came the peculiar electromagnetic effects which were a familiar feature of the famous Rosenheim poltergeist case and others. Electrical objects in the house would function erratically, and the power supply actually failed several times. When he visited his father's workshop machinery would stop or not start, and the firm spent over £3000 on repairs before they made the surprising connection. Witnesses have seen his hands glow at such times.

His distraught parents began taking him to doctors, and so prominent was the boy's unwanted gift that he soon came to the attention of top scientists. Dr Giovanni Ballesio, Dean of Physical Medicine at Rome University said: 'It is wrong to call him an "Electric Boy" because he really doesn't possess any more electricity than anybody else.' Professor Mario Scuncio of the Tivoli Social Medical Centre said the boy was 'perfectly normal'. Dr Massimo Inardi, a celebrated television doctor thought the boy was 'clearly capable of projecting his aggressive powers on outside objects in an extraordinary manner'. The family was undoubtedly relieved when, after an examination, Archbishop Vincenzo Fagiolo pronounced the phenomenon 'not malign', and warned, 'neither must his extraordinary powers be considered miracles'. Meanwhile, a noted parapsychologist, Dr Demetrio Croce, has taken Benedetto under his wing, hoping to channel his 'extrasensory powers of considerable force' into healing and research by teaching the boy how to control the phenomenon. *Sunday Mirror* 21 August 1983.

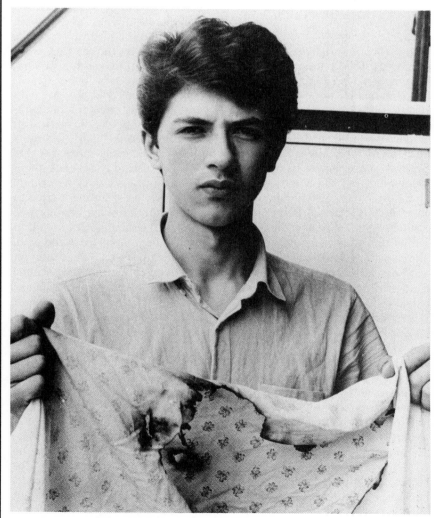

Benedetto Supino holding one of his sheets which had burned through.

Spontaneous Human Combustion

The number of bodies found charred beyond recognition, while very little damage is done nearby, suggests that spontaneous human combustion may be more than myth.

STRANGE FIRES

● Mary Carter, 86, an elderly widow, was found dead in the hall of her flat in Ivor Road, Sparkhill, Birmingham. Although she died from a heart attack, she had severe burns, yet there was no evidence of any fire in the flat, her inquest was told. A fire investigation team concluded that her clothing must have caught fire 'elsewhere' and she had been running for help when she was engulfed by flame. There were candles and matches in some rooms but none near the body. If there was any evidence that these had been alight, or had ignited her clothes, it would not have been labelled a 'fire riddle'. Wolverhampton *Express & Star* 23 April 1985.

● Paul Hayes, a 19-year-old London computer operator, is one of that select band who seem to have survived a spontaneous combustion. What happened to him, as he walked along a quiet road in Stepney Green late on the night of 25 May 1985 remains a mystery to police and medical investigators, because he suddenly and inexplicably burst into flames. From the waist up, he was surrounded by intense flames, as though, in his own words, he had been doused with petrol and set alight. 'It was indescribable ... like being plunged into the heat of a furnace. My arms felt as though they were being prodded by red-hot pokers, from my shoulders to my wrists. My cheeks were red-hot, my ears were numb. My chest felt like boiling water had been poured over it. I thought I could hear my brains bubbling.' Fearing more for his eyes, he instinctively shut them tight and put his hands over them. Screaming and shouting, 'I tried to run, stupidly thinking I could race ahead of the flames.' But he fell to the pavement. In distress and pain, he curled up into a ball. 'I thought I was dying. Images of my parents, my friends, my girlfriend, came to mind.' Then, as suddenly as it began, his half-minute ordeal was over. 'I opened my eyes. There was no flame, no smoke. For a few minutes I lay still, terrified. I began to shiver with shock.' He felt himself gingerly. 'I was numb in some spots, white-hot in others.' Luckily he was only a few streets away from The London Hospital, and he stumbled into casualty, where he received prompt treatment for burns on his hands, forearms, face, neck and ears. Paul does not smoke. London *Standard* 31 May; *National Enquirer* 23 July 1985.

SPONTANEOUS STORIES

● At the inquest on Mrs Lily Smith, a 76-year-old widow of Greenfield Cottage, Hutton-le-Hole, Yorkshire, the Ryedale Coroner, Mr Henry Blakeston, said that her body was so consumed by fire that it was impossible to identify or say how she died. However, since she had been in the habit of bolting herself in her cottage, refusing entry to all except her son, the Coroner was satisfied that the remains were of Mrs Smith, found after a fire at the home on 25 January 1979. The postman raised the alarm that morning, and calling two neighbours and a farmer, they broke in. There was thick smoke but no sign of flames, and they could not find Mrs Smith. A constable was called, and, as he later testified, he found a pair of legs (presumably burned off between thigh and hip) under a wooden dining chair near the fireplace, and on the chair itself, where a body would be sitting, was a heap of charred bones.

By way of explanation a Kirkbymoorside fire officer said Mrs Smith had been in the habit of sitting in front of the fire with her feet on the hearth, and that in his opinion 'something fell either out of the fireplace or down the chimney'. He produced photographs of the scene saying that the fire had eventually gone out 'for lack of oxygen' because of its fierce burning.

Although an open verdict was returned on Mrs Smith's death, the Coroner seemed satisfied with the fire officer's explanation, but I'm afraid it only makes me more curious. The lady's legs were nearest the fire and thus most accessible to any spark or brand leaping from that direction, yet these alone survived the conflagration. It was suggested the fire was so intense that it used up the oxygen and put itself out, yet there is little evidence of other damage in the room. Indeed the fire had been intense enough to reduce Mrs Smith to cinders and yet left the wooden chair on which she sat substantially intact. *Yorkshire Evening Press* 15 February 1979.

● Vicky Gilmour, 19, was in the girls' room of a disco in Darlington, County Durham, when she burst into flames. The burns almost killed her, as friends tried to beat out the flames, and she will need extensive skin grafts to her face and body. In the belief that a cigarette ignited her light Indian cotton dress, a consumer organization tried setting alight pieces of Vicky's dress and other similar dresses with cigarettes – they just smouldered.

In some respects this is similar to the story of Phyllis Newcombe, who in 1938 burst into flames while leaving a ballroom floor, only Phyllis died in hospital later. In this case too, the dress was tested by flicking cigarette butts at it, to no effect. *News of the World* 16 November 1980.

● A week later – 22 November 1980 – the badly-burned body of a man was found at the wheel of a car in a lay-by at High Ercall, on the north edge of Telford, Shropshire. It was suggested he might have committed suicide, but a police spokesman admitted there was little damage to the car itself. *Birmingham Evening Mail* 22 November 1980.

When Mrs Mary Reeser, aged 67, of St Petersburg, Florida, 'departed this life on a pillar of fire', she spontaneously combusted just before the peak of an intense geomagnetic storm on 1 July 1951. The geomagnetic disturbance peaked at a value of 1.7 on the 2nd, while the monthly average for that July was 0.82, less than half this figure. Was there a connection?

The main photograph shows the scant remains of Mrs Reeser and her armchair. It provides evidence of the extraordinarily fierce heat, inexplicably contained. The inset shows Mrs Reeser before this horrific accident.

Plants

Plants are astonishingly resilient and long-lived. Sometimes it almost seems that they may have minds of their own . . .

ONE IN THE EYE

One day in 1976, seven-year-old Julian Fabricus fell down while chasing butterflies in a field. When he returned home his left eye was inflamed and smarting. His mother took him to their family doctor, in Worcester, South Africa – but he could not find the source of the irritation and gave the boy some ointment. In a few days the smarting went.

About a year later Julian complained to his parents that his left eye itched and sometimes his vision was not as clear as it should be. His father looked and saw a white object lodged in the cornea, near the pupil. Oculist Dr Cornelius Kooy, to whom the puzzled parents took the boy, said: 'I saw what looked like a grass seed which had sprouted and grown two little leaves.' The sprout was about 4mm ($\frac{1}{8}$in) long, and pure white. Dr Kooy referred the case to top eye specialist Dr Solomon Abel, of Cape Town, who removed the seed in a 30-minute operation on 20 December 1977. He called in a botanist, who declared the intruder to be of the family *Compositae*, which includes chrysanthemums, thistles and daisies. Dr Abel wrote the case up, and it was published in the September 1979 issue of the AMA journal *Archives of Ophthalmology*. Dr Abel's theory: 'The boy's cornea had been punctured, presumably when he fell in the field, and somehow the seed found its way through the wound and became embedded in the iris. There it lay dormant for a year and then started growing. In order for a plant to grow it needs warmth, moisture and oxygen – all these things were available in Julian's eye.' Framingham *Middlesex News*/UPI 28 September; Omaha *World Herald*/UPI 29 September; *Sunday Mirror* 18 November; *National Enquirer* 20 November; *Weekly News* 15 December 1979; *Awake* 22 February 1980.

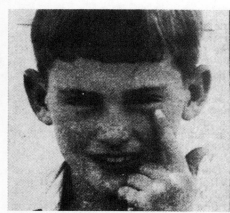
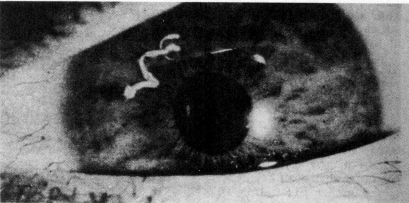

Julian Fabricus and a close-up of the sprout in his cornea. The dark lower end is where the seed entered.

CAN EARTH SEED SPACE?

A few of the hundreds of meteorites picked up in the Antarctic wastes have chemical properties consistent with a Martian origin. Calculations, too, support the notion that a large meteoric impact could propel bits of the Martian surface into space where a tiny fraction would be captured by the earth's gravitational field. Some of these would fall to earth or remain in orbit.

Now the reverse scenario has been investigated numerically. The University of Arizona has simulated what would happen to small chunks of the earth's crust if a large meteor impact excavated a 60-mile-wide crater. 'Phinney's group used a computer to calculate where 1000 particles would go if ejected from earth in random directions, moving about 2.5 km per second faster than the minimum speed necessary to escape. Of the 1000, 291 particles hit Venus, 165 returned to Earth, 20 went to Mercury, 17 to Mars, 14 to Jupiter and 1 to Saturn. Another 492 left the solar system completely, primarily due to gravitational encounters with either Jupiter or Mercury that "slingshot" them on their way.' (Jonathan Eberhart: 'Have Earth Rocks gone to Mars?', *Science News* v135 p. 191, 1989.)

One implication from this analysis is that terrestrial bacteria and spores could well have infected every planet in the solar system, and perhaps even planets in nearby star systems! Conceivably, if other star systems had histories like ours, biological traffic might be quite heavy in interstellar space. In fact extraterrestrial life-forms may be arriving continually.

Andrew Lambert in front of the self-resurrected lime tree blown down in the Great Gale of October 1987.

STUBBORN WEEDS

S eeds brought up from the wreckage of the Spanish galleon *Atocha*, which sank off Key West during a hurricane in 1622, sprouted after 350 years under water. The seeds, preserved by a coating of mud, turned out to be from the local 'beggar tickweed'. The several grape, olive and apricot pits brought to the surface at the same time didn't make it.

Archaeologist Corey Malcolm put the weed seeds in fresh water to prevent their deterioration late in May 1987. After nine days, four of them began to sprout, and Malcolm kept the two survivors in his window box. When reported in the *Kent County Daily Times* (West Warwick), 22 June 1987, the seedlings were two inches high.

Embeddings

Every now and then somebody splits open a stone and finds a frog, or something similar, inside. Of course it's impossible: but it happens.

CONCRETE FROGS

The following account appeared in *Animals* (April 1972, p. 178), and is a letter from Eric Mackley, a gas-fitter of Barnstaple, Devon, to Sir Julian Huxley.

'It became desirable to widen the Barnstaple–Ilfracombe road some years ago, taking in part of the long gardens in front of a row of bungalows which had gas meters housed just inside the front gates; these of course had to be moved back to the new front wall line. The meter-houses were brick-walled but rather massively concrete-floored, and the concrete had to be broken up to allow me to get at the pipes for extension. My mate was at work with a sledge hammer when he dropped it suddenly and said, "That looks like a frog's leg." We both bent down and there was the frog. Being fond of animals the sledge was set aside and I cut the rest of the block carefully. We released 23 perfectly formed but minute frogs which all hopped away to the flower garden ...'

Attempts to explain the phenomenon of entombed amphibians fall into various categories. The editor of *Animals* offered the perennial favourite: that the tiny creatures, or fertilized spawn, fell through minute cracks to hatch and grow. Careful observers – and there have been a few – often discount the idea because of 1) the depth of the cavity in stone or tree, or 2) the readily apparent lack of communicating holes, or 3) the curious detail, often reported, of the cavity and frog or toad being a tight fit, with the former taking the form of the unfortunate within. The editors of *Animals* abandoned their theory when Mr Mackley told them the concrete had been compacted and was without cracks. Mr Mackley's own theory is 'that whoever originally mixed the concrete took up frog spawn with the water from the stagnant stream opposite; the spawn found its way into the middle of the concrete base; and when the tadpoles hatched they cannibalized until the hole was completely filled with small but perfectly formed frogs'. The merits of this theory we leave for the criticism of others, but we would have thought that the concrete would have set around the relatively small mass of the spawn-cluster (if that's the way it happened) long before the critters hatched, not giving them much room. Secondly, they would have to survive the added hazards of the toxicity of liquid concrete and the heat generated by the setting process on top of the rough and tumble of mixing, pouring and compacting. Another interesting point, is the speed with which the little sleepers roused from their torpid state and hopped away 'after over a quarter of a century'.

TOADS IN THE WOODPILE

The commonest form of captive croaker is one imprisoned in stone, but they are also found in isolated cavities deep in the trunk of trees.

● *The Evening Journal* (St Catherines, Ontario) reported on 21 December 1865: 'Recently Mr Angus McDonald cut down a white ash tree, and on splitting it, a live frog was found embedded in the wood. The tree was about 15 inches in diameter, and perfectly sound; the cavity in which the frog had been enclosed appeared as if carved out for its reception. The question of how the frog got there would be an interesting one for naturalists.'

● A similar story in the *Daily Star* 30 May 1905 related that at Pulham St Mary, Norfolk, a toad quickly died after its liberation from an oak tree by a gang of fellers.

Cross-section of the quarry stone tomb where a toad was found alive in Gotland, Sweden, on 8 May 1733.

EMBEDDED FROGS

A gang carving an extension to a railway on New Zealand's North Island was trimming a rock face of sedimentary mudstone, some four metres down, when one man noticed that a cavity in a newly fragmented rock was occupied. Closer inspection revealed an imprisoned frog, which was found to be alive after it was shaken loose onto a shovel. Later that day, a drilling machine uncovered another frog in similar circumstances. A supervisor said neither frog could have fallen with loose rock into the places they were discovered. *New Zealand Herald* (Auckland) 9 December 1982.

FISH IN TREE

In October 1969 farmer Heino Seppi was occupied transporting lumber from the woods of Yrjo Kanto, near Sikasalo, in the Palloneva region of western Finland. The trees had been felled the previous winter and were cut into lengths of a few metres. When Mr Seppi split an aspen log, he found its middle rotten, forming a hollow in which a dried fish over 40 cm long was found. It resembled a perch, and if so it is a large size for a perch. There was no clue as to how the fish got there and all who saw the evidence were baffled. *Vaasa* 17 November 1969.

THE FROG AND PEA PUZZLE

An even stranger case of embedding took place on 9 December 1980, when a farmer, using a mechanical harvester on peafields near Colac, south of Melbourne in New South Wales, stopped to examine his pickings. He was, not surprisingly, astonished to find something other than peas: there were tiny frogs in a few of the pods. In fact four were found half out of the 2-inch-long pods, each with a pea in its mouth. The farmer said the frogs were dead when he found them. 'It looks as though they were born inside the pods, tried to eat their way out, then choked on the peas,' he speculated.

Miracles

Some miracles can be put down to the credulity of believers. But even in the absence of belief, miraculous events still occur . . .

LIBERACE RETURNS

On 10 February 1989 the inhabitants of the tiny town of Fyffe in Alabama witnessed the return to earth of the late glittering pianist Liberace (double-size, 12-foot tall), who descended from a golden banana-shaped spacecraft via a moving stairway and treated the lucky witnesses to a medley of Hollywood show-stoppers, with glowing fingers on a floating piano. Talk of the apparition brought chaos to the town, with 4000 cars jamming the main street on 6 March 1989. An 'American UFO expert' said: 'Too many people have seen strange things for it to be a hoax.' (Portsmouth) *News* + *Daily Star* 7 March 1989.

The six-man crew of a Soviet military transport lost control of their plane in mid-air after a heavy drinking session, reports *International Combats Arms* May 1989.

The crew drank themselves into a stupor and took off without securing a cabin door. As the oxygen level in the plane dropped, all six blacked out while the aircraft 'lurched aimlessly through the air' for more than an hour.

HEAVENLY RIDE

A coachload of 54 Spanish pilgrims, returning from the shrine at the site of the famous Blessed Virgin Mary vision at Fatima, Portugal, were somewhat startled to discover that their driver was not driving – he had his head bowed, eyes closed and hands together in prayer. Yet the bus continued at speeds of up to 50 m.p.h., turning corners, changing gears, winking lights, in a smooth ride for 20 miles before it pulled into the roadside and the driver, Juan Garcia, 50, woke up.

The passengers, including a priest of 40 years standing, Father Cesar Trapiello, drew up an affidavit, now being studied by the Bishop of Leon, who has not rejected it outright. According to the priest, at first there was panic, but it soon became clear the bus 'was not running out of control, but that somebody, some power, had taken over.' Before he woke, the passengers all swear they heard a sombre voice come from the driver's mouth, saying: 'I am your brother, Archangel Michael. God had the grace to drive the bus himself as a test of faith for our brother, the driver.' Garcia himself remembers nothing, except an overwhelming compulsion to pray, and seems to be genuinely unaware of what happened. *Daily Telegraph* 19 October; *Sunday Express* 25 October 1981.

UNCORRUPTED

● **Typical of many cases is that of Nadja Mattei, who died in Rome, aged two years, in 1965. Her mother claims that for 12 years her daughter's voice would come to her in dreams asking to be fetched from her coffin. Early in 1977 the coffin was opened at last and they found the quite uncorrupted body of baby Nadja.** *News of the World* 8 May 1977.

● In Espartinas, near Seville, Spain, a family grave was opened in mid-1977, to inter the body of a local man. The cemetery keeper was, not surprisingly, shocked to find that the body of the man's son was still intact after 40 years. Jose Garcia Morena had died of meningitis in 1937, aged 11, and his brothers deny that he was embalmed. The whole village, who all saw for themselves that night the preserved body in its rotting graveclothes, believe the boy must have been a saint, and have begun agitating for his case to be sent to Rome to begin the long process of canonization. *Reville* 30 September 1977.

MUSLIM SIGNS AND WONDERS

● Appropriately in this time of crisis and upheaval in the Islamic world, the name of Allah is appearing everywhere.

● Farida Kassam, 30, cut open an aubergine at her terraced house in Bakewell Street, Leicester, and found that the seeds spelt out the Arabic inscription 'Yah-Allah', meaning 'Allah is everywhere'. (So said the *Guardian*; the alternative version in the *Leicester Mercury* said it spelt 'Ya-Allah', meaning 'Allah exists'.) 'We were really shocked when we first saw the seeds,' said her husband, Zahid, 32. 'We couldn't believe our eyes. Our insurance man was the first non-Muslim we showed it to and even he could match the writing [with a plate bearing the same words]'.

● Hussain Bhatti, an accountant in Nottingham, had one of the most celebrated aubergines, not only for its clear presentation of the holy words but because his son, who is taking 'A' level chemistry, had the wit to preserve it in a saline solution. Mr Bhatti dismissed any notion of chance. *Daily Mirror + Daily Star* 21 March; *Leicester Mercury* 27 March; *Guardian + Independent* 28 March; *International Herald Tribune* 29 March; *Daily Mirror* 30 March; *Sun + Daily Telegraph* 1 April 1990.

● Meanwhile, in Kenya, on 12 April 1990, a family in Nairobi got an Easter and Ramadan surprise when they cut open an aubergine and found the word Allah in Arabic. A week earlier, a member of the family studying in Britain had had a similar experience. Nairobi *Nation* 14 April 1990.

Hussain Bhatti of Nottingham with his aubergine and a plate both inscribed with 'Allah'.

● On 12 June, the Islamic Salvation Front secured a stunning victory in Algeria's local elections. During an address by the Islamic party leader, the crowd stood up and cried: 'Allah Akhbar!' (God is great), the Islamic radicals' battle cry. To the East, towards Mecca, an unremarkable cloud was being blown into the shape of the Arabic script for Allah. Men fainted on the streets. The journalists' translator wept. *Daily Telegraph + Guardian* 16 June 1990.

Bleeding Statues

Religious icons and statues everywhere seem to drip blood from time to time, almost as often as they appear to cry salty tears.

THE PHILADELPHIA STIGMATIC STATUE

In St Luke's Episcopalian Church, in Eddystone, near Philadelphia, is a 28-inch-high plaster statue of Christ which bleeds from its upraised hands. The bleeding was first noticed the Friday after Easter 1975 and, like the classical stigmatics, it bleeds on Fridays and Holy Days. The first occasion was during a fervent prayer in the home of Mrs Ann Poore, of Philadelphia, who had received the ordinary commercial statue as a gift the previous year. As hundreds of people began turning up to see the figurine, she decided to donate it to the church. Father Olszewski, of St Luke's, says that since it went on display in November 1975 many hundreds have witnessed the flows of blood. He said: 'It stands on a shelf ten feet above the altar, where nobody can touch it. It has bled as long as four hours. I know there can be no trickery. Several times I've seen the palms dry, then, minutes later, observed droplets of blood welling from the wounds.'

Father Olszewski called in Dr Joseph Rovito, a respected Philadelphian physician, to conduct tests on the blood. He said that the blood is 'obviously fresh' when it oozes from the palms, but laboratory analysis shows it to be 'of apparent great age!' 'Fresh blood,' said Dr Rovito, 'contains millions of red cells. The older it gets the fewer red cells – but even after a few weeks there are usually millions of cells left – yet this blood has only an occasional red cell. It is so old we can't even determine the blood type.' Dr Rovito even X-rayed the statue in an attempt to locate hidden reservoirs and the like, but found nothing to account for the appearance of blood on the hands.

Also called in was a Father Lovett, from Corbin City, New Jersey, who studies religious phenomena. He told the *National Enquirer* 20 January 1976 that at first he was 'very sceptical' but was now 'totally convinced' the phenomenon was genuine. 'I've personally taken the hands off the statue – they are held in place by wooden dowels – and examined them. They're solid chalk, nothing else ... and (they) bled profusely even as I watched in astonishment.'

The bleeding statue of Christ in St Luke's Episcopalian Church, near Philadelphia.

Father Olszewski said: 'Sometimes it bleeds more profusely than others – the blood will flow down the plaster robes of the statue in a stream. Incredibly, the blood seldom runs off the statue. Its robes are now encrusted with dried blood.' This detail recalls an observation of tears on some weeping icons, where the tears vanish at the foot of the picture; and of the stigmatic, Domenica Lazzari, d. 1848, from whose skin the dried discharges would vanish, some of these flows of blood having been observed to have flowed *uphill*!

The clergy involved in the Philadelphia stigmatic statue case believe that somehow the blood of Christ is being transported through time to the statue's palms 'to call attention to religion again'. There is no evidence to the contrary!

BLEEDING AND HEALING

A similar sensation centres on a ten-foot-high statue of the Virgin, built in 1979, near the Baguio City Airport, Philippines. Some time in early February 1983 a group of 20 worshippers were drawn 'by an unknown urge' to a small unfinished hillside chapel, where they saw a bright red stream pour from the image of an exposed heart on the statue's breast. The flow was so copious that it splashed and soaked a white sheet placed under the image. Two women claimed visions in which they were given a mandate to heal. The crippled and infirm swarmed there and many cures were reported: muteness, lameness, intestinal ailments, etc. Cures of heart disease and even cancer were claimed. *Guardian* 14 February 1983; *Globe* 24 January 1984.

AND NOW FOR SOMETHING COMPLETELY DIFFERENT

B leeding statues and weeping icons you know about – but are you ready for an iron statue of an Indian goddess that menstruates? This phenomenon is reported in an article on the Mahadeva Temple in the magazine *Probe India* August 1981.

The origin of the story is lost in antiquity. It is said that Parvati visited the area with Shiva, shortly after their marriage, to see the sage Agastya, when suddenly Parvati began to menstruate. According to tradition she separated from her husband for three days meditating on a rock, until she was 'clean again'. A shrine grew up on the site in the reign of King Vanchipuza Tamburan, after blood flowed from the stone when a girl sharpened her sickle upon it. The rock was consecrated according to a tradition which recognizes phallic simulacra as *swayambhu linga* (i.e. spontaneously formed images of Shiva's penis). The temple was alleged to have been first built by a legendary genius of that province, Perunthachan, who is also said to have miraculously found and excavated at the site a metal idol of the goddess Bhagawati. According to the chief priest of the temple, the original building burnt down long ago, but a manuscript by Perunthachan had been found which foretold the fire and the location of a secretly buried replica of the first divine image. The temple today contains the *lingam* stone on the eastern side of its inner courtyard, and the replica idol on the western side.

The writer of the article says that at irregular itervals, on holy days when the temple is closed for reconsecration, the white linen loincloth on the idol is removed for washing. Sometimes – as has happened seven times in the three-year tenure of the present chief priest – the cloth is found stained, and passed to the eldest ladies of the priest's and the ruling family's households for approval. If the ladies announce the goddess has menstruated, she is removed from the temple for three days, then reinstated in fresh clothes at a public festival called *Tripooth Aarat*. Various authorities – a professor and local doctors – are mentioned as believing the statue really menstruates. 'A prominent member of the Rationalists' Association' claimed that the blood was formed by a chemical 'disintegration of granite', until he found out that the idol is made of metal'.

MORE BLEEDING STATUES

T housands of Christians flocked to Rmaich, a Christian village in southern Lebanon just over the border with Israel, to see a small statue of the Virgin Mary said to be seeping blood. The flow was first noticed by the village mukhtar, or headman, in whose house the statue stood, on 18 November 1983, and it was moved to the church so more could see it. Melchite Archbishop Maximos Salloum said that he had been to the church and saw the figure, which has changed colour from red to grey, ooze what appeared to be blood and olive oil. 'It is hard to say this is a miracle, but it is extraordinary,' he said, 'and could reflect the deep pain of the Virgin over the bloodshed of Her beloved sons in Lebanon.' UPI/Plattsburgh *Press Republican* 28 December 1983.

Frog Falls

Frogs are perhaps the commonest object to drop out of the sky, although almost anything does from time to time, as the next few pages reveal.

WHEN PINK FROGS FELL

Falls of pink frogs on the Gloucestershire town of Stroud were recently reported.

The original report appeared on 24 October 1987 (*Daily Mirror* and *Daily Star*), saying that an unnamed elderly lady had reported to the Gloucestershire Trust for Nature Conservancy (GTNC) that 'tiny rose-coloured frogs' had fallen during recent [no date] torrential rain. 'They bounced off umbrellas and pavements and hopped off in their hundreds to nearby streams and gardens,' adds the *Mirror*. An expert leaps to the fore; GTNC naturalist Ian Darling describes them as 'weighing no more than a few ounces and quite harmless'. He explains their pink appearance: 'It seems the frogs are part of an albino strain' whose colour is due to their blood showing through their pale skins.

The *Star* account ends with the note that 'similar' pink frogs were seen in nearby Cirencester about two weeks previously, around about the time Britain was dusted with 'Sahara' sand. The Stroud *Observer* (12 November 1987), however, attributes two sightings to that period, adding that the GTNC were seriously investigating the idea that the frogs arrived with the 'Sahara' dust, possibly 'carried in atmospheric globules of water across land and sea'. This is a refreshing new notion; usually we are asked to believe the creatures were blasted to their dropping points by hurricane-force winds without the benefit of watery vehicles. A sarcastic letter to the *Times* (late February 1988), pointed out that this latter mode of transport would mean a 20-hour journey at 60 m.p.h.

In a fourth incident, pink frogs were spotted in Cheltenham, in the same county. About this time, too, the film *The Love Child* was released, 'the poster for which shows pink frogs falling and the story of which features a band and a song called "The Pink Frogs".'

In early February 1988 the GTNC publicized widely their opinion that the thumbnail-sized frogs were indeed from a desert region, probably the Sahara, and that their pinkness was a camouflage in their sandy habitat. Many reports in the media said the frogs spawned in some Saharan oasis or buried themselves in sand, whence those notorious whirlwinds pluck them. *The Times* (8 February 1988) cites the GTNC as saying the frogs bury themselves to escape the heat and then are dyed pink by crystals in the sand. Already the camouflage theory is contradictory in its suggested mechanism. The account in *Natural World* (Spring 1988), also citing the GTNC, says the frogs 'return to their normal colour when they breed'. This explanatory edifice has, however, been built upon a shaky foundation; there has been no clear evidence of the Saharan genesis of these blushing batrachians.

The GTNC even obtained a photograph of a specimen, and one wonders why their naturalists could not identify the species. Another doubt is the absence of mentions of sand during the Stroud downpour.

MORE RAINING FROGS

● According to the *Bedfordshire Times* (27 July 1979), Mrs Vida McWilliam of Bedford found her garden hopping with little frogs after a fall of rain. It reported that the frogs were about three-quarters-of-an-inch long.

Mrs McWilliam wrote: 'I can't remember the date exactly, but it happened in June 1979. One Sunday we had a really wet day, rain lashing down and windy. It was very damp and humid the next day. On my patio I have a caged-in area (for my cat) and in it, on the tiles, I noticed what

One of the tiny frogs that appeared in the Bedford garden of Mrs McWilliam in June 1979. The coin is just over an inch in diameter.

looked like half-grown tadpoles. To my surprise there were tiny frogs everywhere. I told my family it must have rained frogs that Sunday. Later in the week we went down the garden to cut the lawns. It was amazing; the grass was covered with little green and black frogs – and on the bushes hung spawn. We collected up the frogs and put them safely in the garden with the help of my delighted small grandchildren. All the summer they were carefully watched and made a home under the shed. I'm afraid last year [1980] we only had three left, grown to ordinary size.'

SOME U.S.A. FROG FALLS

The following letters appeared in the *Camden (Arkansas) News* 2 January 1973:

● 'In the summer of 1926, I caddied at a local golf course. There had been a long drought that summer and the fairways were brown and dried up. One afternoon, a sudden storm came up and a terrific thundershower followed. Rain came down in torrents, and with it, a shower of tiny frogs about the size of nickels. They were alive and jumping – thousands of them. The golfers and I couldn't believe our eyes as we watched thousands of frogs

come right down with the rain from the sky.' – W. A. Walker, Evansville, Indiana.

● 'I was raised on a farm in Minnesota, and as a boy I remember a storm coming up. It looked serious, so we ran to the cellar. Afterwards we went outside and saw our chickens eating tiny frogs and fishes.' – F. J. McManus, Laguna Beach, California.

● 'About 35 years ago while I was driving through a thunderstorm near Hershey, Pennsylvania, dozens of tiny frogs came down and pelted the hood of my automobile.' – D. F. Garner, Baltimore, Maryland.

Ice Falls

Ice plummets down on us with terrifying frequency, damaging property and injuring people. 'Experts' say it's from planes. Perhaps . . . perhaps not.

ICE AND HAIL

● At the end of August, or early September 1981, Steven Puckering and Amanda Kaye were on holiday in the south of France at Lac de St Cassien, near Cannes; Steven trying his hand at wind surfing, while 100 yards away Amanda sunbathed on the shore of the lake. Suddenly, out of a calm sky, something struck Steven hard on the head. Although badly stunned, he realized it had been a hailstone the size of a tennis ball. Then down it came – a blizzard of hailstones of frightening sizes. 'One minute I was peacefully sailing over a smooth lake in a temperature of 85 degrees, the next I was in the water in partial darkness, wiping blood from my eyes. I have never been so frightened,' he said. He had lost his balance trying to dodge the hail. In the water he tried to shelter under the sail, but 'the hail was so heavy it pierced the sail, ripping it to shreds'. *Sunday Express* 6 September 1981.

● Perhaps there is nothing exceptionally unusual in tales of hail the size of tennis balls, but what about a block of ice of guestimated weight half a hundredweight? This ice bomb fell on the annexe to the farmhouse of Michael Mogridge, of Dorset, in October 1981.

Mr and Mrs Wildsmith of Pinner, Middlesex, examine their newly acquired car damaged by an 18-inch cube of ice that crashed into it at 5:10pm on 25 March 1974. Mrs Wildsmith is standing on the spot where she was cleaning the car when the ice landed.

Mogridge had just finished milking his cows, and passed through the annexe, where it exploded behind him 'just like a bomb going off'. The huge lump of ice was squatting on the remains of his washing machine. After smashing through a slate roof, it had snapped a six-foot roof beam. The usual 'Fell from a plane' explanation was offered, and, as always, the story ends there. *Sunday Express* 18 October 1981.

WORLD REPORTS

● At 10:30am on 11 March 1978, workers in fields at Becquerel, near Abbeville, France, heard a loud explosion followed by a whizzing sound, like an artillery shell. Following the sound, they came to a fresh, small crater containing a 25-kilo lump of transparent ice with 'greenish depths'. The lump stayed intact for about an hour, despite the heat. *Liberation* (Paris) 13 March 1978; *Le Soir* (Belgium) 16 March 1978.

● At about 4pm on 14 April, at Carbrai, France, some kids training on a football field were startled by something flashing through the air near them. It fell from a clear sky in brilliant sunshine to embed itself in a nearby patch of leeks. On investigation they found a roughly spherical lump of ice, about 45 cm in diameter, weighing about 20 kilos, that started to disintegrate almost immediately. Cambrai is only about 60 miles from Abbeville, the site of the above story almost a month previously. *Nice Matin* (France) 17 April 1978; *Svenska Dagbladet* (Sweden) 20 April 1978.

● In June in Wirral, Cheshire, about mid-morning, Mary Nickson, 95, was sweeping her front bedroom carpet when a frightening crash shook the house and she staggered back as plaster rained down. Through the choking dust she saw a gaping hole in the ceiling near where she had been standing moments before, and on the floor was a 'football-sized' chunk of ice surrounded by more fragments. Police took the ice away for analysis, and later said it contained coffee, sugar and detergent. *Sunday Express* 21 June 1981.

On 28 September, in Yateley, Hampshire, a large ice block hurtled out of the sky into a shattering collision with the front garden of the Pearce family home in Greenleas Close during the afternoon. No estimation of size is made, but it made a three-inch dent in the lawn. Another piece was found under a car 20 feet away. Mrs Joan Brazier, who lived opposite, said: 'It was uncanny. I heard a noise and saw this object coming down at a terrific speed. It plunged through the trees and smashed into the ground. *Fleet News* 2 October; *Farnborough News* 23 October 1981.

Just 11 days later, on 9 October, the Fleet area just to the south of Yateley, had a hailstorm 'of unusual severity', with stones up to quarter of an inch in diameter in one-inch drifts.

Pamela Pearce and son Steven look at the ice-bomb fragments.

● On 24 June, in Anerley, Kent, a block of ice (different accounts compare it to a rugby ball and a football) smashed a two-foot hole in the roof of a house in Stembridge Road, South London, as Philip and Kay Wells watched television downstairs, at 7:50pm. Had the ceiling not stopped the missile it would have landed on the bed of their son Joe, 5, who, with his younger sister, slept through the 'ear-splitting crash'. Kay Wells rescued what she could – an irregular-shaped lump weighing 11 lb 9 oz, which she kept in her fridge. She says it is 'slightly discoloured', and, believing the ice to be waste from a plane, that it 'might have been coffee'. Another piece was found in the garden. *Sunday Express* 10 July; *Daily Telegraph* + *Daily Star* 25 June 1981.

● On 12 March 1982, in Tecumseh, Oklahoma, Lloyd Basden crossed the road to his neighbours opposite, the Hinsons, and told them that earlier that morning he had heard 'a roaring noise' and saw something fall from the sky behind their house. Mr A. C. Hinson went with Masden for a look-see and found a small crater recently knocked into sloping ground about 200 yards north of the house. It contained a block of ice, roughly 30 lb, which had split into several pieces. (Carlisle, Pennsylvania) *Evening Sentinel* + *(Little Rock, Arkansas) Gazette* 16 March; (Tucson, Arizona) *Daily Reporter* + (Boston, Massachusetts) *Herald American* 17 March, all UPI; (Tecumseh) *County-Wide News* 18 March 1982.

Falls

Is it possible that somewhere in the sky there's a kind of 'Sargasso Sea', where objects collect, occasionally raining down on us?

FALLS OF FROZEN DUCKS

Frozen ducks came tumbling out of the sky above Stuttgart, Arkansas. It was thought they had been caught in a tornado, pitched into the sky, 'and like aircraft, got iced over'. The townsfolk had them for dinner. This business of planes and ice seems to be firmly written into the human library of 'explanations'. Neither the *Daily Express* 6 December 1973 nor the *Daily Mail* 8 December 1973 tells us what we really want to know: did they come down plucked and oven-ready? or was it another case of the following? Three deep-frozen seagulls found in the hold of a ship carrying thousands of tons of herrings in ice from Ullapool, Scotland, to Norway, were thawed out ... and promptly flew away. *Daily Express* 24 January 1974.

DIVE BOMB

A man working in his garden in Athelstan Road, Bitterne, near Southampton, looked up to see a five-foot cylinder on an unopened parachute and trailing wires dropping out of the clear sky towards him. Edward Garnham said: 'It exploded twice in mid-air, dived towards my house and hit the ground, where it exploded in flames, wrecking my garden and greenhouse.' Police investigation established that it was a wartime defence device, of the 'aerial mine' sort and made in 1942. 'Where,' they ask in all reasonableness, 'had it come from?' Wherever it came from, it had been there since it was fired into the air between 1942 and 1945. No one will ever know.

CRABS

Morton Street, San Francisco, was the scene of a very strange rain of tiny crustaceans, which came down on the flabbergasted public with a light shower in February 1890. The 'infant crabs', ranging in size from that of a dime up to that of a good-sized Californian oyster, were alive, covering the sidewalk and gutter for 20 feet – some filled the spittoons being washed by a man on a sidewalk. Although 'hundreds' came down on Morton Street, a separate shower of 'infant' crabs that happened between Sansome and Battery at the same time evidently involved only a few. Lima, Ohio, *Daily Republican* 21 February 1890.

MYSTERY SPHERE

A myriad of conflicting reports filled North American papers in mid-April 1974 about a metal sphere, reportedly found on the estate of the Antoine Betz family near Jacksonville, Florida. The object has been compared to the 'Giant Gyros' found in Australia – and it has also been dismissed as only a ball-bearing, such as is used as a check-valve in piping at chemical plants. One aspect that is rarely mentioned is: 'Mrs Betz said her family occasionally hears organ music, although there is no organ in the sprawling home. Doors bang without reason, she says, since the sphere showed up.' *Sentinel Star* (Orlando, Florida) 12 April 1974.

And according to other reports: 'it did strange things, such as rolling around the edges of a table by itself without falling off, and making their dog whimper.' St Louis (Missouri) *Post Dispatch* 16 April 1974. Other sources include: *Miami Herald* 13, 15 + 16 April; *Winnipeg Free Press* 13 April; *Houston Chronicle* 14 + 15 April; *Chicago Tribune* + *San Francisco Chronicle* 15 April; *Sentinel Star* (Orlando, Florida) 15 + 16 April; *San Francisco Examiner* 15 + 16 April; *Chicago Daily News* 16 April 1974.

'A nice, pleasant brain-teaser,' is the way Dr J. Allen Hyneck characterized the mysterious metal sphere when he finally got a look at it. Before he did, publicity about the object prompted many explanations. Anonymous telephone callers suggested: 1) it was a 'giant gyro' such as said to be found in Australia after UFO sightings; 2) it was a tide and current transcriber that is floated on a buoy at sea. The U.S. Navy examined the sphere and concluded it was probably 'a giant bearing used as a check-valve in the piping systems of chemical plants'. At Taos, New Mexico, a sculptor got his measure of attention by claiming the sphere was one he lost while driving through Jacksonville in 1971. He would not divulge the exact origin of the several spheres he said he got for his own use from a friend – but he said they were designed as part of an industrial valve.

Dr James Harder, who ran down to Pascagoula, Mississippi, to look into the UFO activity there, took an interest in the sphere long enough to get quoted in the press: 'Harder said previous sightings of metal spheres were reported in the New England states and off Mississippi "but not one could we get our hands on".'

The Jacksonville sphere was eventually examined by many hands. The U.S. Navy described the object as eight inches in diameter; hollow; empty; high-grade stainless steel to a thickness of half an inch; and with a weight of 21.34 lb. The UFO panel of scientists for a weekly paper studied the ball at a gathering in New Orleans, Louisiana. There, Hynek, Harder and others concluded that it: 1) possesses magnetic poles; 2) contains smaller spheres inside; and 3) is almost perfectly balanced. The last word came from a spokesman for the U.S. Geological Survey, Frank Forrester, who snickered at the activity of the newspaper panel and said the Survey would be 'very receptive to analysing fragments' of the mystery ball. Amid all this action, another Jacksonville resident reached into the back of her garage and produced a similar but slightly smaller metal sphere that had lain there for 15 years. A spokesman for the local St Regis papermill said they recognized that ball as part of a valve used 15 years ago in pipes moving corrosive liquid.

As usual, opinion seems very divided over the source of the sphere and no definite or strongly convincing conclusions have been drawn. You might just want to check your garage to make sure you don't have any spheres there to offer for investigation. *New Orleans Times-Picayune* 23 April; *Atlanta Constitution* 16 April; *Miami Herald* 18 April; *National Enquirer* 26 May 1974.

Wayne Betz, 12, and the mystery metal sphere found on the family estate in Florida.

Fish Falls

Like frogs, fish are always plopping down from the heavens. Sometimes quite a plop: one Chinaman was killed when a three-pound carp landed on his head.

FISH FALL ANSWERS CASTAWAYS' PRAYER

Three fishermen from a tiny Pacific island in the Kiribati group survived 119 days adrift in a 16-foot open boat at the mercy of wind and currents by catching 25 sharks with their bare hands, clubbing them to death, drinking their blood and eating them raw. The ordeal of Take Taka, Tatiete Kannangaki and Bakatarawa Labo, two Protestants and a Catholic, began on 4 April 1986 when their engine broke down within sight of their village. Currents swept them to Naurui, more than 430 miles away. They were finally rescued when a Naurui fisherman noticed birds feeding on fragments of fish devoured by sharks following the barnacle-encrusted vessel. 'One of the most remarkable things they told me,' said Sergeant Paul Aingilea of the Naurui police, 'was that one Saturday night, while they were praying for a different kind of fish because they were sick and tired of shark, something fell into the boat. It was a rare blackish fish which you can never catch trawling. It never comes to the surface, and lives about 620 feet down.' *Daily Telegraph* 25 August 1986.

This story is remarkable, for it is not merely a courageous saga of everyday shark-wrestling folk but has the motifs of the 'answered prayer' and the 'fish fall'. To dismiss the conjunction of these as the product of coincidence would not diminish the wonder of it, still less 'explain' it. In the annals of data on falls, this incident has no rival and contradicts the 'officially' endorsed waterspout theory, by which, it is said, surface water and the fishes in it are sucked up. Still, the sceptics could fall back on the 'bird-dropped-it' notion, and simply ignore the statement, by fishermen, that 'it never comes to the surface', or else suppose the hypothetical bird dived to around 620 feet!

The circumstances of this 'answered prayer' were similar to a case recorded by Increase Mather, in his *Remarkable Providences* (1684), who cites in turn from James Janeways' *Remarkable Sea Deliverances*. The story is of 12 people adrift for five weeks in a long-boat after their ship sank off New England: 'God sent relief to them by causing some flying-fish to fall into the boat, which they ate raw and were well pleased therewith. They also caught a shark, and opening his belly, sucked his blood for drink.' (Mather, 1890 edition, p. 13.)

On the morning of 19 December 1984, drivers on the Santa Monica Freeway, near Crenshaw Boulevard, Los Angeles, were making their way through a rainstorm when 'fish and live crab suddenly appeared at the side of the road. There were no reports of accidents involving a delivery truck – nor distress signals from a fishing trawler far off course in the rain – so California Highway Patrol officers guessed that part of a load fell off a passing restaurant supply truck'. *Los Angeles Times* 20 December; AP 21 December 1984.

These fish suddenly appeared on a Los Angeles freeway during a rainstorm on 19 December 1984.

RAINING FISH

A. D. Ellmers and his wife were standing in their driveway in California, when tiny fish began falling all around them. The two-inch fish were later found to be thread-finned shad, a population of which exists in a reservoir about two miles away. Boston *Globe* 24 August; *Die Welt* 25 August; Portland *Press Herald* 31 August 1984.

Pennies from Heaven

Once more with feeling ... ouch! Sometimes money seems to literally drop out of the sky. Shame it doesn't happen more often.

COINS FALL ON CHURCHYARD

A genuine case of 'Pennies from Heaven' mystified the parishioners of St Elisabeth's Church, Reddish, between Manchester and Stockport. On the morning of 28 May 1981 a young girl claimed to have seen a 50p coin fall 'from nowhere' in front of her as she walked through the churchyard, During the day many pounds worth of copper and silver coins were found by children in the same location. The Rector, Rev Graham Marshall, collected numerous plummeting pence to a value of over £2. Investigation quickly eliminated the obvious theories – the nearby church wall was too high to conceal a practical joker, there were no signs of magpie nests, and a number of coins dropping together ruled out the idea of a bird overhead.

Rev Marshall confirmed all the details. Children would hear the tinkle of coins on the path and turn to discover them. Only in one case did a girl claim to see one falling. Most curious of all, he told us, was that a few coins were found embedded in the ground by their edges. He tried an experiment, hurling a fistful of coins at the ground but they made no impression. Either the coins fell from a great height (which does not square with the gentle tinkle signalling the arrival of most of them), or we are seeing, in the open, the phenomenon of poltergeist projectiles. *Stockport Express* 4 June 1981.

The Rev Graham Marshall sheltering from coin falls at St Elisabeth's, Reddish.

MODERN MANNA RAINS

Several thousand kopecks' worth of silver coins fell on 17 June 1940, during a storm, in the Gorky region of Russia. It was surmised that a treasure had become uncovered in a landslide somewhere, and been picked up by a tornado and gifted to the people of Gorky.

On 8 October 1976 a light plane 'bombed' Rome's Piazza Venezia with banknotes of 500, 1000 and 10,000 denominations. Amazed police were said to be puzzled at being unable to find out who did it and why! *Newport News* (Va) *Daily Press* 10 October 1976; *Reveille* 7 January 1977.

In France, however, a businessman was nabbed for scattering more than £2000, in francs, from the top of a 150-foot crane. He was taken by police to a mental clinic (they get no marks for imagination!) *Reveille* 12 August 1977 ... the incident happened at Nice!

● In the quiet steel-town of Bethlehem, Pennsylvania, police were called when a plumber had to fish out of a service-station toilet more than $3000 in torn $100 bills, on 24 July 1977. On the 26th, a cleaning woman found another $1000 in torn $100 bills clogging a restaurant toilet. Treasury officials say the money does not appear to be counterfeit; and the FBI said the bill-numbers do not match those of recent local robberies. Bafflement reigns! Dallas *Times Herald* 27 July; Dallas *Morning News* 29 July 1977.

● The day after the second lot of bills went down the tube in Bethlehem, on 27 July, a broken sack scattered about $250,000 in $20 bills out of the back unlocked door of an armoured bank truck in the rush-hour in a Philadelphia street. Despite the hectic grabbing that ensued, police proudly claim that at least $242,000 had been recovered. Dallas *Morning News* 28 July 1977.

● A similar incident happened in Nottingham, England, nearly two months later. On 2 September, a security van drove along a street showering loose change from its back. The money was recovered – the men sacked. *Daily Telegraph* 3 September 1977

DISSOLVING CHEQUES

Or maybe we should say checks, as the scam is American. Police cottoned on to the caper in early March 1988. Cheques with an unusual odour and oily feel, which 'sweat and deteriorate', rapidly turning into confetti, were turning up, drawn on accounts in Illinois, California and Tennessee. The scheme: an account is opened with a small amount of money. A large deposit is made with a dissolving cheque, then money is withdrawn before the bank catches on. By 25 March, banks in Chicago and Memphis had lost nearly $70,000. *USA Today* 25 March; *Ashbury Park Press* 4 April 1988.

JAPANESE TREASURE TROVES

For the second time in 5 days, a man hunting for bamboo shoots found a bag containing 100m yen (£434,000) in the same bamboo thicket near Tokyo. The total haul, according to the *Guardian*, was £1,017,316, and the bamboo thicket was near Yokohama. The money turned out to belong to Kazuyasu Noguchi, a company president. Rather than pay tax he had left the money in the bamboos hoping that whoever picked it up would donate it to charity! *Independent* 17 April; *Guardian* 22 August 1989.

● Another lucky Japanese was the garbage collector who found £757,575 when he tried to demolish a safe at a rubbish dump in Yokohama. This later turned out to belong to Haruo Nakanishi, formerly a senior executive of Soka Gakkai, the controversial militant Buddhist group, who had simply left it in a warehouse of a newspaper he published, and forgot about it. The police wanted more details especially when it emerged that the money, takings from a souvenir shop near the cult's main temple, had not been declared for tax. Middlesbrough *Evening Gazette* 30 June; *Guardian* 22 August 1989.

● In most other countries these items would not become news as the finders would not have told anyone. Compare the behaviour of Americans when bags of money fell out of an armoured car on a busy Texan highway during rush hour: there was traffic chaos as motorists scrambled for the cash. Middlesbrough *Evening Gazette* 8 June 1989.

COIN SHOWERS

'Coins have been falling on me from the skies over the past six years,' said Albert Williamson, 71, of Ramsgate in Kent. His neighbour, Kim Moody, 22, said she was recently hit by a shower of coins at a bus stop. 'They came from nowhere,' she said. 'I kept watch on windows and my friend kept an eye on the sky. More fell, but we couldn't see where they came from.' Many were marked with two deep grooves, which suggested they has been fired from a gun. *People* 23 July 1989.

● A shower of hot coins fell on Sophie Gough, 42, and her husband David as they strolled in the graveyard of St Mary's Church, somewhere in England. Some fell on their shoulders, some at their feet. The coins were dated between 1902 and 1953, no longer legal tender. They were quite hot, although it was a cold evening. The church was locked and no aircraft were flying overhead.

Paranormal researcher Richard Benson said that coins had struck visitors in the same graveyard three years earlier. The report in the *Examiner* (U.S.A) 9 January 1990 by Glenn Troelstrup goes on to say: 'Investigators are convinced the hot money is somehow linked to a tragic local ghost nicknamed the Gray Lady of Kenardington. The miserly wife of a wealthy 18th-century landowner, she'd died in childbirth, still clutching the coins she'd been counting.'

The same report goes on to say that coins fell out ot the sky at several churches in the U.S.A. and England in 1981. They fell with a gentle tinkle, as though they had materialized just a few feet from the ground.

Poltergeists

Things that go bump in the night (and in the daytime too) . . . just another apparently inexplicable phenomenon that seems to happen from time to time.

POWER SURGE?

There was terror in the little Suffolk village of Honey Tye, in mid-December 1983. Residents fled their homes as light bulbs exploded, electrical appliances switched themselves on and burnt themselves out. 'It was really weird. We had no idea what was happening,' said Mrs Jackie Pearce of the Red Lion pub. If it had happened in just a single house the story would have been written up as a poltergeist. Meanwhile the Eastern Electricity Board – who had repairmen working in the area at the time (well, where there's a traffic cop there's a holdup, right?) – explained that it was a mystery power surge of another kind. *Sunday Mirror* 18 December 1983.

THE LIFT THAT MOVED ON ITS OWN

In April 1969 Jos Smith led his ten-man team of demolition workers into the 112-year-old Palace Hotel in Birkdale, Lancashire. They had a contract and intended to sleep in the building until the job was done. After about a month they were all sufficiently frightened to move out into lodgings and only work in the daylight. 'I don't blame them,' said Jos. 'Things started to happen soon after we moved in. First of all we were awakened by strange noises in the night. Then the lift would suddenly set off on its own.'

About mid-April Jos ordered all the power to the building and the lift to be cut off – but the lift still glided from floor to floor with its gates opening and closing, and its indicator lights flashing. Electricity Board spokesmen were quoted that the building was isolated – not an amp was going into the place. The men removed the emergency winding handle, but still it moved. Workman Fred Wooley said: 'Nine of us came back one night and as we entered the foyer the lift doors slammed shut and it shot up to the second floor.' The Paralab directory for 1969 has a summary of the case and they mention an 'independent witness', a Mrs K. Templeton, who had gone into the 1000-room hotel looking for antique mirrors. She said: 'While I was talking to the workmen the lift suddenly began to go up. There wasn't any sound from it – it was very eerie. It just glided up about seven feet almost to the next floor and stopped. I ran all the way up to the winding room with one of the workmen, but there was just no way it could have been moved mechanically. The brake was still on.'

A BBC programme ran a report showing a dog that was happy on all floors except the second one – indeed the second floor seems to be the focus of the activity.

The Paralab go on to mention that a decision was made to cut the cables, but the lift did not fall. So they cut through the main shafts, to no avail. It was as perverse in its obstinacy as it was in its previous wilful mobility. It did not fall until it had been continually struck with sledge-hammers for 25 minutes, and then it plunged down the shaft to bury itself four feet into the cellar. This behaviour was naturally found 'unbelievable' by those present.

There is an epilogue of sorts. In the last week of May 1969 the local papers reported 'hundreds of pounds worth of damage' to the building. Why worry, you ask? Well, for example, 200 doors were stacked ready for selling, and during the night they were thrown over a balcony and smashed. Windows were broken, saleable iron balustrades wrecked, and fires started. All this was blamed on vandals, but there were no reports of the vandalism being witnessed; just discovered next morning. *Daily Mail + Daily Mirror* 7 May 1969; *Manchester Evening News* 29 May 1969.

Columbus Despatch **photographer Fred Shannon captured the moment the telephone flew in front of Tina Resch, 14, at her home in Columbus,** **Ohio, on Sunday, 9 March 1984. The disturbances had begun the night before, with lights going on and off, and objects flying about.**

A BOOT THAT WENT BUMP AT THE BEEB

Something went bump in the night at the Beeb. It was a well-aimed left boot belonging to radio news-reader James A. Gordon. He threw it at a ghost that appeared at his bedside in a room provided for nightshift news-readers in the Langham, a BBC administration building.

Gordon fled clutching his trousers and right boot, and spent the rest of the night in his office across the road at Broadcasting House. None of his colleagues laughed when he told them about it – for two other news-readers, Ray Moore and Peter Donaldson, admitted they had the same experience. Moore says: I have seen the figure twice, it is like a bright white light. It is a big thick-set man with his hands behind his back.' Donaldson said: 'I woke up to find a force trying to push me out of bed. The curtains were closed but there was a glowing light inside the room.'

The Langham was once a hotel, and parts of it are centuries old. The ghost is seen only on the third floor, where the overnight accommodation is. 'The whole floor is very moody at night,' says Ray Moore. 'Two of the commission-aires won't go near it after dark. Sometimes if you press the third floor lift button, it goes shooting up to the sixth. But only at night.' *Daily Mirror* 1 August 1973.

A NOTTINGHAM POLT

In May 1987 the Costello family fled from their council house in Aspley, Nottingham, after a series of very disturbing events suggesting a poltergeist.

The Costellos, John, 52, his wife Helen, 51, and their daughters Sharon, 20, Suzie, 18, and Rosie, 13, moved into the house after it had been specially adapted so that Sharon, severely disabled with autism, could live with them. One day in February 1987, when they returned from an outing, they heard the sound of giant 'heart beats' which brought Sharon to her knees. She was in such a state she had to be taken to hospital. Later, there was mournful music, apparently from an electric organ that had been disconnected, and a spirited solo on a three-stringed child's guitar. Windows were smashed, plugs pulled out, while furniture and Sharon's bedclothes moved restlessly around. Spirit-ualist Betty Henswell said there were five 'ghosts' in the house.

Evidence was read in court from Jack Yates, 64, a retired so-licitor's clerk from Yorkshire, who agreed to sleep on the sofa in the living room one night to check their story. The light started to go on and off, and then he felt a force lift him about a foot in the air. This seemed to last for several minutes. He had to use all his strength to come down again. Then he saw a typewriter start to move as if invisible fingers were pressing the keys. The paper started scrunch-ing itself up. On examination, he found *AH AH* [or *ah, ah???*] typed right across it. He also heard scratchings on his bedclothes and strange knockings in the air.

Police and social workers witnessed some weirdness, and a priest came to give an exorcism. When he sprinkled holy water on the stairs, it was chucked back at him. The events continued with the new tenants, James Cotterill, 36, his wife Sandra and their three children. 'Lights flash, locked doors open and white circles with a cross inside appear on the walls,' said Mr Cotterill. *Guardian + Daily Mirror + Sun + Western Mail + Daily Express* 14 April 1988; *Daily Mirror + Western Mail* 19 January 1989.

Ghosts and Visions

The conventional views of ghosts are (1) that they don't exist; or (2) that they represent spirits of the departed. Perhaps neither of these explanations is correct?

The profile of an old man or woman appeared inexplicably on this identity card photo of Wendy Sternberg of Buffalo State College in 1974.

THE AMOROUS GHOST OF WORKSOP

Pretty Beryl Gladwin doesn't get much sleep. Between 4 and 6am, three mornings a week, she is visited by a ghost wearing miner's boots. Her life is made such a misery that her parents are applying for a new home for themselves and their seven children. Beryl, 18, tried sleeping with her parents, but the amorous spook was not deterred. 'First it tugs at the bedclothes and then I feel it get next to me in the bed. It holds my hand and starts kissing me and biting my neck.' The haunting began about the end of February 1975, and after a couple of frightening weeks, the family called in a clairvoyant, Simon Alexander.

Mr Alexander kept a vigil at one of the regular trysting times, and felt a malevolent presence outside the room. 'It tried to make me leave by making me feel ill. I had to fight hard to stay. Then it materialized in the room. It was trying to dodge me and was difficult to get into focus. I could see pit boots clearly, and miner's baggy herringbone trousers held up by a wide belt with a big buckle. It tried to get in with Beryl and kiss her. She was trembling with fear.'

He went on: 'I believe it's the ghost of a miner called Dexter who used to live in the house. He had 12 children of his own, and I'm certain he will make love to Beryl unless something is done soon.' The Gladwins, as seems to be a pattern in council-house hauntings, had only moved into the house six months previously. The church seems unhurried about who gets laid first. The vicar of Worksop, conducting his own investigation, said an exorcism might be a possibility.

Some time after the story appeared, the *People* carried a little note tucked away where few would see it. It read: 'Mr George Dexter, of 31 Windmill Lane Worksop, states that the story we published on March 9 headed "The Ghost that Left Love Bites" was a slur on his dead brother. There was no such intention and we are sorry if the report caused embarrassment to the Dexter family.' You gotta laugh! *News of the World + Sunday Mirror + Sunday People* 9 March; *Sunday People* 11 May 1975.

GHOSTLY GALLANTS

● Mrs June of Marske-by-Sea, near Redcar, Yorkshire, a mature woman with a 10-year-old son, became obsessed with the ouija, which in turn led to automatic writing, the communicating entity being 'a long-dead spirit called Leonardo'. Dead he may have been, but he still knew how to write a good love-letter, and he even claimed to want a child by Mrs June. A few weeks after the automatic writing began, Mrs June saw a floating shadow in the bedroom; then she felt the bedclothes move. Leonardo had arrived ...

and was, it seems, furious to discover she was taking the contraceptive pill. This doesn't seem to have dampened lusty Leonardo's enthusiasm though. Mrs June is quoted: 'I would feel his presence, even his strength of feeling when he wanted to make love. He was a competent lover and must have been on earth. But human love is more satisfying. With spiritual love, there is no warmth of flesh.' *Reville* 24 March 1978.

● Jenny Price, 20, of Shenley Lane, Wedley Castle, Birmingham, clamed complete satisfaction with her own ghostly gallant. Her family had known that the house had a ghost for years, but had never told Jenny about it. The first amorous approach was to the elder daughter, Lorraine, but it merely touched her shoulder. Then, one night when Jenny was sitting up in bed she felt invisible hands round her neck. With great strength, the hands pushed her down on the bed. Frightened, she tried to scream, couldn't, and thought the ghost would strangle her, but then realized the ghost had other intentions. After that she was scared to go to bed in case the attack was repeated, and a week later, it was. She soon realized that the ghost meant her no harm, however, and began looking forward to his visits, which began to take place as often as three times a week . . .

By the time three years had passed the biggest problem appears to have been how to get Jenny out of bed, she being too intent on staying there waiting for her invisible lover to show up.

Jenny's mother, Olive, wanted to get in on the act too, so she swapped beds with her daughter for three weeks. But the randy wraith didn't show up. Olive, however, doesn't think anything immoral's going on. She asked to see the vicar, and he said ghosts probably don't bother with morals. So that makes it okay. Doesn't it? *News of the World* 26 March; *Kansas City Times* 13 April 1978.

LIFT-SHAFT GHOST

Lift engineer Russell Mather was working on a lift-shaft at Kingsley and Forrester Ltd, Gorse Mill, Chadderton, near Manchester, and took a photograph of the shaft. He was unaware of the ghostly shape until the picture was printed. 'You can clearly see a head, arms and legs on some sort of figure,' said his wife Linda. Back at the mill, he was told a story of a little girl being killed after falling down the shaft, but no record of her death could be found. *Bolton Evening News* 6 February 1988.

Inept Crime

Why is it so funny when a criminal makes a cock-up? Somehow one feels that criminals ought to be serious about what they're doing.

CRIMINAL CROPPERS

● David Morris, 21, unemployed, from Beckenham in Kent, was passing the time before a date with his girlfriend when he wrote a note reading: 'I have got a gun in my pocket and I'll shoot it off unless you hand over the money.' He then went into three shops in London Road, West Croydon, London, and passed the note over the counter. At a drug store, a girl assistant refused to accept the note, believing it contained an obscene suggestion, and Morris left. Next door in a hardware shop an Asian assistant looked blankly at Morris, shook his head and said he couldn't read English. Morris then went to a takeaway food shop, but the assistant couldn't read the note without his glasses. Morris asked for the note back, and hung around in the street outside. Arrested soon afterwards, he told the police: 'I've been a twit . . . I only pretended to have a gun.' He was put on probation for two years. *Daily Telegraph + Daily Mail* 20 February 1986.

● 1985 was a classic year for self-incriminating burglars. Stuart Lawrence broke into a shoe shop, leaving behind a bail form from a previous offence. He was jailed for 15 months at York Crown Court in January. A man burgled a Dortmund flat, leaving behind his papers and a razor-sharp passport photo. He was tried in February. Peter Richardson, 33, burgled a house leaving behind a locket with his name and address. He got nine months at Snaresbrook Crown Court in March. Keven Barwick, 35, from Plymouth, broke into a television rental shop during the January blizzards. Footprints from his size eight wellies led straight to his front door. In April, the magistrates gave him three months, suspended for two years. A thief who grabbed an armful of cameras from a Frankfurt photographic shop left behind freshly taken passport photos. He turned himself in in August. In September a man trying to cash stolen travellers cheques in the Yorkshire Bank, Leeds, left his passport behind. *Daily Mirror* 19 January, 23 March, 3 April, 11 September; *Soester Anzeiger* 23 + 24 February; *Royal Guardian* 24 August 1985.

● A burglar broke into a baker's shop in Viblach, Austria. As he crept across the office in the dark, he was attacked by Lola the cockatoo. During the fight, the burglar knocked over a glass tank containing Egor the viper. By torchlight he saw Egor slithering across the floor. At that moment, the baker's pet mynah, Peppino, started his favourite imitation – a doorbell. Terrified, the burglar crashed through a window, cutting himself as he escaped. Baker Robert Koloini, roused by the noise, came downstairs to find chaos, but the £2,000 in his safe still intact. *Sunday Express* 11 August 1985.

CAUGHT NAPPING

● **Thomas Schimmel came home in Texas City, Michigan, to find his pocket watch and rifle missing. He called the police who came to investigate, then headed for bed, where he found the 19-year-old thief fast asleep.**

● **Three youths in Amherst, Nova Scotia, stripped down several cars in a used-car lot overnight and stuffed several hundred dollars worth of parts into the boot of their own car. They fell asleep in the car, only to be awoken by police.**

● **Lazaros Alberis, 25, was discovered in an Athens cinema sleeping over the cash register which he had tried, unsuccessfully, to open with a pair of scissors. *Midnight Globe* 23 January 1979; *The Globe & Mail* (Canada) 5 February; *London Evening News* 7 August 1980.**

TOY GUN ANTICS

● Clive Bunyan burst into a store near Scarborough and brandished a toy revolver. He got the shop assistant to hand over £157 from the till, and fled. He had his motorbike parked for a fast getaway and wore his full-face crash helmet as a mask. He had forgotten, however, that around his helmet in inch-high letters were the words 'Clive Bunyan – Driver'. He was easy to find. *Daily Star* 15 November 1980.

● Edward McAlea of Liverpool went into a jewellers in that city with a stocking mask on, pointed a revolver at three men and warned them, 'This is a stick-up. Get down.' They didn't bother, because they saw a red plastic stopper in the muzzle and realized it was a toy. After a scuffle, McAlea escaped, pulling the mask from his face. *Daily Telegraph* 9 February 1980.

FINGERED

● **During a smash-and-grab raid on a Zurich jeweller, the thief had his finger cut off by broken glass. The police identified the finger from their files and arrested the thief within two hours. Another man had left his finger behind in the mouth of his strangled victim in Ogden, Utah.** *Malden News* **(MA) 11 July 1980.**

LOBSTER WARNING

● 'Never stuff a lobster down your underpants.' A simple maxim, you may think, but one that was overlooked by Boston shoplifter Winston Treadway with unfortunate results. Treadway had already amassed a quantity of stolen food in a trawl around an out-of-the-way supermarket when he spotted a tank full of live seafood. Plucking two lobsters from the water, he stashed them in his underwear and sprinted for the exit – only to pull up short in a nearby alley as the enraged crustacea clamped their claws around his genitals. 'When we saw him he was trying to prise the claws off. He was purple as an aubergine when we got to him,' said police. Having accosted the thief, the cops called for pliers to remove the lobsters. Doctors who confirmed that Treadway had inadvertently performed a DIY vasectomy later told him he might never father children. *Sun* 7 May 1990.

● Altogether more ambitious was Thomas Waddell, a Baltimore man arrested by police with 21 live homing pigeons and five dead ones stuffed down his pants. Waddell aroused the suspicions of officer Ronald Pettie while in process of stealing the pigeons, valued at $300, from neighbour John Styron. 'He looked like the Michelin tyre ad. There were feathers all over the place,' Pettie explained. *News-Tribune* 3 November 1989.

Not Their Day

Bad-luck stories are always cheering for the rest of us. But when somebody suffers extraordinary bad luck, he might be forgiven for feeling persecuted . . .

TWISTS OF FORTUNE

● Bill Helko, 38, was over the moon when he got the winning number in a Californian lottery – the first prize was £412,000. He ordered a Porsche, booked a family holiday in Hawaii and had a champagne dinner with his wife and friends at a swish Hollywood restaurant. When he went to collect his winnings he found that 9097 others had also won first prize, and his share of the jackpot was £45. *Daily Mirror* 23 March 1987.

● Ianni and Anna Deluca had to scrimp for 30 years to pay the mortgage on their house in suburban Milan. After the last payment they held a party and threw the mortgage papers in the fire, which then got out of control and burnt the house down. There was no insurance: that had been sacrificed to meet all those payments. *Sunday Express* 13 December 1987.

● Yugoslav policeman Sinisa Micic, 27, went to a bar to celebrate after winning 20 million *dinars* (about £40,000) in a lottery at Smederevo, near Belgrade, on 20 March 1986. He ordered drinks all round, lurched out of the bar, and was killed by a passing lorry. Tanjug *Emirates News* (Abu Dhabi) 22 March 1986.

● The manager of High Marnham power station on the River Trent decreed that a special flag should be flown to mark the 100th accident-free day, 'our best effort for years'. A security guard was hoisting the flag when the unthinkable happened: the pulley wheel clattered down 20 feet and hit him on the head. *Daily Mirror* 30 September 1987.

● Heart transplant patient, Norman Meredith, 33, was knocked down by a car on his first shopping trip since coming home. He was dragged across the street, in Pontypridd, South Wales, and then the driver got out threatening to punch him. *Daily Mirror* 9 September 1983.

● Convicted murderer Michael Godwin, 28, avoided the electric chair in Columbia, South Carolina, when his sentence was reduced to life on appeal. While sitting naked on the metal commode in his cell he electrocuted himself by biting through a wire while mending the headphones on his television. *Independent + Daily Mirror* 8 March 1988.

BURNING EMBARRASSMENT

● Announcement in a local newspaper in Lingenfield, West Germany: 'We would like to draw attention to the fact that the information evening planned for Saturday in the Weingarten fire station on "Preventative measures for Fighting Fire in House and Home" has had to be postponed. The fire station caught fire on Monday, and must be restored.' *Telegraph* 10 March 1986.

● The fire station in the Black Sea resort of Sukhumi was virtually destroyed by fire while the firemen were in the building playing dominoes. They had ignored three calls, taking them to be false alarms. A fire-extinguishing system at an Italian engineering plant burst into flames; a fire extinguisher factory in Cheltenham caught fire; and two groups of firemen sped out of their station in North Allerton, Yorkshire, went round the building to tackle a blazing fire engine. *Houston Chronicle* 5 June 1974; *Daily Express* 21 March 1979 + 20 March 1980; *Sun* 12 April 1985.

UP IN SMOKE

● Relatives at the cremation of retired farmer Eddie Oakley, 78, asked for a tape of Ella Fitzgerald's classic 'Every Time We Say Goodbye' to be played. Instead, the Stourbridge Crematorium played 'Smoke Gets in Your Eyes'. *Daily Star* 31 October 1989.

KWAAK!

BAD TASTE

● Staff at the Center for Devices and Radiological Health, part of the Food and Drug Administration in Washington, held a Christmas party on Friday, 14 December 1984. More than half the party-goers had nausea and other symptoms of food poisoning by the following Monday. *St Louis Post-Dispatch* 25 December 1984.

● In New York, wine merchant Bill Sokolin was celebrating his acquisition of a bottle of 1787 Chateau Margaux which once belonged to U.S. President Thomas Jefferson. As Bill was proudly showing the antique claret to admiring friends a waiter brushed past and the inevitable happened. Bill wept openly as the wine, now valued at £400,000, smashed on the floor. When he tasted a salvaged mouthful, he also had to admit that it was 'not very good'. *Sun* 26 April 1989.

TIMELY COLLAPSE

During a ceremony at the Kemper Arena, Kansas City, at which the building's designer, Helmut Jahn, was to receive a citation from the president of the American Institute of Architects, watched by 1000 of the Institute's members, the roof of the twelve-million-dollar building fell in. Twenty-six architects were hospitalized. So much for the pros. *Architects Journal* 13 August 1979.

BACKFIRINGS

Rob Manes, who works for the Kansas Game Commission and teaches hunters how to bag game safely, was accidentally shot (not fatally) by another safety expert, Gene Brehm. Manes was wearing an orange cap with 'Kansas Safe Hunter' printed on the front. The accident happened near a town called Pratt. *News of the World* 15 February 1987.

● The imitation duck-calls made by Dimitris Thomasinas, 19, to lure birds his way when he went shooting in Salonika were so life-like that two of his colleagues fired at the bushes where he was hiding and shot him dead. *Telegraph* 28 January 1985.

● On a hot, sticky night in Palermo, Sicily, Salvatore Rosella opened the windows of his apartment, but the noise from his neighbour's children was driving him and his wife mad. Countless times he had told them to keep quiet to no effect, so he grabbed his pistol intending to frighten them into silence. When he banged on the neighbour's door an argument developed. Antonella Rosella leaned out of the window to tell her neighbour to shut up. Salvatore lost control and threatened to shoot the neighbours, and fired the gun into the air. He shot his wife! *Sunday Express* 18 September 1983.

Strange Lights

Lights in the sky are usually classified as 'UFOs' and dismissed. Others are defined as meteorological curiosities. But some remain difficult to explain.

BRAZILIAN SPOOKLIGHTS

Cynthia Newby Luce writes:

'I live in a remote Brazilian mountain village – a stranger in a strange land. I thought I was lucky to pay only $2600 for 66 acres, plus a spring with superb water. The locals were laughing at the stupid 'gringo' who paid so much for a piece of haunted land!

'Soon I was cautiously asked if I'd seen the '*Mae de Ouro*' (mother of gold). Finally someone explained to me that for at least 150 years people had been seeing a light, usually a yellow-orange glowing ball slightly smaller than a volley ball, making a slow pass across the face of the hill. It usually passed behind the house I had built. Since this is a land full of semi-legends of ghosts, and the local voodoo-type religion (Macumba, Umbanda, Condomble) entails a type of very tangible possession, I dismissed the discreet enquiries with a shrug. In my subsequent extensive travels throughout Brazil I have found the *Mae de Ouro* legend to be ubiquitous and ingrained in the culture. One follows the *Mae de Ouro* and the first body of water it crosses – river, creak or stream – is where one should look for gold. And gold is found often enough to keep interest and belief in the phenomenon alive.

'The first time I saw the light on my land was one evening in June 1980 around 7:45pm. There were five witnesses: my daughter aged eight, myself, two maids and the gardener. A yellow-orange glowing ball, slightly smaller than a standard volley ball, passed from east to west with the wavering flight of a butterfly above five feet off the ground. It was about 30 feet away from us and was passing between the garage and the house. It made a wide curving turn and headed off towards the stables and vegetable garden near the spring. My gardener, fascinated, went after it. Foolishly he reached out to touch it. The ball faded away to nothing as he put out his hand, then reappeared about 15 feet ahead of him. He came back to the house rather unnerved because the phenomenon seemed to him to have intelligence.

'I have not personally seen the light again, but my servants have seen it numerous times in the past seven years. It even swooped down on my cook as she hung out some clothes early one evening, and nearly hit her head. The phenomenon seems to prefer the colder dry months, but I have also recorded its appearance in the hot wet season (November through April). It has even appeared in light rain.

'The villagers have become more interested in unravelling the mystery since I've been so voluble in an effort to dispel any superstitious attitudes, telling them that physicists and researchers all over the world are interested in what is widely seen as a natural phenomenon. Hardly a month passes now without at least one villager telling me of a sighting. The colour is usually reported as yellow-orange, but sometimes as blue-white; it usually, but not always, travels from east to west; and the size also varies. Reported size is to some degree, of course, dependent upon distance; from my hill to the village is about 1200 feet as the crow flies.

'After talking to a geologist friend with first-hand knowledge of the phenomenon, I've been trying to borrow or rent a metal or mineral dectector to see whether the underlying rock, which is mostly granite, has a vein of iron which, by itself or in combination with the numerous springs, may influence the appearance of the phenomenon. I might add that this area is probably the least likely in the world to experience earthquakes, and the methane hypothesis I've also found to be invalid.'

WEST COAST METEORS?

A puff of brown smoke and a brilliant silver glow lit up the sky for less than ten seconds over 400 miles of northern California and southern Oregon at 2:50pm, Friday, 20 July 1984. John Melvin, a Prairie Creek State Park ranger, said the object (a meteor?) could have been 50 miles from him and 5000 feet high. Dozens of people called authorities and radio stations from as far away as Medfield, Oregon, 90 miles north-east of Prairie Creek, and San Francisco, 330 miles to the south.

Gilbert Sena, a coastguard helicopter pilot flying at about 1500 feet near Eureka, 270 miles north of San Francisco, also saw the object, which appeared to be 7000 feet above sea level, and going up! Duluth, Minnesota, *News-Tribune Herald* 22 July 1984.

On the following Friday, a strange spark-tailed white and orange something splashed down a thousand yards south of Lummi Island in the Puget Sound, off Washington State. The event was reported to the Coast Guard at 3:45am, 27 July, by the *Steeva Ten*, a 42-foot fishing vessel. The object made two 'U' turns before splashdown, and sent up a plume of water 100 feet high. A flash in the sky was noted at the same time by a tugboat about five miles to the south.

The Coast Guard investigated, but found no debris. Checks with other authorities turned up no reports of missing planes or space junk crashing in the area. The object sank in water 270 feet deep in Rosario Strait, an area of intense currents, which made it difficult to do a survey, according to the Coast Guard station at Bellingham, Washington, which sent a boat to the scene. At 5:05am the Coast Guard vessel reported a large lighted object in the sky, which quickly passed out of view. St Louis *Post-Dispatch* 28 July.

METEORIC FALL

F rom midnight to dawn on 11–13 August 1977, the public was told in advance, sky-watchers would be able to see many fiery 'shooting stars' throughtout the world, as lumps of rock and ice from the close passage of Comet Temple-Swift burned up in the atmosphere. *Daily Telegraph* 3 August 1977.

● On 12 August 1977 a mystery light was seen in Sussex believed at the time to be a plane crashing into the sea or a shooting star; and there were several witnesses to UFOs at Russ Green, Essex. It's possible that those lights were cometary debris.

Later that year, a meteor 'as big as a house' trailed across the southern U.S.A. *Texarkana Gazette + Northwest Arkansas Times + Log Cabin Democrat* (Arkansas) *+ Marshall News Messenger* (Texas) 19 October 1977.

CHINA LIGHTS

A t 9:07 pm on 26 August 1988, a luminous spot the shape of a duck's egg with a bright comet-like tail rose from the north-west horizon, and spiralled slowly across the sky over north-east China. As it moved towards the constellation Ursa Major, it began to diffuse and form a large ring, with tiny bluish spots of light on the outer rim. The phenomenon reappeared every other day, and lasted for about 30 minutes each time ... possibly appearing about three or four times in all. The local paper described it as an Aurora Borealis. *China Pictorial* April 1989.

Does Grey Matter?

Is your brain really necessary? It seems not, according to some of the stories related here.

BRAINS – WHO NEEDS THEM?

A 20-year-old French house-wife discovered that the cause of her severe headaches was a .22 bullet her husband fired at her as she slept. Evelyne Muxart, of Saint-Etienne, near Lyons, woke up one night in May 1983 to find a little blood in her hair. She washed her hair then went back to bed with her husband. But when her headaches continued for ten days she went to hospital, where X-rays showed the bullet in her skull. It was removed, and her husband charged with attempted murder. *Guardian* 18 June 1983.

QUALITY NOT QUANTITY

Phineas P. Gage, 25, was a railway foreman in the U.S.A., when on 13 September 1847, while placing a charge in a hole, a premature explosion drove the tamping-iron through his skull. The 13-lb, $1\frac{1}{4}$-inch diameter, 3-feet-7-inch-long rod entered point-first and passed completely through. He lost parts of his skull and some brain matter, but a few hours later was still rational enough to ask after his work. For several days he discharged bone and brain bits through his mouth, then passed into delirium and lost vision in one eye. Gage recovered rapidly, and even tried for his old job. His employers rejected him not because he wasn't fit, but because 'the most efficient and capable foreman' had changed into a truculent, brutish, untrustworthy simpleton. His friends said he was 'no longer Gage'. *American Journal of Medical Science* (Philadelphia) July 1859; *British Medical Journal* 21 April 1888; *Boston Medical & Surgical Journal* 18.

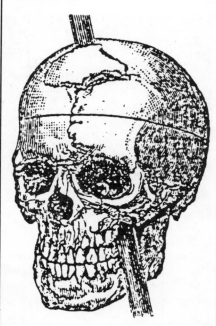

The skull of Phineas Gage.

In most cases of similar serious accidents where the injury is survived, there is some recovery, mentally and physically, though very rarely does that recovery approximate to the pre-accident normality. The question raised is just how much of our brain matter is essential to normal functioning at any time? The answer must be that we simply don't know much about the living brain function in its 'global' mode (to use computer jargon).

Part of the answer may be the discover of the ability to relocate specific brain functions in other parts of the brain, but whether this means that the available matter is shared out in a new proportion, or that there are unused or 'spare' areas of matter which can be cultivated in the event of accident to other parts, is not yet fully understood. This versatility was shown dramatically in a documentary called 'Is your brain really necessary?' ITV 11 May 1982, 10:45pm, in which several patients were described who had 'no detectable brain' or minimal brain tissue; facts confirmed by the latest brain-scanning techniques. These techniques also helped to show that some functions had relocated in the remaining brain tissue. A few examples from that programme follow:

● Sharon, during a routine check on a brain fluid valve, was discovered to have a huge cavity where brain tissues should have been. A Professor Lorber said her brain had disappeared or become paper-thin in the frontal cortex region. She was otherwise functioning normally.

● Roger had only five per cent of his brain left, but still got a first-class degree in mathematics. The whole area where speech and feelings are usually located was missing.

● Stephen's absence of brain was demonstrated by holding a light behind his head, which glowed like a dull pink goldfish bowl. He nevertheless obtained five 'O' levels. Later his brain was found to have 'returned' or 'regrown' or 'reflated' – in any case, he was back to normal.

The results, said Professor Lorber, suggest that it is quality, not quantity, which counts in the old grey stuff. Weird!

Cases of this kind have been turning up at autopsies for years, and reported in the appropriate medical journals, but have been disregarded, perhaps because they are so destructive of established beliefs about the relationship between consciousness and the human brain. Although the reduction in the normal quantity of brain tissue in these individuals ranges from a few per cent to 95 per cent or more, there seems to be no correlation between the amount of residual tissue and IQ. The subject named Roger, referred to in the television documentary, who has no more than five per cent of the normal amount of brain tissue and a first-class degree in mathematics, has an IQ of 126.

Kaye Vandal holds her adopted son Andrew, born without a brain in 1984.

A BOY OF LITTLE BRAIN

Doctors said they doubted he would live out the year, when Andrew was born on 12 July 1984. In 1989 he was celebrating his fifth birthday, and set to celebrate more. In the early stages of Andrew's foetal life, a cyst on the stem of his brain prevented the rest of it forming, a disease known as hydrancephaly, which leaves his cranial cavity containing nothing but fluid. Dr Robert Leshner, professor of paediatric neurology at the Medical College of Virgina, said there is no known cure and the prognosis is poor. Andrew was adopted by Kaye Vandal, a paediatric nurse, of Wallingford, Connecticut, who is devoted to 'giving him the best quality of life for however long he lives'. Kaye has two other adopted children with the same condition, one of them a girl of 12.

Kaye says Andrew has a 'glowing, outgoing, bubbly personality' and laughs, giggles and smiles, actions the doctors said he would never perform. The question of whether Andrew is experiencing amusement divides Kaye from the doctors: she believes he grows and responds, while the doctors point out he has no cerebellum or cerebrum, the parts that allegedly allow us to think and co-ordinate movement. Andrew cannot walk, but scoots about on his back. He has no speech and is cortically blind (images are seen but not interpreted). South Bend *Tribune* + Maryland *The Capital* 13 July; Omaha *World Herald* + Atlanta *Journal* + *Constitution* 14 July 1989.

Headbangers

Sometimes it seems that human beings are like machines: a thump in the right place, and we start working properly again.

REVERSAL PUZZLE

The curious case of 'PM', a geology student in the University of Pavia in Italy, who can read and write backwards, was reported by neurosurgeons in Acta *Neurologica Belgica* in October 1986. The 25-year-old student gained the remarkable ability after the removal of a tumour 'as large as a fist' from the right side of his brain in 1970, an operation which left him partially paralysed and epileptic. Dr P. Tosca of the university's department of neurology noticed that 'PM' could speak backwards as student told how the first thing he said after he woke from the operation was 'artsenif' (the Italian for window is 'finestra'). The paper in the Belgian journal recalls the hypothesis that the brain stores visual images and other information in one hemisphere and mirror images in the other. It is suggested that the operation somehow liberated the mirror images stored in the non-dominant hemisphere, thus causing the amazing side-effect. *Daily Telegraph* 23 October 1986.

HAIR RESTORERS

● Allan Goldring, 66, a Battle of Britain pilot from Lancing in Sussex, began to grow a new head of hair in January 1987 after 12 years of baldness. His wife Chris, a natural medicine practitioner, had persuaded him to wash his head twice a week in a shampoo made from peat, and twice a day to rub in a tonic made from plants, minerals and mud from an Austrian lake. After three months the treatment appeared to have worked ... or at any rate his hair started to grow for some reason, or none. *Daily Mirror* 23 January; The *People* 1 February 1987.

● Farmer John Coombs in Wiltshire was pleasantly surprised when he discovered early in 1984 that his hair was returning after his head had been licked by his cows. Guy Tolson, 52, a farmer from Ghent in Belgium, who had been bald for 25 years, read about this and smeared damp salt on his head so one of his cows would like it. This he did for six weeks, after which, amazingly, he also grew a full head of hair. Tolson told astonished reporters all about it at a press conference called by a dermatologist. *Weekly World News* 9 December 1986.

EYE TEETH!

● Gun Thoresson, 43, who had been blind since she was 20, went to her dentist in Burea, northern Sweden, where her sight was restored after three heavily filled molars were extracted. The explanation may lie in 'oral galvanism' – a small electric current set up in the mouth between two dissimilar metals. *New Scientist* 27 July; *Mail on Sunday* 13 November 1983.

● Ian Kirby, 20, from Hindhead, Surrey, had been told he would never see again after gradually going blind at the age of 15. In December 1984 he went into hospital and had his wisdom teeth removed, after which he could see again, although he still could not distinguish colours. But his sight was improving every day. *Daily Mail* 2 January; *Daily Telegraph* 3 January 1985.

RETURN OF SIGHT

● Joan Hornby, of Walney Island, Cumbria, had been blind since she was six months old. At the age of 18 she accidentally stepped into a hot bath before running any cold water into it. She gave a yell and found that she could see. *Weekend* 26 April–2 May 1978.

LIGHTNING RECOVERY

● Edwin Robinson gradually lost his sight and hearing after an accident in February 1971, when he jacknifed his tractor-trailer rig to avoid hitting a skidding car, and suffered a severe head injury. On 4 June 1980, Robinson, by now 62, was out looking for his pet chicken, Took-Took, near his home in Falmouth, a suburb of Portland in Maine, and took shelter under a tree during an afternoon thunderstorm. He was knocked to the ground by lightning, came to after 20 minutes, and went into the house to take a nap. After a while, he found his central vision was back although he couldn't move his eyes; and the next morning he could hear perfectly without his hearing aid (which, in any case, had been burnt out by the lightning). He had survived the lightning because he was wearing rubber-soled shoes. A week or two later, when he was in New York for an appearance on ABC-TV's 'Good Morning, America', he said his scalp 'felt funny. I felt like I had whiskers on my head.' As a young man he had thick, bushy hair, but he had been bald for 35 years. Now his hair was returning! By the end of August he had a full head of hair and excellent sight and hearing. Medical 'experts' predictably asserted, without examining him, that Robinson had been suffering from hysterical blindness and deafness. 'I can't see it. It couldn't have lasted this long,' said Robinson's ophthalmologist, Dr Albert Moulton of Portland. 'From the physical findings originally, he was definitely blind.' Omaha (Nebraska) *World Herald* 7 June, 27 August; Lincoln (Nebraska) *Journal* 7 June, 4 July, 14 July 1980.

● Bernt Bostrom, 43, from Sweden, had been blind in one eye since birth. Suffering from backache, he visited an osteopath who noticed a vertebra at the base of his skull was out of alignment and pushed it back. The following day Bostrom could see with his blind eye. It was thought that the vertebra had moved during his birth, trapping a nerve and causing the blindness. *Daily Mirror + Star* 15 April 1988.

● Maurice Elder went blind because of diabetes. Laser treatment failed, and specialists said the chances of him ever seeing again were remote. In May 1989, the 54-year-old ex-businessman was dozing in an armchair at his home in Shawlands, Glasgow. Startled by a loud bang outside his window, he jumped to his feet and found that he could see. *Sunday Mail* 11 June 1989.

● Henry Wahlberg of Stromsund in Sweden dived into a lake from a bridge when he was a boy. A fishhook got caught in his left eye and virtually blinded him. Many years later he was strolling in the woods and bent down to pick up a tree root. A branch struck him in his bad eye, and the next day he found that his sight was restored: 'I could even read the small print in the newspaper. I was never able to do that before.' *Sydsvenska Dagbladet* 17 September 1981.

SHOT BACK TO HEARING

● Rene Bouchard was going deaf, and several doctors in Paris told him there was no cure. Resolved on suicide, he clapped a pistol to his head and pulled the trigger. He failed to kill himself, but his hearing returned. *Reveille* 10 December 1976.

WALL BANGS RESTORE SENSES

● Yvonne Brown, 18, lost her sight through eye disease at the age of 11. Her boyfriend walked out because he couldn't cope with her blindness, she banged her head on the wall in despair, and her sight returned. They were married in Hereford. *Houston Chronicle* 7 November 1983.

● After three years of deafness, 12-year-old Claire Booth's hearing returned when she banged her head on the wall during an argument with her mother at their home in Harvey Road, Congleton, Cheshire. *Sun + Daily Telegraph* 17 November 1983.

● Joe Sardler, 32, from North Carolina, lost the sight in one eye because of optic nerve atrophy when he was 14 months old. He became blind in the other eye in about 1975. On 11 March 1981 he went to the basement to wash some clothes for his wife, tripped over a dog and hit his head on the wall. When he came to, he could see the furnace; the eye which had ceased to function six years earlier was working again. Omaha *World Herald* 14 March 1981.

GUIDE DOGS IN A NEW ROLE!

● Jon Lawrence, 43, a bank employee from Maidstone, Kent, had been blind for four years because of a nerve complaint. On 26 May 1975 he was walking downstairs when he tripped over his guide dog Omar and hit his head on the wall, restoring his sight. *Daily Mirror* 31 May 1975.

● Bob Aubrey, 50, from Ottawa, had been blind for eight years from the hereditary Lebere's optic disease. While heading to open a door, he tripped over his guide dog, jarred himself and found he could see. Schenectady *Gazette* 22 August 1979.

Hard to Swallow

We're accustomed to finding grit in a sandwich or even an insect on a lettuce. But some of the things that present themselves as food are a lot harder to take ...

SNACK SURPRISES

● A dead mouse came with the Seals' skimmed milk in Somerset. Beryl Seal poured it into a cup of coffee after her husband had had a bowl of cereal. Owen's Dairies of Frome were fined £100 with £325 costs.

● Jane Etheridge found a two-inch spider sticking out of her cod batter in Birmingham. Food firm Ross Young was fined £400 with £75 costs.

● A lizard's head an inch long made its way to Coventry, Warwickshire, in a pack of California raisins, where it was found by Jayne Wiltshire. *Today* 27 May; *Daily Telegraph + Sun* 14 June 1989.

● September was a bad month for snacks in the East End of London. Mark Campbell found a Chinaman's molar in a bag of peanuts which his father had bought in South Woodford, Essex. Rowntree got a £100 fine with £176.88 costs. The molar looked so like a nut that it had escaped the notice of rigorous processing, colour sorting and the trained eye of six inspectors in Scunthorpe. *Daily Mirror* 9 September 1988.

● A few days later, Chris Ezekiel and Debbie Brown dipped into a bag of crisps in Chris's mother's house in Marshfield Street on the Isle of Dogs when Debbie screamed and threw the packet away. She had discovered what appeared to be a human eye. *East London Advertiser* 16 September 1988.

● The following month, Ray Tilbury of East Devon Shellfish found a set of Icelandic false teeth in a batch of prawns at Exmouth, Devon. *Daily Telegraph* 15 October 1988.

● On 22 November 1989 Tony Rooman (or Roomans) of Tunbridge Wells in Kent thought he had found a dead rat in a bottle of milk delivered by Unigate Dairies. He and his wife Sue handed the bottle to the local environmental health officer. *Daily Star + Edinburgh Evening News* 23 December 1989. The next day they had become Tony and Sue Umens of Lamberhurst in Kent, and the 'rat' was revealed as a piece of cardboard with 'three pints please' written on it. A Unigate spokesman said 'it is a mystery how this object got into the bottle', though we guess it was through the hole at the top. *Cardiff Western Mail* 24 November 1989.

● The following week, Northern Dairies Ltd in Yorkshire were fined £1000 after one of their pints was found to contain a piece of cardboard with 'No milk today' written on it. *Daily Star* 29 November 1989.

BELLY BANKS

● A buffalo recently acquired by a peasant farmer in the Indian state of Haryana swallowed all his wife's gold ornaments. Despite tearful entreaties, the farmer refused to slaughter the beast. Nine years later, in April 1989, the buffalo finally expired, and after a feverish search, a vet recovered the booty from its body. Its glitter had dimmed, but its value had soared with inflation. *Daily Telegraph* 1 May 1989.

● On 12 December 1987, the Yugoslav Tanjug news agency carried the story of farmer Alet Hajdarevic, who slaughtered one of his cows and found a wallet in its belly containing 2000 Yugoslav dinars (about $1.60) and 2000 West German marks. *Sunday Journal-Star + Newport News + Virginia Daily Press* 13 December 1987.

● The wife of Sioux Indian, Benny Left Hand, was cutting up a chicken she had recently killed, and discovered the kind of chicken nugget you *won't* find at

McDonald's. Mrs Left Hand was in her kitchen on Standing Rock reservation, when 'she felt something hard in the chicken's gut, like a stone,' said Benny. 'She cut it open and that thing popped out.' That thing was a nugget of gold, about an ounce in weight, and with an estimated value of $500. The Left Hands have no idea how it came to be there, and add that since the news got out there have already been attempts to steal their other chickens. Beaumont *Enterprise* 26 August 1985.

BERRIED IN A TOMATO

Keith Bennett of Ruardean, Gloucestershire, was amazed one weekend in September 1982 to find a strawberry had grown inside one of the tomatoes in his greenhouse. **His daughter cut the tomato to make a sandwich and got quite a shock. Local gardeners said they had never come across anything like it before.**

TOO RICH TO EAT

George Veriopoulos, an Orthodox priest, was preparing to tuck into a dish of *kefalaki*, to the Greeks a delicacy but boiled sheep's head to you and me. He did a double-take as he noticed that the bottom half of the sheep's teeth were made of gold. He scraped away more flesh and saw gold along the jawbone as well. He was given the young sheep by his sister and her husband to celebrate the birth of their first child. The feast was forgotten as Father George put the head into a bag and rushed off to see a jeweller. Sure enough the gold was 14-karat and had an estimated value of about £3000. He phoned his brother-in-law, Nicos Kotsovos, who said: 'I rushed out to check the rest of my sheep, but there was not a trace of gold among the whole flock of 400.' A local vet was stumped as to how the gold could have been deposited in such quantities in coin-sized areas of the teeth and bones. Other farmers have suggested the sheep chewed grass covered with gold dust from a nearby small gold mine.

The Greek Ministry of Agriculture investigated and found the story of the gold-bearing teeth true, and unique, and also inexplicable. Their chief vet, Andreas Anastasovitis, rejected the farmers' theory on another count: such a deposition of gold would take years, and this sheep was only eight months old. 'There is also gold in the jawbone. How do you explain that?' Meanwhile, farmers have adopted a new ritual; peering into the mouths of their flocks while their wives actually pan the sheep's milk for the golden sparkle. *Sunday Express* 10 June; *Globe* 21 August 1984.

Haunted Houses

Some properties just seem to have 'something' about them that makes them different from the rest . . .

THE HOUSE OF BLOOD

Jean-Marc Belmer, a lorry driver aged 30, and his wife Lucie, 23, redecorated their new home at Saint Quentin in Picardy, France, in August 1985. The following January they noticed tiny red droplets all over the walls and carpet of the living room, which they cleaned off. At the beginning of February the droplets reappeared. That night, Jean-Marc left on a job at 3am and an hour later Lucie heard the sound of crashing crockery in the kitchen. Terrified that someone had broken in, she locked herself in the bedroom, but in the morning she found that nothing was broken or out of place. The following day the couple woke to find their pillows and the kitchen table dotted with tiny red stains. Though scared, they spent one more night in the house. In the morning, the stains were back all over the bed, and even on their pyjamas. The Belmers moved to Jean-Marc's parents' house with their Spaniel Pataud, who had refused to enter the Saint Quentin house for several weeks. Forensic experts said the stains were dried blood. *Sunday Express* 14 February 1986.

THE HOUSE OF HORROR

Mrs Penelope Gallerneault, 26, lived in a flat in the Victorian-Gothic country house of Oakley Court, on the banks of the river Thames at Bray, Berkshire. The family were warned by friends before they moved in that the place was spooky, and frequently used by Hammer Films as a location for 'Dracula' or 'Frankenstein'. And in the three years they were there, she and her husband and children suffered many tragedies. Her marriage broke up and two of her four children are dead.

The horror began in the summer of 1972. 'I started to see people walking in the grounds wearing hoods,' she says. Then one morning she found a box on their doorstep – and, inside, the body of one of her cats, with its neck broken. And in December her two-year-old son, William, died. Mrs Gallerneault was running him a bath when the phone went. When she returned he was floating in the water. 'I realize that many people might try to blame me for being careless, but that is just not the case. In a rambling old house like that, there are so many precautions you have to take.' Then early last month, her son Edward, who was just two, was left in his playpen in the grounds. Somehow he got out, toddled down to the river, fell in and drowned.

The other residents of Oakley Court remember two more deaths. A man fell from a pleasure steamer in 1971 and drowned in the same stretch of river as young Edward. And an old lady, whose body lay in her flat in the Court, was found dead in November 1972 after at least a week. Mrs Gallerneault said, 'The house has an aura of evil and I could never go back there. Horror films being made there seem like a joke. I'm sure evil has rubbed off on the place.' The Rev. Sebastian Jones, curate of St Michael's Church, Bray, added: 'Oakley Court is definitely "spooky" and I would not want to stay there myself. Evil can generate evil, and the grounds would be an ideal place to practise black magic.' The police, called in at every stage, are mystified too. A senior policeman said: 'There have been some strange happenings at the house, which have never been explained. We made regular patrols after complaints about witches, and things seem to have quietened down now. We never discovered how Mrs Gallerneault's cats died or who killed them. *News of the World* 30 September 1973.

ANOTHER HOUSE OF BLOOD

At around 11:30pm on 8 September 1987, Minnie Clyde Winston, 77, stepped out of her bath at 1114 Fountain Drive, southwest Atlanta, Georgia, to find the floor oozing blood 'like a spinkler'. She also found blood in the kitchen, living room, bedroom, all the halls and the basement. She and her husband William, 79, a retired porter for the National Screen Service Company, had been married for 44 years, and had rented and lived in the six-room brick house for 22 years. William had gone to bed at 9.30 after locking the doors and activating a security system. Neither he nor his wife heard any intruders, they didn't have any pets, and the house was free from mice and cockroaches.

The following morning they called the police. The homicide detective Steve Cartwright found 'copious amounts of blood' spattered on walls and floors in five rooms. The stains ranged in size from a dime to a silver dollar. In the basement, spots were found under a TV, on a dirt floor and in narrow spaces virtually impossible for a person to reach. *Express-News + New York Daily News* 10 September; *Constitution* 19 + 11 September; *The New York Times* 12 September 1987.

AN INGENIOUS PLOT

A rich widow of 81, Catherine Noodyke, married dashing Neal Faasen, 44, in 1980. Her life soon turned into a nightmare. Crazy voices would babble in the pre-dawn darkness. Household objects such as cutlery, carpets and rugs would move on their own. After five years of marriage, Faasen dumped his wife, having fleeced her of over two million dollars. A court action was brought by her family, accusing Faasen of fraud. It was claimed he had engineered the strange effects to drive his wife insane. *Sunday Express* 25 August 1985.

Castle Grant, Nairn, reputedly haunted by Barbara Grant who died in the tower in the sixteenth century after being imprisoned by her father for refusing to marry a man she did not love.

Occult Crime

Some crimes seem only to be explicable in supernatural terms . . .

BUILDING BRIDGES

A new category of occult crime is the felonious stealing and carrying away of bridges. Two cases, one from Gwynedd and the other from Uruguay, are both dated late in July 1987.

As part of a job-creation scheme, Gwynedd county council ordered the construction of a wooden footbridge over the River Penrhos, between Pwllheli and Llanbedrog in North Wales. The £1200 bridge was completed on 11 May; at the end of the month its remains were found on the river bed. According to the *Guardian* 23 July 1987, 'it had not fallen, it had been pushed'.

The council got tough. At a further cost of £1500, they replaced the wooden structure with a steel bridge weighing several tons. It was a real beauty, 18 feet long and fitted with gates at either end. At the end of July it vanished – disappeared and could not be found. 'It isn't often we have to investigate the theft of a bridge,' remarked Detective Chief Inspector Irfon Evans, predictably. 'The bridge was bolted together,' confirmed a police spokesman. 'It would have to be dismantled, loaded and carried away . . . obviously it would have needed a heavy vehicle.' Dark rumours blamed local land-owners who had opposed the project.

That explanation could be accepted, but consider this: in the *Independent* of 24 July 1987 one can read of the disappearance of a 160-foot iron bridge which spanned the Santa Lucua Chico river where it flowed through the town of Florida, Uruguay. Not a bolt was left behind.

BEYOND EXPLANATION

● **An un-named 21-year-old woman lost half an ear during the night of 15/16 September 1985, says a UPI wire story of the 16th. The woman was woken by a sharp pain to find 'blood all over her sheets' but no sign of an intruder or break-in. Police at her Mesa, Arizona, home said there was 'just no logical explanation'.**

● Samantha Huffmaster, 12, was upstairs getting ready for bed while her parents were watching television downstairs. There was a scream and the parents rushed upstairs to find their daughter lying in a pool of blood. She died an hour later in hospital in Cherokee Village, Arkansas. Samantha had been killed by a .45 automatic pistol lying on a chair in a bedroom next to hers. The gun had gone off for no apparent reason and the bullet travelled through the chair, through the dividing wall and then struck her in the side killing her. A spokesman for the sherriff's office said, 'That gun went off all by itself . . . We can't understand it.' *Sunday Express* 26 January 1986.

'HOUDINI GANG' RAID STRONGROOM

£143,000 disappeared from a strongroom at New York's Kennedy Airport on 12 April 1967, and an FBI spokesman confessed their bafflement. Somehow, whoever pulled this off, got past armed guards, a double-locked steel door, into the strongroom and out again, without being seen and without leaving a mark or clue anywhere. The theft, if that is what it was, was discovered when an armoured truck came to take the money to a Manhattan bank. The matter was said to be under investigation. *Daily Mirror* 13 April 1967.

MASS HYPNOTISM

● **A shop owner and 20 customers in Sciacca, Sicily, were put into a trance by two Indians who stared into their eyes and gesticulated, before raiding the till. London *Evening Standard* 9 December 1987.**

A ONE-LEGGED GHOST

Police answered a burglar-alarm call from the home of Mr Kenneth Broadhead in Ashill, near Thetford, Norfolk, and found the house supernaturally secure, with nothing stolen. But what did make their hair stand on end was the single row of footprints – all made by the same foot – across the floor of a room ending up against a solid brick wall. Then the ghost apparently dematerialized through a door and set off a burglar-alarm. A senior police officer mentioned the tradition of a one-legged Jesuit priest ghost at the house, but added: 'Why set off an alarm when you can just melt through a door?' No other details were available. *Daily Mirror* 13 February 1974.

POWERS OF SORCERY?

● In the otherwise sober study of prisoners in Fort Leavenworth prison (*My Six Convicts*, New York 1951), Donald Wilson, a professor of psychology, describes a prisoner called Hadad (a pseudonym) who managed to escape from handcuffs, straitjackets and cells at will, apparently passing through solid walls. Part Hindu Indian and part Senegalese, he said he had studied at Oxford, although his records could not be verified. This man also feigned death for three days to impress Wilson, and 'cured' the epileptics in the prison by some form of remote hypnotism. He left prison whenever he wished, but returned because, he said, he was on a mission, and he would depart 'this sphere' when it was complete; he offered Wilson and Gordon, the prison physician, the power to be 'ageless and timeless'.

● Yilderay Abdullah, 18, was serving time in Birmingham's Winston Green Prison for impersonating a police officer. In January 1985 he walked unchallenged through the gates, pretending to be another prisoner who was due to be released. The other prisoner was of a different colour and build; his clothes were several sizes too small for Abdullah. Thirty-six hours later he turned up at the prison asking to be let back in! *Daily Mirror* 28 January, 30 May 1985.

● 'Dangerous criminal' Zulkkifli Kenyon was wounded when he was arrested in Sumatra. He was left handcuffed in a locked hospital room with two guards on the door, but was later discovered missing. He had left his handcuffs behind. *Daily Mirror* 28 May 1986.

● Two teachers from East Jakarta were on a bus when a man got on, shook their hands and read their palms. He asked them for their money and jewellery which they gave him. He then asked them if they had done this willingly and they said they had. A few minutes later, the man got off the bus. The teachers were not aware of what had happened until the driver of the illegal bus asked them to get off only half way to their destination. *Jakarta Post* 15 January 1986.

YORKSHIRE MYSTERY

● Someone, or something, uprooted four concrete lamp-posts one night on a housing estate in Barnsley. Said local councillor Philip Hadfield: 'We are absolutely baffled. We can't imagine the strength of someone who can uproot a lamp-post. It's not the result of car crashes but someone physically lifting the lamp-posts out. Whoever is responsible is either a complete fool or very disturbed.' *Daily Mirror* 14 December 1989.

Homing Rings

Some objects, usually rings or other jewellery, but not always, seem to want to return to their owners. How, and why?

TEETH AND GLASSES

● Roy Peters, 55, of Bristol was swimming in 15 feet of water at Beer in Devon when he opened his mouth and his top false teeth fell out and sank. When he went back to the resort (we are not told how much later this was) he found that a set of dentures had been washed up in a gale and handed in to the beach café. He tried them on and found they were his. *Reveille* 4 February 1977.

● Bill Lees lost his glasses in the sea off Benidorm in Spain when he dived off a pedalo. He only realized later that he must have been wearing them when he dived in. During the night he had a feeling he knew exactly where they were. His daughter bought some diving goggles and they rowed out and found them in about 15 feet of water. *Sunday Express* 13 November 1971?

OF CASH AND WALLETS

● 'For years I carried in my purse a lucky sixpence with my initials on it', wrote Mrs M. Coyle of Glasgow (*Sun* 19 August 1971). 'The day before I went to Ireland on holiday, I accidentally spent it. Two days later, in a small Irish village, I had the sixpence back in change.'

HOMING BOOKS

Mrs S. C. M. Hill of London wrote to the *Sunday People* (27 July 1980): 'My mother bought some children's books at a jumble sale, intending to read them to my young niece when she came to stay. Later when she examined one of the books more closely, she saw my name and address on the fly-leaf, written by me when I was five, 25 years ago. There was also a half-finished letter that I had been writing to an aunt.'

SWALLOWED WATCHES

Brian Potter's uncle Dennis owned a small farm. One day a cow nuzzled against his stomach, took his fob-chain in his mouth and swallowed it, watch and all. Later that year (which year is unspecified) the farmer died. Several summers later Brian found the watch, next to a fresh cow pat. It was still going, though it was four hours slow. *Daily Mirror* 6 November 1979.

● Two years after farmer Ferdi Parker lost an antique wedding ring, it was found in a cow's stomach by a vet, during an autopsy on the animal. *Sunday Express + News of the World* 28 March 1982.

DIGITAL BOTCH

An un-named Aussie farm-worker was overjoyed when he heard that two severed fingers – lost 23 years earlier in a tractor accident in Bendigo, Victoria – had turned up pickled and sealed in a Vegemite jar. But a spanner was thrown in the works of a planned reunion of digger and digits when Michael Ellis, the man who recovered the freelancing fingers, contested ownership on the grounds that he had grown 'emotionally attached' to them. London *Evening Standard* 17 May 1990.

RETURN FROM EARTH

● Mrs Jane Hicks was helping her husband on their farm a mile from Land's End, when she lost her wedding ring. It was discovered 40 years later as her son was ploughing the field. *Sunday Express* 2 May 1982.

● Mrs Marlene Carvell was celebrating the finding of her wedding ring, yesterday, lost 20 years previously in the garden of her Northants home. *Daily Telegraph* 15 May 1982.

● Albert Thornton, weeding at his home in Surrey, found his wife's wedding ring, lost 15 years before. It was their silver wedding anniversary! *Sunday Mirror* 18 July 1982.

HOME FROM THE SEA

● Joseph Cross, of Newport News, lost his ring in 1980 while crossing Hampton Roads. It was knocked off his hand and sank into the channel waters during a storm. Two weeks ago it was noticed inside a fish, caught for a restaurant in Charlottesville, and its owner traced through an inscription. *Houston Chronicle* 5 March 1982.

● Mrs G. Gudebrod of Hillingdon, California, lost her wedding ring on a beach picnic. A year later, her husband brought home a crab caught on the same beach. Mrs Gudebrod found her ring fixed to one of the crab's claws. *Weekend* 14–20 May 1980.

● In 1897 the dock and harbour master of Newport, Monmouth-shire, married a Miss Hunter of Newport. They spent their honeymoon at Dawlish in Devon, where she lost her gold bracelet in the sea. They revisited the beach in 1925, and while sitting in deck-chairs, spotted a glint of gold in the sand as the tide went out. It was the lost bracelet. *Sunday Express* 13 July 1975.

● Tony Green was angry when his wife lost her wedding ring during a holiday at Barmouth, North Wales. Three weeks later they returned to Barmouth, from their home in Stourport, to collect sea-shells . . . and found the ring. *Daily Express* 22 September 1982.

MONKFISH RETURNS SPECTACLES

Gosselin Delius, 38, from Brussels, lost his spectacles overboard in September 1988 while sailing off Folkestone, Kent, in a force seven wind. Later, he read in a newspaper that Belgian fisherman Yan Gezelle had found a pair of spectacles as he was gutting a 13-lb monkfish – supposedly eaten by the fish. He rang the fisherman, checked that the code number (374191) tallied, and recovered his spectacles, which were slightly bent but otherwise fine. **Portsmouth Evening News** + **Daily Express** 11 October 1988.

The Crying Boy

The story of the jinx on these tacky but obviously popular paintings is an interesting example of how the tabloid press treats inexplicable phenomena.

FEARS FOR TEARS

The Crying Boy (TCB) exists in a number of different versions, all of them mass-produced 'paintings'. On 4 September 1985 *The Sun* reported that there was a jinx on TCBs. A Yorkshire fireman, Peter Hall, was quoted as saying that copies of TCB were frequently found at the scenes of fires, and usually untouched by flames. He and his colleagues were serious about this enough to promise that they would never allow the painting into their own homes. Peter's own brother, Ron Hall, had refused to take the firemen's warning, and while fire damaged the kitchen and living-room of Ron's Swallownest, South Yorkshire, home, the TCB on the living-room wall was not harmed. Ron's son put his boot through it in revenge, and his wife banned its replacement.

The next day's *Sun* (5 September 1985) said they had 'a flood' of calls in response to the TCB story, and presented four cases. Dora Mann, of Mitcham, Surrey, said 'Only six months after I bought the picture my house was completely gutted by fire. All my paintings were destroyed, except the one of the crying boy.'; Sandra Craske, of Kilburn, said that she, her sister-in-law, and a friend had all had fires since buying the picture. She had also seen the TCB print swing from side to side. Linda Fleming, of Leeds, and Jane McCutcheon, of Nottingham, both had fires in which the print escaped. Janet Wyatt, of Wroxall, Isle of Wight, said she tried to burn her two copies after reading of the jinx, but they would not catch fire. Other stories followed thick and fast; and are abbreviated below . . .

● **Brian Parks, of Boughtor, Notts, was destroying his copy after a fire put his wife and two children in hospital.** *Sun* **9 September 1985.**

● **Grace Murray, of Oxford, taken to Stoke Mandeville hospital with severe burns. TCB 'almost undamaged' in fire in her home.** *Sun + Daily Star* **9 October 1985.**

● **The Parillo Pizza Palace, Great Yarmouth, destroyed by fire. TCB undamaged.** *Sun* **21 October 1985, which invited readers to send in their 'cursed' copies for destruction.**

● **Kevin Godber and family, of Herringthorpe, South Yorks, lose home to a fire. TCB 'unmarked' while pictures on either side of it were destroyed.** *Daily Mail* **24 October 1985.**

● **Explosion destroys the Amos family house, in Heswall, Merseyside. Two TCBs, in living-room and dining-room, unharmed. They are unceremoniously destroyed by Mr Amos.** *Sun* **25 October 1985.**

● **House in Telford partially damaged by fire. The owner, ex-fireman Fred Trower, refuses to blame his TCB, hung in the hall. 'Obviously, if there was another fire it would go. I'm not that open-minded,' he adds.** *Shropshire Star* **26 October 1985.**

● **Six months after restaurant-owner George Beer installs two TCBs in his Holsworthy establishment, they are severely damaged by two separate fires a year apart. Both times the prints were unsinged. He doesn't blame them, and wouldn't part with them.** *Western Morning News* **26 October 1985.**

● *Sun* **26 October 1985 reports on accumulating pictures for mass burning. Various improbable stories: a male stripper's fire-eating act goes wrong after he taunts his wife's TCB; one woman blamed the death of her three sons and husband on the picture. Dr Peter Baldry of City University, London, cited saying no reason why the pictures shouldn't burn. Roy Vickery, secretary of the Folklore Society, speculates whether the artist mistreated his model resulting in a vengeful curse.**

Unscathed TCB found by student tenant Nick (second from right) after fire destroyed everything else in the cellar of a house in July 1984.

● Stella Brown, of Portsmouth, burns two TCBs successfully, blaming them for a long run of bad luck and family health problems. Her son trips while fetching water to put the fire out! *Portsmouth News* 30 October 1985.

● After hearing of the curse of the TCB, Richard Reynolds and his wife, of Falmouth, dumped their two TCBs upon a bonfire that was being made for Guy Fawkes' night. Twice they had given them away to friends, only to have them returned. *West Briton* 31 October 1985.

● *Sun* 31 October 1985 – 'thousands' of TCBs burned. Supervising fire officer Barry Davis cracks: 'We all listened for muffled cries, but all we heard was the crackle of paintings burning.' Sandra Jane Moore said her home was flooded after drawing punk hair on her friend's TCB. Mrs Woodward, of Forest Hill, blames TCB for death of her son, daughter, husband and mother.

● *Guardian* 1 November 1985: entertaining write-up of the *Sun*'s big bonfire, tells that *Sun* editor Kelvin McKenzie, who believes in the picture's curse, 'went bananas' when some wag hung a TCB in his office. It also notes the refusal of several fire brigades to join in the burning.

● Malcolm Vaughn's living-room blazed after he destroyed a neighbour's TCB in Churchdown, Gloucestershire. *Sun* 12 November 1985.

● Death of 67-year-old William Armitage in the fire that swept through his Weston-super-Mare, Avon home. The TCB was intact, lying on the floor near the pensioner's body. One fireman said: 'When you actually come across the picture in a gutted room, it is most odd.' Sun 24 February 1986.

● The Daily Mirror (Letters, 5 March 1986) advised one frightened old lady who owned such a picture to ignore the rumours, dismissing the succession of disaster claims as 'coincidence'.

● A columnist in the Western Morning News (11 March 1986) spoke of a neighbour's son in 'great anxiety' because he had slipped with a knife and accidentally slashed his mother's TCB.

● Bob Cherry of Glasgow claimed that a TCB has brought him nothing but good luck. One day when his car broke-down in a lay-by, he noticed a TCB propped up by a dustbin. When he put the picture in his car, the old banger started first time, 'and I haven't had any bother since'. Within a week he had three wins: £20 at bingo, £4 on the pools and £11 on a fruit machine. *Sun* 20 March 1986.

TCBs meet flaming end, October 1985.

Explosions

There's nothing very mysterious about explosions in general. But some bangs are stranger – and funnier – than most . . .

EXPLODING TVs

The Russian paper *Isvestia* – cited by *The Independent* 14 November 1986 – carried a report about a woman whose Raduga television set exploded as she watched, adding that she shouldn't have been surprised because 'more than 400 exploded last year in Leningrad alone'. The chief technician responsible for the Raduga wondered what all the fuss was about. Yes, he agreed the Raduga sometimes catches fire, 'but then so do other television sets such as Foton, Sadko and Rubin'.

EXPLODING CAT

Peppi, a cat adored and spoiled for eight years at Anmer Lodge old folks' home in Stanmore, London, went for his usual nap on a chair in the day lounge. 'There was a terrific bang and a flash and he flew several feet into the air,' said Mrs Irene McSweeney, the deputy. Some believed Peppi was enveloped in a 'blue-flame'. Firemen, called to investigate, could find no obvious cause for the blast, and blamed 'a build-up of static on the cat's fur'. If that is so, why hadn't it happened before? *Daily Telegraph*; *Sun* 28 November 1986.

EXPLODING PEOPLE

In Clement-Ferrand, France, a corpse was blown apart, and a crematorium oven severely damaged, when the cardiac pacemaker of the deceased exploded. *Bild* 28 January 1988.

The following January, an 82-year-old cancer victim exploded while under electrosurgery in Nottingham hospital. 'It was a definite explosion that was heard in the next room,' said the surgeon, Mr Earnshaw. 'It was frightening, but quite spectacular.' He put it down to a mixture of stomach gases, including methane, ignited by sparks. He told the *British Medical Journal* it was only the second case. *Daily Mirror* 17 January 1989.

EXPLODING COAL

● In January 1985 blacksmith Les Edwards, 65, stoked his living-room fire, and shovelled more coal into the grate. A detonator had been delivered with the coal and it went off in his face. He was covered in blood and temporarily blinded and deafened. Nearly four years later the National Coal Board admitted negligence. *Daily Mirror* 16 November 1988.

EXPLODING TOMATOES

The New Zealand Health Department warned South Islanders against potentially explosive cans of Italian peeled tomatoes bearing the appropriate brand name *Flamma Vesuviana*. Acid from the tomatoes had corroded poor-quality tin plating inside the cans, producing hydrogen. Hot weather would then detonate them. *Wellington Evening Post* 3 August 1988.

EXPLODING SNAIL

● Karen J. Prouty, 36, was about to take her second bite of a bubbling order of escargot in a Syracuse, New York, restaurant on 26 February 1988, when one of the snails exploded, burning her around the right eye. She was blinded for about 90 minutes, and was treated in the city's university hospital. *Detroit Free Press* 28 February; *Canberra Times* 29 February 1988.

EXPLODING NAPPIES

● Two suspicious packages aboard a TWA plane necessitated an emergency landing and evacuation at Mid-Continent Airport, Wichita, Kansas. The packs were removed and blown up before being recognized as soiled nappies. Houston *Chronicle* 21 July 1986.

EXPLODING TELEPHONES

● At 3:15am on Easter eve, 25 March 1989, an explosion wrecked a public phone box near the police station in Pontybodkin near Mold in North Wales. Dozens of people were woken by the bang, which shattered all the glass and destroyed the fuse box and the plastic casing which houses the wires coming up from the ground. Police, Wales Gas men and British Telecom failed to explain the incident. The village does not have natural gas and no traces of methane were found either, although the area is riddled with old mine workings. 'People at Pontybodkin are demanding answers' thundered local councillor Selwyn Roberts. *Daily Post* 27 + 29 March; *Western Mail* 29 March 1989.

● **A Swedish company recalled 30,000 of its mobile telephones after reports that three of them blew up. The phone, called Hotline, is only sold in Scandinavia, Switzerland and Malaysia. *Daily Record* 27 May 1988.**

EXPLODING CHICKENS

About 26,000 dead chickens, buried in a 20-foot pit, exploded scattering pieces of putrid poultry all over Larry Mohler's chicken ranch in Sheridan, Oregon. They had died in vast numbers during a heat wave at the beginning of June 1986, and he needed a bulldozer to dispose of them. Twelve hours later 'the dirt we piled on top of them started bubbling and moving' with the build-up of gases. Then it blew up. 'We had a miniature St Helens,' said Mohler. Milwaukee *Journal* + Houston *Chronicle* + Pawtuxet Valley *Daily Times* + London *Evening Standard* 5 June 1986.

EXPLODING LAVATORY

Hilton Martin, 41, was cleaning his lavatory in Satellite Beach, near Cape Canaveral in Florida. He used Comet brand cleanser in the tank, and hung a Sani-Flush block inside. As the water started bubbling the telephone rang. He rushed to answer it, but it stopped before he could pick it up. Then he heard behind him a noise 'like a hand grenade going off'. Lavatory and tank were blown up.

Fire officials were stumped, but someone suggested the calcium hypochloride in Sani-Flush had combined explosively with hydrocarbons in Comet. Spokespeople for both products denied that this was possible. *Huntsville Times + Duluth News-Tribune + Herald + Shropshire Star* 20 September; *Times + Daily Star* 21 September 1985.

Feral Children

Children brought up by animals have been known since Romulus and Remus, and perhaps before. Here are some recent examples . . .

THE NEW 'WOLF CHILDREN'

In June 1973 a boy aged about 12 was found living with monkeys in the jungles of southern Sri Lanka. He was named Tissa after the village near where he was found. The boy cannot speak, but barks and yelps, crawls on all fours and, when at ease, reclines in a monkey-like posture. And in August Italian paediatricians and psychiatrists have debated whether Rocco (named after the rocky crag in the Abruzzi mountains where he was found) really was brought up by wolves. He too is speechless, grunts in a 'half-wolf, half-goat' way, and bites and claws at anyone who shows him affection.

Exotic as these children are, there is considerable doubt as to whether these 'animal' characteristics are really animal at all. Usually, it seems, 'wolf' children, perhaps mentally deficient and physically handicapped, have been abandoned by their parents when they find the child too much of a handful. These children spend little time in the wild – they would be incapable of surviving for very long. They walk on all fours, not because they are imitating animals they have lived with, but because their bones allow them to walk no other way. The same applies with their speech: they have small brains and so are capable of only monosyllabic grunts and growls.

Possibly most interesting are those who were abandoned, not because of something wrong with them, but because their parents for economic or emotional reasons of their own, simply cannot cope with children. In these cases it seems that the children really may live in close proximity to, if not actually with, wild animals and imitate their habits.

These children, although they may not be able to talk when found, who may even lap milk from a plate like a dog, readily adapt to civilization and do learn how to talk, eat and wear clothes, sometimes within months. Unfortunately, this does not apply to Tissa and Rocco, who both appear to be mentally retarded. *Sunday Times* 26 August 1973.

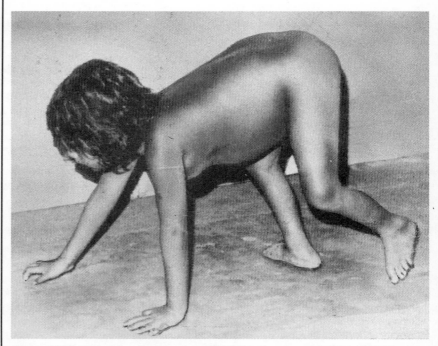

This child, found in the jungles of Sri Lanka, is probably autistic.

THE DEATH OF A WOLF BOY

According to the United News of India (UNI), a wolf boy called Ramu died in Prem Nivas, Mother Theresa's Home for the Destitute and Dying in Lucknow on 18 (or 20?) February 1985. He had developed cramps two weeks earlier and did not respond to treatment. The report said that he had been captured in a forest in 1976, aged about ten, in the company of three wolf cubs. He was on all fours, had matted hair, nails like claws, and his palms, elbows and knees were calloused like the pads of a wolf's paws. He ate raw meat, and after his capture, he would sneak out and attack chickens. He learned to wash and wear clothes, but never to speak. Houston *Chronicle* 23 + 27 February; *Shropshire Star* + *The News* (Portsmouth) + *Express & Star* 23 February; *Seattle Times* + *Le Republicain Lorrain* + *Observer* + *Sunday Mail* + *Cincinnati Enquirer* 24 February; Belleville *News-Democrat* 26 February 1985.

Reuters had reported on 20 April 1968: 'Ramu the Wolf Boy, found naked in a third-class waiting room at Lucknow station 14 years ago, died today in Lucknow hospital...' *Washington Post* + *Sunday Express* 21 April 1968. When found in 1954 he was about ten years old, had deformed limbs, uttered animal cries, and ate raw meat by snatching at it with his teeth. He spent the next 14 years at the hospital and probably died of a chronic respiratory infection. There are photo-features on this child in the *Illustrated London News* (27 February 1954) and the *Sunday* magazine (Calcutta) (4 March 1979).

The 'Ramu' who died this year is probably the child found in May 1972, aged about four, in the forest of Musafirkhana, about 20 miles from Sultanpur in Uttar Pradesh. Narsingh Bahadur Singh, a *thakur* (landowner) from the village of Narayanpur, found him playing with four or five wolf cubs, with no she-wolf in sight. Narsingh caught him and was bitten, so he trussed him up with a cotton towel, lashed him to his bicycle and rode home. The boy had very dark skin, luminous clear eyes like fireflies, long hooked fingernails, uneven sharp teeth, matted hair and calluses on his palms, elbows and knees. Some of the villagers said he had been reared by a she-bear and named him Bhaloo (like Baloo the bear in Kipling's *Jungle Book*), but Narsingh called him Shamdeo.

It was said around Narayanpur that Narsingh was no samaritan really, that he was only picking up free labour for his 30 *bighas* of land. In 1961 he had rescued an infant, practically a foetus, from a drain, and taken him home. Naming him Ramdeo, he brought him up, but although he was physically sturdy, he was a congenital idiot and an epileptic. Still, he had a few uses about the house.

Shamdeo cowered from people, played with dogs, and at night he had to be prevented from following the jackals that howled round the village. At first, Narsingh took him with him every day to work – he ran a tea stall in a railway depot. Large crowds frequently gathered to see the boy, who obliged them with occasional outbursts of jungle behaviour. He once pounced on a chicken, disembowelled it with his teeth, and ate it, entrails and all. Narsingh was later to deny indignantly that he charged money to see the boy. Some claimed him as their own. One such was Pallar, a washerman from a neighbouring village, whose child had been kidnapped in infancy. He changed his mind when he saw the growling, spitting creature on all fours. Shamdeo's limbs began straightening out with regular mustard oil massages, and after five months he began to stand. Two years later he was doing useful jobs like taking straw to the cows. He was weaned off raw meat, and took to eating earth for a while, but eventually came to terms with a diet of rice, dal and chappatis. He never managed to talk, but learned some sign language, like crossing his thumbs and flapping his palms – his symbol for 'chicken' or 'food'.

In 1978 he was discovered by nuns, Sisters of the Little Flower of Bethlehem from the Stella Maris Convent in Sultanpur. Sisters Clarice and Lyta were in Narayanpur to visit two of their pupils, and, hearing about Shamdeo, went to see him. They told their superior, Father Joseph de Souza, who had him brought to the convent on Good Friday. The following day he was taken to Prem Nivas, Mother Theresa's Home for the Destitute and Dying in Lucknow, where the nuns renamed him Pascal. He soon made friends with a dog, but one day took its ear in his mouth and bit it. At first he ripped off his clothes, but within a week he began to settle down. He learned the Indian salutation of palms pressed together, the *namaste*. He had to be watched with other children. Sometimes, without warning, he would flick his fingers into their eyes. He liked to travel round the garden sitting upright in the back of a bicycle rickshaw.

Most of these details come from the report by C. Y. Gopinath in *Sunday* magazine, Calcutta (4 March 1979).

Mommy Dearest

Contrary to what we think we know, there seems to be almost no age, old or young, at which a mother cannot conceive a child.

VIRGIN BIRTH?

A human egg has defied scientific convention and divided without waiting for fertilization by a sperm. The egg, from a woman receiving treatment in the fertility clinic at Monash University, Melbourne, did so 12 hours after removal from the woman. It spent the intervening time well away from any fertilizing agent.

Although the egg stopped after the first division, a host of interesting possibilities have been raised. Virgin birth, and the potential existence of daughters who are clones of their mother, are just two of the implications doctors will have to ponder. Dr Donna Howlett said: 'God only knows what happened.' Just so! *Guardian* 21 November 1985.

CHICAGO'S YOUNGEST MOTHER

An unnamed girl became the youngest mother, at the age of ten years and eight months, to give birth naturally in Chicago, and the second youngest in the United States, when she was delivered of a 6 lb 4 oz girl on 5 April, at the city's famous Cook County Hospital. The record holder was four months younger who had a Caesarian section in 1964. UPI Harrisburg *Evening News* 6 April; *Daily Telegraph* 7 April 1984.

The above reports mention that the all-time youngest mother title is held by a Peruvian girl in 1939, Lina Medina, who at five years seven months gave birth to a boy of about 6 lb, but the reports get several things wrong: one says Lina was six and a half, and both say her baby was stillborn. In the *Examiner* (?) for 20 December 1983, we read that Lina became her doctor's secretary, and her son, named Gerado after the doctor, was a brilliant scholar and became a successful accountant. Lina's mother believed the girl had been bitten by a magic snake which holds power over women who sleep in the open air, as Lina often did; while her father supposed that she was the victim of a mountain pool with legendary fertility properties in which women bathed who wished to be pregnant. Lina often swam there.

Coincidentally, Lina was brought to doctors in Chicago in 1940, home of the latest young mother; but where the father of Lina's baby was never discovered, the man responsible for the latest Chicago prodigy was being sought by police. The girl had been raped and the two suspects were her uncle and a babysitter's husband.

ANOTHER VIRGIN BIRTH

An astonishing chain of events has resulted in a teenage girl, born without a vagina, giving birth (presumably by Caesarian section) in Lesotho, Southern Africa. Unable to have sex in the usual way, the 15-year-old girl was having oral sex with her boyfriend when, at his climax, an ex-boyfriend burst in, catching them *in fellatio delicto* (you might say). The intruder fell upon the girl, stabbing her repeatedly.

One of these blows pierced her stomach and fallopian tubes, allowing some of the ingested sperm to seep into the opened tubes. Thus she became pregnant; although the report does not say whether the foetus developed in her womb or in the abdominal cavity (the damage to the fallopian tubes making an ectopic pregnancy entirely possible).

'It's bizarre, but absolutely true,' says Dr Douweouwe Verkuyl, author of a report on the case in the prestigious *British Journal of Obstetrics and Gynaecology*, cited in *News of the World* 30 October 1988. 'Being born without a vagina is a very rare condition,' he says, presumably referring to females. 'But the fact that the girl's son resembles the father guarantees that oral sex caused the birth.'

OLDEST MOTHERS

● On 14 March 1988, 71-year-old Aisatu Olorunnibola of Nigeria was safely delivered of a girl. She had sought the help of a witchdoctor after her previous pregnancies ended in miscarriage. She claims she only stopped menstruating at the age of 65. *Swazi Observer* 10 November 1988.

● Leontina Albina of Colina, Chile, was already a noted Guinness record-holder for fecundity as well as age. In 1981 she was credited with 55 registered births but she has had more babies since then. At our report date she claimed to be 59 years old, but the Guinness reckoning puts her age at 62. Her husband, Gerado, is aged between 73 and 80. She was just 12 when she had her first baby; now she has 59 children, six of whom died at birth or shortly after.

Most of the children came in twos and threes: 'I was a triplet myself,' she said. Her greatest problem is in remembering their names; a problem not made any easier when, perhaps out of forgetfulness, many share the same name. Cleveland (Ohio) *Plain Dealer* 8 May 1988.

● **The most prolific mother on record is said to be the wife of a Russian peasant, Feodor Vassilyev, who had 69 children between 1825 and 1865.**

● **Grandmother Kathleen Campbell of Cotmanhay, Derbyshire, was said to be Britain's oldest mother at 55 and 130 days, beating a previous record by Winifred Wilson of Eccles, Manchester, who gave birth aged 55 and three days in 1936. *News of the World* 30 August 1987.**

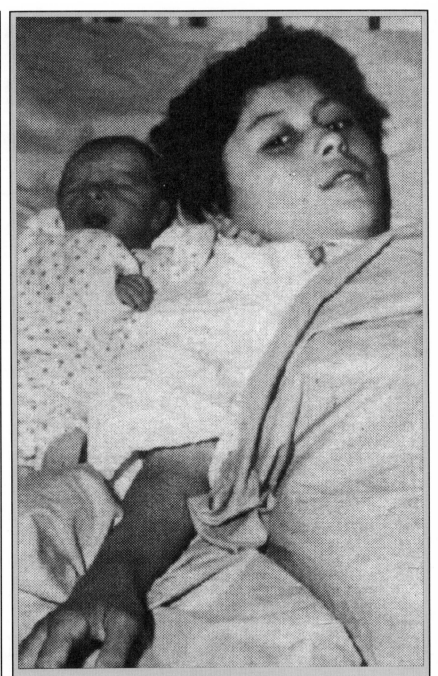

MOTHER AGED NINE

Selma Bozcan, aged 9 years and 25 days, gave birth to a 5-lb baby boy by Caesarean section at a state-run clinic in western Turkey, on 12 March 1990. She was able to breast-feed it. *Daily Telegraph* + *Sun* + *Daily Express* + *Daily Mirror* + *Edinburgh Evening News* + *Glasgow Herald* + *Hull Daily Mail* + *The News* (Portsmouth) 15 March 1990.

Surprise! Surprise!

The birth of a child is usually an expected event, by the mother at any rate. Or is it?

MEDICAL MIX-UPS

An article interviewing a few women who have had unsuspected pregnancies appeared in *Woman's Own* 15 February 1985. Author Lucia Green solicited an opinion from Dr Colin Brewer, of London's Westminster Hospital, and a former research fellow for the Pregnancy Advisory Bureau. He implied that the number of women who did not know they were pregnant was surprisingly high. Not all were 'young girls trying to fool themselves' that it wasn't happening. He said there were several good reasons why the incidence might be high: that not every woman has morning sickness; that if a woman's periods are slight or irregular, she may not realize they had stopped; that not all women's breasts enlarge during pregnancy; and that sometimes overweight women can carry underweight babies undetected.

UNCONSCIOUS BIRTHS

● An unnamed 18-year-old girl, at a boarding school in Iceland, seemingly gave birth to a baby boy in her sleep. The infant's cries were heard by a girl in the next room, who found the mother still sleeping with the baby between her legs. The girl insists she is a virgin, and there was some discussion in the reports about virgin birth, although almost everyone had doubts about the girl's claim. Almost as curious, given the difficulties of keeping a secret in such surroundings, is that the pregnancy went full term undetected. *Sydsvenska Dagbladet* 21 November; *Arbetet* 24 November 1985.

● In Spain, Gloria Maria Grases, 32, knew that she was pregnant, but the stomach cramps she felt one night during the eighth month she attributed to the peppers in her evening meal and she went to bed. Her husband Enrique recalls: 'That night I was reading a book and fell asleep in the chair. I awoke at 4 am and went to the bedroom. When I turned back the covers on the bed, I couldn't believe my eyes. Maria was on her back, and I could see the baby's head. I thought I was going to have a heart attack. I knew it was too late to call a doctor, so I helped the baby out. My hands were trembling when I cut the umbilical cord. But I did it and woke up Maria with my shouts.' Mrs Grases said: 'I didn't feel pain or anything. The baby was born while I slept.' *Weekly World News* 17 June 1986.

MORE SURPRISES

● Belle Glade, Florida: 6-ft 1-in Mary West, 16, put on a little weight and didn't play as well as usual for her school basketball team. She was given a medical check-up which resulted in a clean bill of health, and included a negative result to a pregnancy test. Four weeks later she played in an important championship match. 31 hours after that, she gave birth to a 6 lb 2 oz baby girl, Cassandra. She gave birth at home, with only her 11-year-old sister present, and though she felt pains before the birth, thought they were just 'ordinary cramps'. *Nigeria Falls Review* etc 10 March 1980.

● In London, Margaret Porter, 35, thought too much Christmas food had given her stomach-ache. It got worse, so she went to hospital, and gave birth to a boy. Another total surprise, as she and her husband had been trying to have a baby for 14 years, and had given up hope. *Daily Mirror* 6 January 1981.

● In Genoa, Italy, Doctors operating on an unnamed pregnant woman for an apparent tumour found her healthy baby had developed outside the womb, among the intestines. The baby boy was delivered by Caesarian. *Guardian* 6 April 1983.

UNSUSPECTED PREGNANCIES

● Lana Griffiths, 40-year-old mother of two, landlady of a Plymouth pub, thought she wanted to spend a penny, but gave birth to a 7 lb boy in the pub's toilet. She had no idea she was pregnant: 'I was skinny with a 24-inch waist.' The first her husband, Ned, knew of it was as he waited outside the toilet and she called through the window to him. *Daily Mail* + Portsmouth *News* 5 August 1985.

● Rhonda Budak, 22, of Helena, Montana, made a pre-dawn trip to hospital seeking relief for excruciating 'gas pains'. She had become quite overweight and was even teased about being pregnant, but was convinced she was not. Her doctor had advised her against having a baby until her abdominal problem was sorted out. Five minutes after reaching the hospital she gave birth to a 6 lb 15 oz girl, Marquette. *Weekly World News* 1 October 1985.

● Ann Newey, 37, of Barlaston, Staffordshire, thought she had appendicitis, and she was rushed to hospital where baby David was born. When she found she was putting on weight, she went on a slimming course. During the pregnancy she also smoked, drank, ate what she liked and even went on a tour of Europe. On the day of the labour she had even worked overtime at her job. 'Doctors tell me I made a complete mockery of antenatal care,' she said. *Daily Mirror* + *Daily Mail* 16 December 1985.

● At Falun, in Dalarna, Sweden, a woman who claims to have taken the Pill without fail, gave birth to a surprise girl, three weeks premature. She had seen her doctor about stomach pains and was awaiting a hospital appointment for further examination. No-one suspected she was pregnant until she collapsed in pain, phoned for an ambulance, and then gave birth. 'It happened so quickly. Suddenly I had this little child beside me on the floor. It was like I was dreaming,' she said. *Sydsvenska Dagbladet* 12 January 1986.

● **Lois Grimsley, of Enterprise, Alabama, gave birth to a surprise son, Marcus, on her bedroom floor. She protested to doctors that there was 'no chance she could be pregnant'. Nevertheless, she seemed happy with the outcome. Harrisburg** *Evening News* **19 February 1986.**

● Gwen Wilson, 47-year-old mother of four, went to the bathroom after returning from shopping and doubled up with pain on the floor. Suddenly she gave birth to a 5 lb 6 oz girl. 'Everything happened so quickly, I had no time to call for help. It's a good job I had reached home or the baby, Janet, would have been born in a shop.' This was the second time she had not realized she was pregnant. 'I just thought I was overweight both times,' she said at her home in Leek, Staffordshire. By coincidence, husband Howard was downstairs telling the other children about the unexpected arrival of their sister Helen 11 years previously, when they heard Gwen scream upstairs. Then she called down: 'I've done it again . . .' *Daily Mail* + *Daily Mirror* 27 February 1986.

● The most extreme of the recent cases happened to Julieta Lopez-Flores, a 29-year-old immigrant from Guatemala who lived with the Kazab household, in Miami, looking after their young children. For the previous two days, Julieta felt 'slight' pains in her stomach which she dismissed as 'a female problem'. That morning, after the Kazabs had left, the pain got worse and she went into the bathroom. 'I looked down into the toilet bowl and saw a fully developed child.' After her initial shock, she 'lifted the little thing out, walked with it through the kitchen and got a pair of scissors. I saw a bottle of Johnny Walker scotch and poured some over the scissors to disinfect them. I went back to the bathroom, and cut the baby's cord. I was so scared I almost passed out. I smacked the baby's bottom until she cried, and I put her in the bathtub.' But the ordeal was not over: 'Five minutes later, I had the urge to push again, and [another] baby was born the same way. I was almost numb from shock. Two babies . . . and I hadn't even known they were on the way.' Julieta bathed the babies, wrapped them and put them under a blanket. Then she cleaned up the bathroom, put on clean clothes and lay down to rest. Boy, were the Kazabs surprised when they came home an hour later! Julieta said: 'I'd never seen a baby being born before, but I remembered things I'd read and seen on television. It all seemed so natural.' *Globe* 24 December 1985.

ENCORE

● **A 16-year-old Nairobi schoolgirl collapsed during a biology class, complaining of stomach pains. To the amazement of her fellow students and teacher she gave a live demonstration of how babies are born. London** *Evening Standard* **11 July 1986.**

Over-reactions

Some people just seem to take things too far . . .

FATAL ARGUMENTS

● **A 29-year-old admirer of Imelda Marcos stabbed his 35-year-old brother to death and seriously wounded a drinking companion during an argument over whether Mrs Marcos was prettier than the Princess of Wales, the Philippine news agency reported on 12 June.** *Daily Telegraph* **13 June 1987.**

● **A man was accidentally killed in Thonburi, Thailand, in a fight with his friend over which came first, the chicken or the egg. He said it was the egg.** *Sunday Times* **15 January 1978.**

● Reuters relayed an item that appeared in the Philippine *Daily Inquirer* and rang a distant bell. Two men were shot dead when they argued that the chicken came before the egg. Two proponents for the egg coming first took out their pistols and shot the men after one of them, thinking his view had won, made an obscene gesture. *Middlesbrough Evening Gazette* 8 June; *Independent* 9 June 1987. More details were given in *The Orcadian* 11 June. The victims were Georgio Santos and Tomas Ja, barbers from the town of Tamban, and the gunmen were Jose Martas and Francisco Ferre. In this version, Tomas Ja cried out: 'You are fools! What I say proves that the chicken came first!' No mention of an obscene gesture.

● **Nathan Hicks, 35, upset because his younger brother, Herbert, had used six rolls of lavatory paper in two days, shot and killed him, said police in St Louis. He was charged with second degree murder.** *Middlesbrough Evening Gazette* **9 December;** *Guardian* **10 December 1986.**

● A senior executive officer at the Department of Employment, a man of 'impeccable character', strangled his Austrian wife at the dining table in December 1985 after an argument over the place on it for the German mustard. Thomas Corlett, 58, had been married to Erika, 63, for 15 years. 'It was her fault,' he told the police. 'I always placed my newspaper on one side of my plate, the mustard on the other. But she moved my paper and put the mustard in its place instead, saying, "That's where I want it, and that's where I will put it." She started shouting and kept on and on about the paper. She raised her hand and I thought she was going to hit me. I just grabbed her by the throat and we fell to the floor.' He was jailed for three years. *Daily Telegraph* 9, 10, 15 July 1987.

SLIGHTED MAN GOES BERSERK
Farmer Pantelis Vizonis, 54, of Palea Vigla in north-west Greece was in a local taverna when a friend jokingly accused him of never buying a round of drinks. Vizonis left and returned with a shot gun with which he shot dead two friends and the owner. He returned home and shot his wife and two other friends who had unsuccessfully tried to restrain him. *Daily Telegraph* 18 March 1985.

THE MORDEN ICEMAN

● Stephen Reader thought a new Ice Age was coming and would only work at night or in freezer centres. He went for a holiday in Resolute Bay in North Canada in January 1989, but it wasn't cold enough for his taste. He planned to go to Alaska, but instead ended up in Iceland. Five days after he set off for Klanders mountain in January 1990, his frozen body was found huddled in a ditch beside a track leading to the mountain. Reader, 25, from Morden in south-west London, had bare feet and was dressed only in a tracksuit.

Social worker Keith Beard told the inquest at Westminster Coroner's Court that Reader's behaviour 'was out of the ordi-

nary. He had a fixation with the cold for the last three years. He would not touch warm food. If you gave him a warm meal he would place it in the refrigerator until it was frozen solid. Then he would eat it.' He had known Reader for ten years since the latter was put into care for an arson offence. He said Reader had never talked of committing suicide. *Daily Post + Daily Telegraph + Daily Mirror + Evening Leader* (Mold, Clwyd) 27 April 1990.

● A similar death occurred in late September. Music teacher Ghislaine Sanchez, 37, climbed a 6000-foot glacier on Mont Blanc, sat down to meditate in the nude, and froze to death. *Sun* 11 October 1990.

TAKING IT TOO FAR

Philip Pyne, 51, of Romford, Essex, nailed himself to a bench outside the Gloucester Hotel on the esplanade at Weymouth, Dorset, to draw attention and prevent his falling off after a heavy drinking session. He put six nails through each leg of his trousers, and some actually penetrated his flesh. Police found him at 5 in the morning. The fire brigade was called to lift Mr Pyne plus bench into an ambulance. The nails were removed in hospital; he was lucky none of them had hit a major blood vessel or bone. *Evening Leader* (N. Wales) 24 August; *Daily Mirror + Guardian + Independent + Daily Post + Scotsman* 25 August 1990.

● **In Virginia Beach, Virginia, an intruder entered a woman's unlocked apartment while she was sleeping and forcibly covered her face and clothed body with chocolate and vanilla cake frosting. He reportedly told his victim that she should have known this would happen if she left her doors unlocked.** *Playboy* **November 1981.**

● **Told to get lost by an irate housewife who answered their knock on the door, two vacuum-cleaner saleswomen in Ljunby, Sweden, saw red. Instead of leaving, they vacuumed every carpet in the house, while accusing the owner of failing to keep it clean. The struggle to evict them took three hours.** *Guardian* **31 March 1990.**

Crop Circles

If crop circles are a natural phenomenon, why didn't anyone notice them until relatively recently?

CIRCULAR ARGUMENTS

Mysterious geometric patterns have been appearing in the fields of Wessex, the grain belt of south-western England, over the last ten summers. Typically, they are neatly flattened circles. The crops are swirled in often complex spiral patterns, in several interwoven layers with the tautness of thatch. The stems are almost never damaged and the crop continues to ripen till harvest. The edges are well-defined.

To begin with, the circles caught the interest of a few meteorologists and chroniclers of anomalies, and formed an occasional filler during the silly season; but each summer brought greater numbers and intensified study. Ninety-four circles were recorded in 1988 and 270 in 1989, when three books appeared on the subject. Over 400 have been recorded in 1990, and patterns of unprecedented complexity and beauty have appeared.

There is a general impression among circle enthusiasts (or *cereologists* as they have been dubbed), that the field patterns are evolving in complexity, from single circles to multi-ringed circles and geometric clusters. One of the classics, first noted in Wessex in the 1970s, is the five-circle pattern,

one large circle surrounded by four smaller ones like the dots on dice. The 1990 season, for the first time, saw rectangular and triangular shapes.

The nation's newspapers and bar-rooms have been gripped with circle fever. Unlike many old 'paranormal' perennials no-one could deny that there was something that needed explaining: the evidence was there on the ground for all to see. In July 1990 it seemed every cartoonist in the land used them as a political or social metaphor; soon the circles started to appear in advertisements. Now they have firmly entered national consciousness.

CONCEPTUAL ARTISTS/HOAXERS

Numerous attempts by crusading sceptics and newspapermen have failed abysmally to mimic the crop circle phenomenon, which is widely perceived as a hoax. Stakes have been driven into the ground pieces of wood on ropes rotated along the ground and various other methods have been tried; but the crop stems are always broken, evidence of arrival at the circle remains and the complex swirling patterns cannot be reproduced. If it *is* some kind of practical joke, then the organization behind it outstrips the Mafia, KGB and Illuminati combined.

The White Horse hill-figure at Westbury, Wiltshire, photographed from a crop circle, August 1987.

The five crop circles at Westbury which appeared on 3 July 1983. The wheat was not broken or crushed but 'swept' in a clockwise spiral from the centre and the circle edges were clearly defined.

THE WEATHER

One of the first people to take an interest in the circles back in 1980 was Dr Terence Meaden, founder of the Tornado and Storm Research Organization. His first thought was some kind of whirlwind. Ordinary whirlwinds, of course, result in random damage. They can last from a few seconds to a few minutes and can vary in size from 3 feet to 65 feet.

Over the last decade, he has rejected his first choice – stationary fair-weather whirlwinds – in favour of something he calls a 'plasma vortex', an unusual atmospheric disturbance caused by winds passing over high ground and creating a spinning ball of air highly charged with electricity, perhaps related to the ball lightning phenomenon. This plunges down, leaving its uniform mark.

LITTLE GREEN MEN

The other original investigators of the Wessex crop phenomena were the UFO buffs. They were familiar with the swirled depressions in crops and grass noted in Australia, U.S.A. and South Africa in the 1960s and nicknamed 'UFO nests'. The circles, it was thought, were the landing traces of flying saucers. As 'ufology' got more sophisticated, and enthusiasts abandoned the 'nuts and bolts' hypothesis (UFOs were craft from other planets), for more subtle theories (UFOs are some kind of psychic or meteorological phenomenon, or are analogous to radio interference, the wavelength of another universe bleeding into our own), so the explanation developed. Today they are seen as a message from an unknown intelligence.

TECHNOLOGY

It has been suggested that helicopters are responsible; but the downdraught from a helicopter flattens crops in a tapering effect, not a spiral.

A retired soldier wrote to a British newspaper to say that his squad formed crop circles in the 1960s with an aerial that sent out electromagnetic radio waves. There are large army encampments on Salisbury Plain in the heart of Wessex, and many people believe that the circles are evidence of secret weapon testing by the Ministry of Defence. There are several rumours that the telephones of crop circle researchers are being tapped, reinforcing the belief that the Government is somehow involved. The Government denies this.

The Hole Story

How does a chunk of earth weighing perhaps a ton suddenly uproot itself and fly 75 feet through the air? Whirlwinds? Earthquakes? UFOs?

On 18 October 1984, Rick and Pete Timm were rounding up cows on their father's wheat farm, near Grand Coulee, Washington, when they found an irregularly shaped hole, about 10 feet by 7 feet and about 2 feet deep on land adjacent to a wheat field. The Timms had harvested the area in mid-September, and the hole had certainly not been there then. To their greater astonishment a large plug of earth, the same size and shape as the hole, rested on the ground 75 feet away (see diagram). The plug had obviously been taken from the hole because between the two were 'dribblings' of stones and earth which had dropped to the ground as the plug travelled through the air. But there was no sign upon the hole or plug, or on the surrounding ground, that it had been mechanically made, or somehow rolled or dragged.

Puzzled, the Timms called in Don Aubertin, director of mining for the Colville Indians, whose reservation is near the site. Aubertin speculated initially about a meteoric impact, but changed his mind after visiting the site with Bill Utterbach, a geologist retained by the Colvilles. Aubertin said: 'The hole was not a crater. It had vertical walls and a fairly flat bottom. It was almost as though it had been cut out with a gigantic cookie cutter.' But this image, and the suggestion that the hole was made by a helicopter-borne grab, are disproved, if disproof were needed, by the fact that roots dangled intact from the vertical sides of both the hole and the displaced slab. Digging underneath the displaced block showed undisturbed vegetation, and plants on top of the plug showed it had been set down the right way up. Although a whirlwind might have the vertical suction needed, can it account for the general neatness of the action?

It was clear that some force had torn – not cut – the three-ton plug from the hole, transported the mass through the air without breaking it up (some say because the plug had a dense root mass), and set it down (gently?) at a slight angle relative to the hole; but what force, how and why? When contacted, a spokesman for the Smithsonian's Scientific Event Alert Network said they knew of no similar phenomenon. Alas, in the weeks that followed the site was trampled by cows, and the evidence – particularly the plug – rapidly disintegrated beyond further scientific value.

However, some light can be shed on this enigma from other directions. A geologist with the Bureau of Reclamation at Grand Coulee Dam, Greg W. Behrens, spoke of the 'interesting' geology of the area. The hole sits in a depression in a plateau at 2,360 feet above sea level, probably scraped out by an ice-sheet many thousands of years ago. The wheat field is dotted with 'huge' boulders left behind when the ice-sheet retreated, and known locally as 'haystack rocks' (though some are larger than haystacks). Near the mystery site is what Behrens calls a 'kettle', a geologist's term for a place where an underground mass of ice has melted, causing the ground overhead to collapse. The mystery hole was quite different from a 'kettle'. More interesting, says Behrens, is the fact that a small quake (3.0 Richter) occurred about 20 miles south west of the mystery site at 8:24pm on 9 October, just nine days prior to the discovery by the Timms boys. While Behrens was prepared to consider the possibility of converging shock-waves, which might have popped the divot out of its hole whip-crack fashion, another geologist, Stephen D. Malone of the University of Washington, was quoted as saying this was 'very, very unlikely'. Although the tremor was felt in towns in the area, it was not noticed at the Timms' farmhouse a few miles from the mystery site. Seattle (Washington) *Times* 23 November 1984.

The *APRO Bulletin* 32:10 (February 1985) mentions three possibly similar cases:

1) Following a 3.5 Richter quake in northern Utah, a strange cruciform hole was found, about 14 feet in diameter, with clods of topsoil hurled some 14 feet beyond the limits of the feature, landing overturned. The Utah Geological & Mineral Survey report describes the mark as 'mysterious'. (UGMS *Survey Notes* February 1979.)

2) The case of 'The Impossible Hole', given in Aimé Michel's *Flying Saucers and the Straight Line Mystery* (1957), page 132. Following the sighting of a glowing object in a field in front of her house at 8:00pm on 4 October 1954, Madame Yvette Fourneret, of Poncey-sur-l'Ignon, France, investigated an egg-shaped hole about 3 feet 6 inches on the main axis; halfway down the hole was wider than at ground level. On the fresh earth in the hole white worms wriggled, and scattered all around were clods 10–12 inches across. Similar clods dangled on the sides of the hole attached by roots. In the centre of the hole lay a plant with a very long root, the end of which was still *in situ* in the soil at the bottom, and all its exposed roots were quite undamaged. Michel says that it looked as if the earth had been sucked out by a giant vacuum.

3) Following observations of a shape – and colour – changing UFO, which also seemed like a searchlight beam in South Africa, on 11 November 1972, chunks of tar were found ripped out of a tennis court belonging to one of the witnesses. Although no damage was done to the surrounding high fence, chunks of tar were found caught in the fencing, and later on a nearby hillside. A subterranean gas explosion was post-

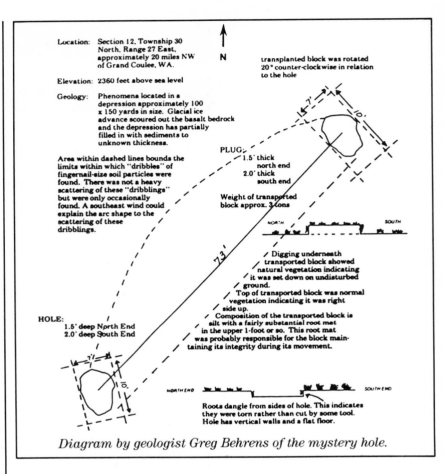

Diagram by geologist Greg Behrens of the mystery hole.

ulated to account for the upward and outward projection of tar chunks, but this was inconsistent with other facts. A whirlwind was similarly disposed of as the culprit. Interestingly, guards on a nearby petrol dump told police they had seen small red lights circling in the tennis court area just before a 'strange incandescent light' lit up the whole area (*APRO Bulletin* January–February 1973).

In Fort's *Books* reference is made to Humbolt's account of the Riobamba quake in which the vertical motion was so strong a graveyard was demolished and 'bodies were tossed several hundred feet in the air'.

From the records of the Tudor annalist, Stowe, as quoted by Harold Wilkins in *Mysteries Solved and Unsolved* (1958), comes the following quote: 'a piece of earth suddenly quitted its place of former time, and was transferred and transported forty yards to another paddock, in which there were alders and willows. It stopped the high road leading to the little town of Cerne. Yet the same hedges which surrounded it still enclose it today, and trees that were there are still standing. The place this bit of land occupied is now a great Hole.' Stowe says this event took place on Sunday 3 January 1582, at The Hermitage 'in the valley of the Cerf Blanc', in Dorset.

Swarms and Migrations

From time to time animals, particularly insects, gather in great numbers. Why they do this is often unclear, but the results are usually pretty spectacular . . .

TOADS AND SNAKES ON THE MOVE

● 'Voracious toads the size of dinner plates' are spreading rapidly across Northern Australia. The Cane Toads were introduced to Queensland from Hawaii 50 years ago, to combat sugar cane destroying pests. Now they have become a major pest themselves, eating almost anything, and are even suspected of hitching lifts in cars to speed their migration. Local conservationist, Bill Freeland, says: 'Toads have appeared up to 60 miles ahead of the main toad front. The bloody things eat some sorts of native wildlife into extinction.' Reuter. *Times* 5 July; *The Scotsman* 6 July 1985. Latest news: scientists have failed to come up with a poison to stop them. *Sunday People* 16 February 1986.

● Carpet snakes are seen 'ankle-deep' at Inwood, Manitoba, which now sees an annual migration to and from nearby limestone pits and swamps. The half-dozen limestone pits now contain, between September and May, the world's largest concentration of reptiles. A single hole may spawn 10,000 snakes, which mate in the late spring sun and then migrate to the swamps to hunt frogs. The journey of several dozen miles can take up to two weeks. Some residents of Inwood have got used to finding hundreds of these harmless snakes in their cellars, and one family made friends with one which lived in their shower. An annual two-week 'snake picking' season recently netted 50,000. In May, up to 100 males will strive to twist themselves around a single female, and the writhing cabbage-sized ball will flow to and fro, over rocks and up into trees, for up to two hours, until the female has mated. The mating season has become a major tourist attraction, as the pits literally seethe with rippling clots of frenzied snakes. *Wall Street Journal* 11 June 1985.

ANTS ON RAMPAGE

● A column of killer ants a mile long and half a mile wide marched on the Brazilian town of Goiania and devoured several people – including the Chief of Police. Sixty firemen with flamethrowers took 16 hours to drive the ants back into the jungle. *Sunday People* 9 December 1973.

● In Sri Lanka, a vast army of ants, numbering 'billions', is advancing on Sri Jayawardenapura. Power supplies are cut off as the insecticide-resistant ants short-circuit switches and wires. *Sunday Express* 1 September 1985.

TURTLE ORGY

The greatest gathering of sea turtles seen for years appeared on Raine Island, part of Australia's Great Barrier Reef, staying for what was luridly described as 'a mass egg-laying orgy'. Between 50,000 and 150,000 female green turtles appeared, laying up to 1000 eggs each. 11,500 turtles were counted in one night alone. The U.S.A.'s 'leading turtle researcher' commented: 'It's just incredible. We've seen large concentrations of other species at times in the Caribbean, but not this big.' *Detroit News* 4 December 1984.

GHOST SPIDERS IN THE SKY

Millions of spiders floated across the sky in parts of South-Eastern Australia on strands of webbing. Huge areas are covered with the thick snow-like webs – and whole clouds of webs, some thousands of feet high, often blot out the sky. At the same time there were 'freak' storms along the East coast of Australia – there may or may not be any connection, but those web-clouds couldn't have stayed up if they started to collect water. *Daily Express* 27 May 1974.

A PLAGUE ON BRITAIN

● Some very unusual visitors have arrived on these shores: live Saharan locusts. Five were found in Cornwall, the first such invasion there for 34 years. In Devon, three were found in the environs of Plymouth, and several at Newquay. Three were found in the Scilly Isles. All were coloured *pink*, which signifies that they were immature specimens. Tony Harman of the Canterbury Field Studies Centre estimated the final tally was about 40 locusts discovered in the West Country. *Mail on Sunday* 30 October; *Daily Telegraph* + *Western Morning News* 31 October; *Kentish Gazette* 25 November 1988.

● One was found on the wall of a house in Herne Bay, Kent; the only known find of a locust in this county. It was identified as *Schistocerca gregaria gregaria*, the Desert Locust, and had a wingspan of 13 cm. *Kentish Gazette* 25 November 1988.'

● There is a possibility that some or all of the locusts might not have been blown from the Sahara, but from a source nearer home – France. According to E. M. Venables' column 'Selborne Notes' in the *West Sussex Gazette* (18 August 1988), the Red-Legged locust had been long established in the Loire valley before World War II. The local farmers kept them under control successfully, so that they never reached the swarming phase; but then came the German occupation which prevented the farmers from taking their usual precautions. Shortly after the Germans were expelled from France, the locusts swarmed and within two days had reached southern England. The incident helped establish the Anti-Locust Research Centre in London.

● It is fairly well known that the Saharan dust, grit and sand, entrained in the lower atmosphere by high winds, generally head in two directions, northwards towards Britain and westwards as far as the Caribbean. At the same time as the invasion of Britain and the Middle Eastern swarmings, and shortly after Hurricane Gilbert caused the worst damage to Jamaica and the Cayman Islands in modern times (2nd week September 1988), a Brazilian agricultural official was expressing great concern over the sudden appearance of large numbers of African locusts in north Brazil, Surinam and Venezuela. It is known for African locusts to be blown into the Atlantic Ocean, said Evaristo Miranda. Usually they perish, but this horde seems to have survived the 3500 km transit, taking 20 days. He feared that they could easily adapt to conditions in South America and establish themselves. Tanzania *Daily News* 5 November 1988.

Naturalist Tony Harman of Canterbury holds the specimen of Desert Locust found on a wall at Herne Bay, Kent, in November 1988.

Freak Animals

Freaks are surprisingly common, it seems — so if this is true, then why do we find them so disturbing? Here are a few of the less unpleasant ones . . .

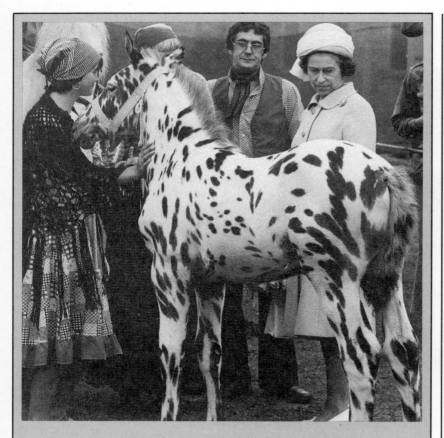

QUEEN SPOTS HORSE

Queen Elizabeth II examines 'Zebradia', a foal which looks more like a zebra than a horse. Zebradia's parents were a white mare called 'Spotty' and a pure-bred Cleveland bay stallion, 'Wheelgates Bill'. A year after Zebradia's birth in 1976 another zebra-like filly 'Elizabeth Anne' was born to the same pair. Their owner has been offered as much as £1000 for 'Zebradia'. 'Have they been decorated?' quipped the Duke of Edinburgh.

ABNORMAL GOAT OR UNICORN?

Lancelot, a year-old Angora goat, sports a 10-inch horn in the middle of his forehead. His owners claim they bred him using an ancient secret for unicorns. But animal scientists say the horn is just a rare abnormality. Either way, he attracts lots of interest at the San Francisco Marine World zoo park.

LEGS OF LAMB

A five-legged lamb and its normal twin were born to a Border Leicester Cross ewe, on 15 March 1982, at Cwm Farm, Forden, owned by Mr G. O. Evans, near Welshpool, in Powys, Wales. The strange animal is shown here, right. The vet who was brought in to remove the leg confirmed that it was in fact two legs, as evidenced by the double foot, joined together. It/they were not connected to the animal's pelvis, merely attached to its lower abdomen by flexible tissue.

TWO-FACED KITTY

You're not seeing double – this kitten was born with two faces. Dan Lizza of Latrobe, Pennsylvania, did a double-take when he first saw her and named her Gemini, the star sign meaning twins. The other three kittens in the litter were normal.

Animal Sabotage

When an animal appears to be trying to sabotage a piece of human equipment quite deliberately, something strange is going on.

RABBIT AND SQUIRREL SUBVERSION

● At Ellsworth Air Force Base, South Dakota, rabbits and squirrels caused chaos in the secured weapons area by setting off security alarms. The rabbits were also breeding like crazy and burrowing into missile mounds, causing cave-ins. The Air Force were intending to go hunting . . . with bows and arrows! *Toronto Sun* 11 May 1980.

● The ancient monument of Stonehenge is in danger of falling down due to the burrowing of a vast army of rabbits. Officials are digging a wire fence into the ground to keep the invaders out. *Daily Express* 4 July 1980.

● Air-raid sirens were set off in Toronto, apparently due to squirrels gnawing through circuit wires (one of these days, a rodent's going to start World War III!). *Toronto Sun* 30 May 1980.

● In New York State, hundreds of paranoids were convinced their phones were bugged . . . the cause of the mystery crackling turned out to be squirrels sharpening their teeth on the wires. Five miles of cable needed replacing. *Daily Mail* 8 August 1979.

BIRD BLASTS

● Eight hours of traffic chaos in Yarmouth, Isle of Wight, followed the action of a seagull which shot a turd straight onto the electronic eye of a new 2-million-pound swing bridge, putting it out of action. *The People* 21 May 1989.

● Thousands of commuters from Liverpool Street Station, London, were delayed 20 minutes after a pigeon flew into overhead power lines between Gidea Park and Shenfield, causing a break in electricity. *Evening Standard* 19 October 1979.

● A crow flew into power lines in Japan, halting 20 high-speed trains and causing widespread chaos. *Daily Mirror* 9 April 1980.

● An owl pecked through the cooling cable and blew a 132,000-volt cable near Black Carr Woods, Bradford, causing £13,000 damage. *Daily Star* 5 August 1980.

● A kestrel perched on an overhead railway power cable as a train passed underneath caused a short-circuit, blowing masonry from an overhead footbridge and halting mainline services at Crewe, Cheshire, for more than an hour. *Daily Telegraph* 27 December 1979.

LONE RANGERS

● Canadian firemen responded to an alarm call from the fire-detector at the home of Mervyn Orr, but there were no flames. Instead, they opened the detector and found a spider which had spun its web between the ionization chambers and set off the alarm. *Toronto Star* 27 November 1979.

● Herbert the Trigger-fish burrowed into the sand at the bottom of his 400-gallon tank, in a West Midlands pet shop, and the coral reefing in his tank collapsed; heating elements fell against the half-inch-thick glass; the six-foot tank shattered causing £5000 of damage (Herbert survived). *Daily Mirror* 30 October 1979.

CAT AND DOG STORIES

● Cindy the cat managed to climb up an electricity pylon, causing workmen to black out the village of Streatley, Luton, for 20 minutes while they rescued her. *Weekly News* 5 April 1980.

● The Piccadilly Line of the London Underground was brought to a halt when a dog went for a walk . . . for six miles along the tunnels from Wood Green and Holborn stations. *Daily Telegraph* 29 December 1979.

FISHY PROBLEMS

● On 30 September 1984 thousands of jellyfish shut down two nuclear reactors at St Lucia, Florida. Huge swarms of the little wobbly critters are not unknown in these waters and this is not the first time they had clogged the plants' cooling systems' water filters. Duluth *Herald & News-Tribune* 1 September; *Daily Telegraph* 3 September 1984.

● A Norwegian supertanker, the *Moscliff*, was held up for 22 hours in the English Channel when it ran into a huge shoal of mackerel. The ship's engine stopped automatically when thousands of mackerel were squeezed through the strainers of the cooling system intake. About a ton of minced mackerel had to be removed before the ship could get underway again. London *Evening Standard* 10 January 1980.

COMPUTER SABOTEURS

From Japan is the news that the third most common cause of computer failure in that country is *rats*. It seems that the critters are attracted to the power supply hums and end up gnawing cables and urinating over the remaining wiring. So serious is the problem that a rat-catcher was commissioned to invent a suitably technological rat-trap. It consists of an ultrasound generator (duplicating the power supply hum) and an automatic vacuum device to suck the rodent into a lethal carbon dioxide chamber. However, the trap's own sound generator is attracting snakes and spiders. This story came from *Computer Fraud & Security Bulletin*, cited in *Computing* magazine 11 October 1984.

MASS ATTACKS OF MICE AND RATS

● The San Ofre nuclear power station, California, was closed down by mice which shorted the electrical system. *Daily Mirror* 12 November 1979.

In Arlingsaas, Sweden, a van carrying hundreds of mice to a hospital for experiments never made it. The cunning little devils would keep *breathing* . . . until the windscreen steamed up, and the van went off the road! *Daily Telegraph* 27 November 1979.

● Hordes of rats, apparently breeding for nine years in an excavated lot in Manhattan, suddenly swarmed out to bite women and jump on cars, gnawing windscreen wipers and vinyl roofs. Health officials fenced off the site and put down poison. *Niagara Falls Review* 12 May 1979.

Animal Attacks

Wild animals are not usually hostile towards humans, but occasionally they turn against us and launch deliberate attacks for no obvious reason. Why?

COYOTE ATTACKS WORRY TOWN

In New Mexico, two girls were attacked by a coyote as they slept in sleeping-bags in their front yard. The father of one of the girls, James R. Conn, said: 'I can name incident after incident of people and animals attacked by coyotes here lately. Conn said the attack on the girls ceased when a neighbour heard their screams and came to investigate. 'The neighbour said the coyote backed off when it saw him. But it just walked out into the middle of the street and calmly stood there, just watching to see what would happen.'

Police say they see coyotes on city streets in early morning hours. 'They'll come right up to the car, just like a pet dog. They aren't afraid of people at all,' said Police Sergeant J. R. Keane. George Adamson of the State Fish & Game Department said that in 34 years with the agency he had never heard of a coyote attacking a human before. He theorized the behaviour might be attributed to lack of food, the encroachment of humans into their former habitation, and predator control laws that restrict methods of killing coyotes. Milwaukee (Wisconsin) *Journal* 14 April 1974.

FEATHERED DIVE-BOMBERS

● Kevin Graham, of Tweedmouth, Northumberland, was crossing Tweed Bridge, Berwick, when he was attacked by screaming dive-bombing seagulls. Shouting and waving his arms, he made his way to a couple on the other side, also under attack, and the three ran for cover. They were shaken up but unpecked. Several other people said they had been flapped at while crossing the bridge. Local authorities put it down to birds nesting in the structure who feel threatened – but normally seagulls are quite harmless. *Weekly News* 10 August 1974.

● Terry Hauf took to the fields south of Yoder, Wyoming to hunt for game birds. He stopped to look at the sky, and the next thing he knew he was lying dazed and wounded on the ground – and 15 feet away sat an eagle also a bit dazed. The bird came out of the sky to strike him, cutting his head and seriously injuring his right eye. When he got up to go for aid, the bird 'took off at a kind of trot'. An official from the Wyoming Game & Fish Department said that it was 'extremely abnormal behaviour' for an eagle to attack a human. Denver (Colorado) *Post* 22 November 1974.

● On 14 January 1975 a jackdaw hailed a group of schoolchildren at Leighton Buzzard (yeah!) Bedfordshire, with a friendly, 'Hello Jack, my name's Mary.' But no-one was deceived. In the previous two weeks it had swooped on five children at Beaudessert Infants' School, cutting them about the face and hands. Mothers were also attacked as they collected their kids – and teachers armed with sticks were needed to escort children to the outside toilets in the playground. A police marksman was called, but missed. The next day (16th) the gunman had another go, and this time successfully blasted the pest out of his tree. As an exercise in public relations, however, the triumph was immediately soured. The gunman went to pick up the bird, and found its wings still fluttering as he held it up for all to see. Mothers screamed and children began crying. As the police drove off, one mother shouted: 'You rotten lot, why didn't you catch it?' *Daily Mirror + Sun + Daily Mail* 15 & 16 January 1975.

'The Strange Nations Slain by the Lions of Samaria', one of Gustave Doré's illustrations of the Bible (1866).

Fair Game

When an animal counter-attacks a hunter, it seems only fair, though sometimes rather hard to explain.

GAME GETS ITS OWN BACK

A 73-year-old retired businessman, Francis Wearne, was out shooting pheasants on Dartmoor with a 79-year-old friend. A bird popped out of the hedges, and Mr Wearne fired as the bird passed low overhead. The shot bounced off the bird and hit the luckless hunter in the eye, which shortly became bruised and swollen. He was admitted to Torbay Hospital, Torquay, for observation, but died during the night. A police spokesman said: 'It appears that the pellet entered his eyelid and touched the brain, causing a fatal blood clot.' His widow commented: 'It was a chance in a million.' *Daily Mirror* 23 November 1973.

● Someone or something Up There seems to be chucking things at people. Maryland Secretary of State Fred Wineland was aiming at his second goose when the first one he'd shot fell on him from 100 feet up. He was knocked out, cracked four ribs, and his dignity was badly bruised. *Daily Mail* 29 November 1973.

● From New England comes a report that hunters are suffering acute frustration because the grouse are committing suicide before they can be peppered with lead. For a week, tales of kamikaze birds were being told: flights through or into the sides of barns, walls and windows. Explanations have been ventured from being drunk on fermenting fruit or hallucinating on fungus, to the theory that they are responding to some unselfish stimulus to thin out over-populated flocks. *Daily Mail* 2 November 1972. (You notice how the most obvious theory is always overlooked? That out of pique a plot may be hatching to turn the tables, to deprive the hunters of their explosive depravity.)

James Twomey, a Nottingham chiropodist, was waiting for his next client when in walked a cockerel with swollen feet. Said Mr Twomey: 'My street door is always open in the daytime. Suddenly the cock came in, limped around, and looked at me with his head on one side. It's quite fantastic that of all the houses on the road it should seek refuge in a chiropodist's. Somebody had obviously tried to fatten it up ... and the feet were swollen through having run a long way. *Daily Mail* 8 December 1972.

● Perhaps pheasants were feeling particularly peeved at the end of November – leastways they had a few tales to tell wherever pheasants gather at the end of the day to tell their tales. Some people, like Peter Cowtan, just come right out asking for it – striding around on a Berkshire moor with an ample, russet-coloured pheasant-like beard. Before the day was out somebody had shot half his beard clean off his face; miraculously, he was unharmed. *Daily Express* 29 November 1973.

DOGS GET THEIR MAN

● Farmer George Hadjinicolaides and his faithful dog Flox chased a fox into its lair in northern Greece. He laid his shotgun against a tree and prepared a small fire to smoke the fox out. Flox knocked over the gun and it fired, hitting Hadjinicolaides in the stomach and legs. Portland *Press-Herald* 1 September 1977.

● Three men on a pigeon hunt at Horsholm failed to bag any game and laid down their shotguns to discuss the day's events. One of the dogs ambled towards his 52-year-old master, trod on the trigger of a gun and loosed off both barrels. The man was seriously injured, while the dog suffered a broken claw. *Daily Telegraph* 23 September 1986.

● Roger Surroca, 37, of Pinet, central France, placed his shotgun on the passenger seat of his car after a day's hunting. His alsatian Napoleon leapt into the car, hit the trigger and shot his master dead. *Daily Mail* 25 August 1987.

● As dawn broke, Michael Martin, 24, was pulling his boat up to the bank of misty Lough Ree in Ireland, on the opening day of the duck-shooting season. His labrador Lindy stepped on the trigger of his single-barrelled shotgun and shot her master in the leg. *Times* + *Daily Mirror* 3 September 1987.

FISH BITE BACK

Lou Wiezai, 71, reeled in his line on the fishing boat *Royal Star*, about 250 miles south of the tip of Mexico's Baja California on 1 March 1987, when a large wahoo, a game fish in the mackerel family, leaped out of the water and sank its razor-sharp teeth into his left hand and forearm, cutting him to the bone. Pawtuxet Valley *Daily Times* 2 March 1987.

● A spotted brown ray with large wing-like fins, with an estimated weight of 250 lb, soared out of the water and landed on Carlton Carroll, five, of Tallahassee, knocking him unconscious aboard a boat in the Gulf of Mexico where he was fishing with his father. His father and a friend were able to lift the ray, with a wingspan as large as the boat, and slide it back into the water. Toronto *Star* + Lincoln *Journal* 6 July 1987.

● Fisherman Anthony Fernando, 21, died off Sri Lanka when a swordfish-like garfish leaped from the water and speared his neck. *Sun* 9 March 1988.

OTHER GAME

● Ron Canny, 45, was crouching in a ditch on one side of a field near Osage, Iowa, while his two sons-in-law flushed about seven deer from the other side of the field at about 4:30pm. One of the deer tried to jump the ditch and landed on Canny, breaking his neck. Lincoln *Journal* 28 December 1987.

● Gilbert Fenwick, 39, of Low Row, Swaledale, was out shooting grouse on Lord Bolton's estate at Wensley, near Leyburn, in the Yorkshire Dales. He had shot one grouse and was aiming eagerly at a second when the first bird, weighing one and a half pounds, hit him in the face at 60 m.p.h. He was knocked unconscious and flung backwards into the heather. The eight other huntsmen rushed to his aid and he left the moor half an hour later nursing a cut lip and two black eyes. 'I ate it for dinner three nights later and it was delicious,' he said later. A spokesman for the British Field Sports Society said it was the first time he had heard of this happening. *Daily Telegraph* + *Wolverhampton Express & Star* 21 December 1987.

● A few days later, Chapman Pincher, the spy writer, wrote in saying that the same thing had happened to him. The dead grouse broke his nose when he was in a grouse-butt on Sir Thomas Sopwith's moor at Arkengarthdale in Yorkshire in 1961. *Daily Telegraph* 24 December 1987.

● A dead pheasant weighing three and a half pounds struck the wife of the man who shot it on an estate in Hampshire. The 50-year-old woman was sitting on her shooting stick leaning against a fence when the bird hit her in the back, rupturing her spleen. *Daily Mirror* 1 January; *Daily Telegraph* 2 January 1988.

Bird shooting hunter: 19th-century woodcut from 'The World Turned Upside Down'.

Not so Dumb?

It's convenient to think of animals as stupid and inferior. But sometimes they do things that make it hard for us to maintain our arrogant attitudes.

ANIMAL RESCUES

● Lottie Stevens, 18, and a friend were on a fishing trip near the Pacific island nation of Vanuatu when their boat capsized on 15 January 1990. His friend died, and after four days he decided to swim to safety. He claimed he was saved by a stingray, which carried him 450 miles over 13 days despite shark attacks. He was washed up on the shores of New Caledonia on 7 February. Reporting the story, Radio Vanuatu remembered how a woman was saved by a shark four years previously. Bangor (ME) *Daily News* 8 February; *Today* 10 February 1990.

● Near Augusta, on Western Australia's south-west coast, two boats manned by members of the Mosman Sea Scouts were on a summer camp exercise at the mouth of the Blackwood River. In an attempt to retrieve a lost oar, their leader, Vollert Asmussen, 41, his son Bjorn and a friend were swamped when their dingy was hit by a wave. Strong currents swept them out into the Indian Ocean, and as they held onto their capsized dingy they became aware of a large whale in the waters close to them. 'It circled us for about an hour,' said Asmussen, 'which is not a nice feeling. It was a huge

hill of meat.' Tiring of waiting for the men to take up the invitation to play, perhaps, the whale tried a different game; it tried disappearing from view and surfacing beneath them. 'It went under us and it touched my feet. I stood on him,' Asmussen said, 'but he kept rising. I folded my legs and knelt on him.'

This was enough, it seems, for as luck would have it, Alan Wood, of Augusta, was on the shore, looking for whales with a telescope when he saw the three men's heads bobbing up and down. 'They were very, very lucky,' he said, 'It was the calmest day we have had, otherwise I might not have seen them.' He called a neighbour and the sea scouts were finally rescued. *Canberra Times* 21 September 1985.

ANIMAL ODDITIES

● **Katrina the cat came back from the dead in Pleasanton, California, after being put down by lethal injection. The corpse was put in a deep freeze, but two days later Katrina strolled back into her old home a couple of miles away, showing no ill-effects. Dr Richard Elliott, who gave the injection, could think of no explanation. *USA Today* 29 July 1983.**

FELINE REINCARNATION? Since strolling into a Buddhist temple in Kuala Lumpur in early 1989, this tabby was noticed apparently praying.

CLEVER BIRDS

John B. Brice, writing to *The Times* (10 September 1985) said: 'Recent observations of the travelling habits of some of London's pigeons suggest a level of intelligence hitherto unsuspected. Using the District Line, I have seen pigeons boarding the Underground trains at Edgware Road station and later alighting at various points along the line.'

TURTLE SAVIOUR

Mrs Candelaria Villanueva, 52, was on board the *Aloha* when it caught fire and sank 600 miles south of Manila in the Philippines. She said she had been floating for more than 12 hours (with a life-jacket) when a giant sea turtle appeared beneath her. She was spotted on 4 June, having been in the water 48 hours, by a Philippine navy vessel, *Kalantia*, who thought she was clinging to an oil-drum. 'Someone threw her a life ring. The moment she transferred her hold to the ring, the drum sank. We did not realize it was a giant turtle until we started hauling up the woman, for the turtle was beneath her, apparently propping her up. It even circled the area twice before disappearing into the depths of the sea, as if to reassure itself that its former rider was in good hands.' Mrs Villanueva said that *another*, tiny turtle climbed on her back. 'The small turtle bit me gently every time I felt drowsy. Maybe it wanted to prevent me from submerging my head in the water and drowning.' *News of the World* 28 July 1974; Knoxville (Tennessee) *News-Sentinel* 24 June 1974.

FOX TALES

● A hungry fox was killed by a gaggle of geese after it broke into their pen to eat them. George Norton and his wife Sue, who run the Binton Social Club at Stratford-upon-Avon, Warwickshire, found the dead vixen the morning after hearing a commotion at the bottom of the garden. Said Mrs Norton: 'The fox couldn't have stood much of a chance. All we found was a bite on one goose. The rest were fine, but the vixen's body was covered in vicious peck marks and wounds.' A spokeswoman for the National Farmers Union had never heard of geese killing a fox, but said she was not surprised. 'They are extremely strong and can break a man's leg with their wings. Farmers often use them to protect their land.' *Daily Telegraph* 17 February 1990.

● Around Easter time, farmers of Penmaenmawr in Wales sought out the lair of a fox that had killed two lambs. In the hole they found remains of geese, ducks, hens and lambs. They shot the vixen and five young, but the fox escaped. In the weeks following, Diawl Goch, or Red Devil, as the locals dubbed him, carved a swathe of vengeance through a dozen flocks, devouring more than 60 lambs. Every night, sheep farmers patrolled their pastures to protect their livestock. One farmer said: 'This is by far our worst-ever lambing season because of this vicious, avenging fox. We never dreamed it would react like this when we killed its family.' *Sun + Daily Express* 29 April 1990.

THE CATS OF WAR

The following letter from Mrs B. N. Harris of Harrogate in Yorkshire appeared in the *Sunday Express* on 17 July 1977:

'During the wartime evacuation from London we were housed in Tiverton Road, Exeter – the straight road out into the country. In the early evening before the tragic raid which so devastated the city, there was an unbelievable exodus of cats padding in a gentle stream past our windows towards Tiverton. Knowing nothing about cats we watched in great surprise, wondering why. Before morning – sadly – we knew.'

Fishy Stories

Like anything else it seems, the slippery world of fish is full of surprises . . .

DOG FOOD

On 8 October 1987, Moscow radio reported that a fisherman's dog disappeared while swimming across a river in northern Siberia. Moments later the fisherman cast his net and hauled in a massive pike, weighing 114.6 pounds with a tail sticking out of its jaws. He cut it open and his dog struggled out, none the worse for wear. [R] *Sandwell Express & Star + Aberdeen Press & Journal* 9 October 1987.

STRAYING SWORDFISH

● **An eight-foot-three-inch-long swordfish normally found in warm, clear waters, was washed up, dead or dying, on the beach at Clevedon, near Bristol, on the Bristol Channel. Bristol *Evening Post* 31 October 1984.**

PIRANHA-EATING TROUT

At the Tropiquaria aquarium in Watchet, Somerset, an eight-lb trout was found in a tank of piranhas, and ate six of the smaller fish before it could be hauled out. Owner Sarah Griffiths saw the trout leap three feet from its tank into the adjoining one. Bristol *Evening Post + Western Daily Press + Daily Telegraph* 31 May; *Weekly World News* 11 July 1989.

MARLIN MYSTERY

Stanley Clarke and his son, Alan, were swimming in the River Leven, at Ulveston, Cumbria, when an enormous silver-blue fish leapt out of the water, twisting in mid-air, several hundred yards ahead of them. Investigating from the safety of the riverbank, they noticed the fish leap again and again, but more astonishing was its huge swordfish-like spike. Eventually, it hurled itself onto rocks, and the Clarkes saw that it was badly gashed about the gills and dying. They killed it quickly. It was identified (from a photograph) by the British Museum of Natural History as a white marlin, an ocean fish common off the coasts from Africa to Portugal and never before recorded further north than Brittany. The Clarks had witnessed its death-throes in fresh water – but just how and why did this 58-lb, six-foot denizen of more tropical waters find its way a couple of miles inland in a relatively shallow (4-ft) lakeland river? One fish expert thought the marlin might have come, not from North Africa, but from the North Carolina coast, where they teem in August, via the good old Gulf Stream. *Sunday Express* 18 September 1983.

FISH THAT GOT AWAY

A crack squad of police frogmen have been called into action . . . to track down thousands of very slippery characters: escapers that appear to have disappeared from a special 'top security prison' – a 14-foot deep pool. The pool, which belongs to a works angling club at Smethwick, Staffordshire, was stocked with thousands of roach, perch, bream and gudgeon three years ago. Members looked forward to some heavy work with rod and reel – but all they have caught are a few 'tiddlers'.

The club is the Guest, Keen & Nettlefold Sports & Recreation Club in Thimblemill Road, Smethwick. Committee member Bill Blick, 40, said yesterday: 'We can't understand where the fish have gone. So we asked the police to help.' Mr Blick of St Katherine's Road, Smethwick, added: 'We expected to be pulling out fish weighing at least a pound. But we are lucky if a sixteen-man fishing team weighs in with a catch of several ounces.' Chief Inspector Cocayne said, 'Samples of pool-water have been sent to the public analyst.' A frogman added: 'If there are any big fish in the pool we haven't seen them. The biggest are three inches long.'

MONSTER STURGEON

A 900-lb sturgeon 11 feet long was found dead in Lake Washington, Seattle, on 5 November 1987. The monstrous fish was believed to be over 80 years old and may have died of old age, according to Washington state fisheries official Tony Floor. Tales of a gigantic duck-eating monster had circulated at the lake for a number of years. Sturgeon specialist Gail Kreitman told journalists that fish of this breed can live to be 100 and grow to be more than 20 feet long. Some specimens have weighed more than one ton, she said, but no sturgeon is capable of eating ducks. How many other lake monsters have been built on monstrous fish? *Albuquerque Journal* + *Orange County Register* 7 November 1987.

DISAPPEARING TROUT

Mr C. W. Foster rears trout in a brick pit at the Marina, Barrow Haven, near Barton-on-Humber, Lincolnshire. There were 8000 fish, all between 10 and 12 inches long, averaging 1 lb each – total value £400. When he came to feed them (which he did daily) on the afternoon of 1 May 1974, they were gone. Police were called and after much bafflement announced their theory that 'several people' must have been involved, with large nets, between 1pm and 4pm that very day. They don't explain how this could have been done without leaving obvious signs (like water and fish-scales all over the place), or without being seen or heard. And that would be that, if there were not a note in the next day's papers, to the effect that detectives returning to the scene of the 'crime' casually threw some food into the pit, and lo! the trout were back; all 8000 of them 'miraculously reappeared'. This was headlined in the paper as 'Detectives Trace Trout'. Hah! Red faces all round. The only thing Foster could say was that the fish must have been sleeping when he threw the food in, or ill – both factors that would have normally occurred to anyone who breeds fish. But for them to be sleeping at their routine feeding would itself have been unusual, and 'they appear to be alive and well enough now'. One would also expect a fish-breeder to tell the difference between a pit-full of $3\frac{1}{2}$ tons of trout from an empty one. Scunthorpe *Evening Telegraph* $2+3$ May 1974.

Elephants

Big and slow is how we see them, because we're so small and thick. In fact elephants have huge brains, amazing senses, and sophisticated communications.

ELEPHANT SUBSONICS

It was not until 1985, that it was discovered elephants, alone among land-mammals, emit subsonic signals. These are between 14 and 25 hertz, below the threshold of human hearing. Katherine Payne, a research fellow of the New York Zoological Society, was observing elephants at Washington Park Zoo in Oregan when she felt unusual throbbing sensations in the air that lasted from 10 to 15 seconds. 'They felt something like the vibrations from the lowest note on a big pipe organ, or the slight shock wave one can feel from far-off thunder,' she recalled.

Using advanced acoustic measuring devices, Payne and her colleagues established that the sounds corresponded to a trembling on the elephants' foreheads at the point where the nasal passages enter the skull, a trembling that also accompanies audible vocal calls such as rumbles or purring sounds. Subsequent observations of African elephants in Amboseli National Park in Kenya and of Asian elephants in zoos in Oregon and Florida have indicated that the subsonic calls convey a variety of messages. When a calf screams, several adult females move towards it and start vocalizing in low frequencies. Adults utter many subsonic calls as they begin to move as a group, or as they guide a stray baby back to its mother. *New York Times* 11 February; *Daily Telegraph* 12 February; *Saudi Gazette* 13 February; St Louis (Missouri) *Post-Dispatch* 25 February 1986.

MISCELLANEA

● **A herd of elephants was devouring a sugar cane crop in Terai, India, and a hedge was set on fire to drive them away. The elephants got water from a nearby stream, put out the fire, and returned to the feast.** *The Times* **14 August 1954.**

● **150 elephants broke into an illegal still in West Bengal, drank a lot of moonshine liquor, and then proceeded to kill five people, injure twelve others, demolish seven concrete buildings, twenty huts and several acres of corn.** *San Francisco Chronicle* **20 July 1974.**

● **An ivory poacher shot a bull elephant in the forest near Putalem in northern Sri Lanka. As he moved in to saw off the tusks, another elephant knocked him down and the whole herd trampled on him until he was dead.** *Sunday Express* **19 November 1978.**

THE SUMATRAN ELEPHANT WARS

Back in April 1983, about half of the 230 elephants forcibly moved from south Sumatra forests to make way for a settlement broke through an electrified fence and started trekking home across the Air Sugihan area, destroying crops as they went. In January 1984, an elephant herd strayed from a northern Sumatran reserve and ran wild through 25 acres of marijuana, sending the growers fleeing. In December 1983, 20 elephants carried out their 20th raid since September, attacking a village and coconut trees. *Daily Telegraph + Sun* 5 April 1983; *Daily Telegraph* 4 + 31 January; London *Standard* 30 January 1984.

ELEPHANT ARTISTRY

Ruby, an Asian elephant at Phoenix Zoo, Arizona, has learnt to paint. Her keepers, noticing that Ruby sometimes picked up sticks and made scratch marks in the dirt, gave her an artist's paintbrush to doodle with. Ruby chooses with her trunk from a palette of eight colours but she shows a strong preference for red, blue and yellow. So do elephants see in colour?

Kangaroos

One thing we know for certain about kangaroos is that they live in Australia and nowhere else. So why do they keep popping up in our back yards?

FRENCH KANGAROO CAPERS

Some time around 17 June 1986, an anonymous motorist saw what he later described as a kangaroo jumping onto the road, near Morange-Silvange in the Moselle region of France, and bounding into a nearby wood. Inquiries were made at a new zoo, near Hagondange, which was just two weeks from its public opening: their shipment of wallabies had not yet arrived, so the mystery beast was not one of theirs. Two employees from that zoo went to investigate, and were reported to have seen the creature themselves. It was about a metre high, and jumping on its hind legs, and lurking in bushes. Several local youngsters said they had seen *two* kangaroos the previous day.

The Gendarmerie said they had received no reports of kangaroos escaping from a circus or anywhere else, and they appealed to the increasing numbers of sightseers to tell them if they saw anything. The kangaroos were not seen again, but a hunter told the gendarmes that he had spotted a small deer with deformed (shortened) front legs (the result of an injury, he supposed). The poor, lame animal was skipping and hopping in its flight.

ABOUNDING BOUNDERS

● In the first week in January 1985 William Phillips, of Westward Ho!, Devon, discovered a great number of prints in his garden in Beech Road. He was convinced they were made by a wallaby because 'they were long, deep and in pairs, which indicated that they were made by an animal jumping with two feet together'. A local animal welfare 'expert', asked by the newspaper to examine the tracks, pronounced them to be made by a large rabbit. *Bideford Gazette* 4 January 1985.

● On 14 August, at Crowmarsh, Oxfordshire, student Greg Caswell was driving home late from a party when he saw a wallaby (a kangaroo in some reports) bounding along the Benson to Crowmarsh road on the pavement outside the South Oxfordshire district council offices. He got out and chased it but it was too quick for him. A Wallingford policeman also chased and lost it. Earlier that evening a cyclist was knocked off his bike by what might be the same animal, which then bounced off across the fields. No clues as to the origin of this mystery marsupial.

The next day, in another part of Oxfordshire, there was a further surprising sighting. Not a marsupial but a hippo found sniffing roses in a garden at Little Tew. It was caught and returned by Banbury police to Chipperfield Circus which was quartered at Heythrop, two miles away. Emma, the two-year-old hippo, had been left in a field at dawn, but escaped by a river. There is no obvious connection with the wallaby; the circus hadn't lost one, although a spokesman said darkly: 'There've been one or two missing recently.' 'Two or three' wallabies are known to have escaped from the McAlpine estate at Fawley, near Henley, about eight miles down the road from Crowmarsh, before Christmas 1984, but they were all believed to have been killed in road accidents before. *Oxford Mail* 15, 19 August; *Daily Mail + Daily Express + Sun* 16 August; Oxford *Times* 30 August 1985.

● On 21 August, at Chipping Camden, Gloucestershire, Mrs Julia Brooks, of Hoo Lane, was putting out scraps for birds in her garden when she was understandably shocked to see them eaten by 'a wallaby'. *Daily Mirror* 22 August 1985. If this is the same animal as the Crowmarsh wallaby, it had travelled no less than 33 miles to the north-west, across Oxford itself, without being seen.

● On 24 or 25 August, at Crowmarsh, Oxfordshire, a wallaby was found drowned in a private pool near Wallingford; it is thought to be the same one seen on 14 August. Oxford *Mail* + *Daily Telegraph* + *Sun* 28 August 1985.

● On 25 August, at Charlbury, Oxfordshire, workers on the Cornbury Park estate saw a kangaroo in nearby fields. One man thought it was a deer at first and got within 50 yards, then it reared up and jumped towards him. The witnesses are insistent that they saw a kangaroo and not a wallaby. They describe it as 'between five and six feet tall and grey-coloured'. Charlbury is about 15 miles southeast of Chipping Campden, between that town and Oxford. If the Crowmarsh animal had travelled to Chipping Campden it would have passed through or close to Charlbury – but this sighting comes after the drowning at Crowmarsh. One possibility is that the Chipping Campden and Charlbury animals are the same, but then it was a wallaby and not a kangaroo that Mrs Brooks is supposed to have seen. Back at Charlbury, there was another sighting by more estate workers coming home from a pub. Oxford *Mail* 27 August; Oxford *Times* 30 August 1985.

The Oxford *Mail* for 17 September 1985 says that a police constable, Jon Badrick, of Chipping Norton police, had been assigned to track down the creature. He reveals that the animal is most likely a wallaby that once belonged to Mr Dennis Washington, who keeps several wallabies at Middle Barton. It is not said whether any of Mr Washington's animals had escaped, and if so, when.

WALLY MAKES WALLIES OF THEM

The police net closes in but once again Wally the runaway wallaby is too fast for them. The men from Chipping Norton police station in Oxfordshire had been tailing the meandering marsupial since he escaped from a private zoo several weeks before. On 5 October 1985 they thought they'd cornered him near the railway line at Finstock Halt. But Wally caught them flat-footed as he skipped off into nearby bushes.

Out of Place

Kangaroos are not the only things that turn up where they're not supposed to . . .

BREAKFAST SURPRISE

Greg Bliss of Bundaberg, Queensland, Australia, had bought a dozen eggs from the local store, and they had been in his fridge for four days. He had not adjusted the heat to incubation temperature. Planning an omelette, Mr Bliss had cracked some eggs into a mixing bowl. One of them yielded a gecko, a night lizard, which immediately began to scurry about in the egg white. Mr Bliss opened every egg he had in case the geckos had spread; but there was only one.

Ray Byrnes, director of the Department of Primary Industries, pig and poultry branch, said from Brisbane that he had no record of anything like it happening before. He said that a hen's egg took 25 to 26 hours to form. The yoke was shed from the ovum and travelled down the oviduct. Several layers of egg white were secreted onto the yolk until, at the final portion of the oviduct, the two layers of membrane were added. Then there was a 15 to 16 hour period when the shell was deposited and hardened. *Bundaberg News–Mail* 16 February 1987.

WILD BOARS BACK IN BRITAIN

A wild boar was hit and killed by a vehicle on a forestry road on the estate of the Earl of Cawdor, near Nairn in Scotland. The wild boar has not been seen outside captivity in Scotland since the 19th century – this one was a year old. The Highland Wildlife Park, near Aviemore, about 40 miles from Nairn, has a breeding pair, but they and their offspring are all accounted for. The Park's director of information, Wille Newlands, said no others are known to be in private collections and that it was apparently impossible for the dead boar to have come from 'original Scottish stock'. All concerned remained baffled. *Daily Telegraph* 16 March 1976.

At least three wild boars appeared in Hampshire in the autumn of 1972. About 9:30 pm, on 5 August, a man knocked on the door of Detective Constable Bernard Startup's house, in Linden Avenue, Oldham, to tell him there was a wild boar in his front garden, eating his young fir trees. As they watched, it over-reached itself and fell into a fishpond. Bernard quickly blocked his driveway with his car, turned on the headlights, and dashed inside to phone for help. Some of his colleagues arrived and they tried to lassoo the beast, but it escaped into the road. The policemen trapped it in another garden with their cars and successfully roped it – then a vet tranquillized it. The 200-lb boar, with two-inch tusks, was eventually taken in by Marwell Zoological Park, where an expert said that, officially, boars have been extinct in England for at least 400 years. The police phoned around and no zoo or private collectors in the south had any boars missing. *Aldershot (Midweek) News* 8 August 1972.

A few days later, on the 10th, a woman living at Up Nately, near Odiham, saw 'a big black animal' which looked like a boar, dash into woods near her home. She phoned the police who arrived with tracker dogs. All they found were some tracks, and the dogs followed the spoor into the woods and along the banks of a canal – but didn't find the animal. *Aldershot (Midweek) News* 15 August 1972.

On 16 August, a man saw 'a funny looking pig' in a field near Odiham. 'It had a long tail with a sort of tassle on the end and it was dark grey with a kind of pointed head.' It ran off into nearby woods – and a police search later found no sign of it. *Aldershot (Weekend) News* 18 August 1972.

SURPRISE BIRDS

● A decomposing ostrich was washed up on the Scilly island of Bryher. 'There is not much left of it, a large head and a few feathers, a beak and a spinal cord,' said Richard Pearce, who found it. A few yards away were the rotting remains of what might have been a leatherback turtle. *Western Morning News* 10 October 1986.

● A woman horse rider told police at the beginning of August that she had spotted a six-foot, emu-like bird in woods near Lifton in Devon. She claimed it had jumped out in front of her and tried to attack. *Independent* 2 August 1990.

ROAD SHARK

● A jaywalking shark was struck by a car as it crossed a San Francisco street. The shark either entered the city's sewers at high tide, or fell off a truck en route to the fish market. *Daily Express* 11 August 1973.

PUZZLING FINDS

A 300-year-old mummified head, with hair and teeth intact, has been found – on its own – in a phone box in London. Strange tattooings suggest it once belonged to a Maori chief.

Some absent-minded collector of curiosities could have mislaid it, of course; but it was probably swiped from a medical school museum. *Sun* 21 January 1984.

● Jennifer Cobb found a live scorpion while she was vacuuming the living-room carpet in her Banbury Park, Torquay, home. She offers a novel origin – the luggage of foreign students. *Sun* 27 June 1983.

● A giant fruit-bat from New Guinea with a three-foot wingspan was found clinging to a car radiator in the middle of Exeter in Devon. Taken to the RSPCA kennels, it tucked into bananas and apples. Origin 'a total mystery'. *ITN News* + *Daily Mirror* + *Shropshire Star* 3 October 1984.

This huge snake was hauled out from under a house in Fort Lauderdale where it had been living for a month in summer 1989.

SNAKE DISCOVERIES

● A two-foot garter snake was discovered hidden behind the wallpaper in a Manchester flat, said the *People* of 6 August 1989, while the *Daily Mirror* 8 August reported that a girl sunbathing in Brighton had been frightened by a six-foot black mangrove snake which slithered onto her balcony. After the girl had raised the alarm it was captured by zoo officials, who said it had 'escaped some time ago'.

● Much larger still was the snake caught in Fort Lauderdale, Florida, after a group of men hauled it from the house it had been living under for a month. The 17-stone, 20-foot python might have been a pet released into the wild 'several years ago', suggested snake wrangler Todd Hardwick, the man who caught it. *Sun* 19 August 1989.

Under Their Noses

Sometimes a thing you've been looking for turns up in the most unexpected place: right in front of you.

STUNNING PROOF

British naturalist Dick Watling's year-long search in Fiji for Macgillivray's Petrel, thought to be extinct, ended when it crashed on his head.

The one and only record of this small black-and-brown bird before May 1984 was in 1855, when a survey ship caught one on the island of Gau, midway between Fiji's two main islands. It was stuffed and is now in a London museum.

Mr Watling lured the bird in from the sea at night, using torches and amplified recordings. It crashed on his head and after examining the dazed bird he let it go. 'I can't take a specimen until I know how many there are,' he told *Reuters. Evening Standard* 10 May 1984.

FAIR COP

● Christopher Logan, 49, charged with impersonating a policeman, escaped from Bow Street Court – by impersonating a policeman. *Sun* 10 October 1985.

● Police in Indianapolis allowed a woman accused of passing $100,000-worth of bad cheques to post bail with a cheque. It bounced. *Scotsman* 12 March 1986.

LOST FATHER FOUND IN A LIBRARY

Wilf Hewitt, 86, a widower from Southport, wanted to look through an electoral roll in Southport library, and asked the woman opposite whether she was going to be long. Vivien Fletoridis replied that she was looking for a man named Hewitt. She was his daughter, who he had not seen for 46 years. Wilf had had a wartime love affair with Vivien's mother, who had died in 1983. Their daughter was adopted in 1941 and went to Australia with her foster parents in 1954. In July 1987 she travelled 13,000 miles to track down her family. She traced her two brothers and sister through an agency, and then set out to find her father. *Daily Express* 24 July 1987.

A TURN-UP FOR THE BOOKS

Officials at the Philadelphia State Library discovered a book left in a manila envelope on 30 December 1985. It was a volume of *Townsend's Collection*, published in 1657, detailing the Cromwellian laws passed in the previous year, and was one of the books purchased for the General Assembly under the direction of Benjamin Franklin, some time between 1745 and the Revolution. The book had vanished from the library some time between 1823 and 1900.

THERE ALL THE TIME

The Director of Greece's National Archaeological Museum, Nicholas Yacouris, startled the world by announcing that 'wondrous . . . archaeological pieces of art . . . almost priceless' have been found – 15th-century BC stone seals; jewellery; weapons; much very valuable Mycenean stuff like a compass and ivory model of a war galleon, and a curious piece of armour plating for a warrior's heel (as Achilles could have done with). And where should they find this fabulous hoard? – that's right, *in their basement*, lying in 'layers' of forgotten crates, unopened since the digs in the 19th century. Many of the bits and pieces they found were the missing parts of items already on open exhibition, e.g. Yacouris mentions a fifth-century BC engraved stone head of a sea-monster that was found to fit a gap below the goddess Amphitrite on the Parthenon's upper western pediment. Houston (Texas) *Chronicle* 27 June 1974.

ANT EERIER

Kathryn S. Fuller, President of the World Wildlife Fund, noticed ants crawling across her desk in her Washington office. For weeks they appeared mysteriously, as if from nowhere. Later she traced them to a South and Central American potted palm in her office.

One day, Professor Edward Wilson, an authority on ants, came to call. He could not immediately identify the tiny yellow insects, except to say they belonged to a large New World genus. He later declared that they appeared to be a species previously unknown to science, and suggested they be called *Pheidole Fullericola* (the ant living with Fuller). *The Times* + *Gloucestershire Echo* 16 October; *Independent* 17 October 1990.

LOST FINDS FOUND

The spring of 1988 brought the controversial rediscovery of Egyptian relics lost for half a century, connected with Lord Carnarvon – who, with Howard Carter, was responsible for excavating the tomb of Tutankhamun.

The discovery was made at Highclere, the Carnarvon family seat near Newbury, Berkshire. The current Lord Carnarvon, grandson of Carter's collaborator, was making an inventory of the mansion's contents with the aid of retired butler Robert Taylor. It was Taylor who revealed the relics, unseen since 1936, in cupboards located in a closed-off passage. The 300 objects, excavated between 1905 and 1914, included a carved and painted wooden face of Amenophis III,

possibly Tutankhamun's grandfather, figurines from the same monarch's tomb, jewellery from Balamun in the Nile delta and figurines and funerary items from seventh-century BC Thebes.

Quite naturally, as the export of antiquities is illegal in Egypt, the authorities there started making noises about their return. And predictably enough the right-wing British popular press expressed outrage at Egypt's reaction. *Daily Mail* 8 March 1988.

The relics, unsurprisingly, have stayed exactly where they were rediscovered, and are now on display at Highclere – which, it might be added, is now open to the public and has doubtless benefited considerably from the sudden publicity about the surprising find in most national dailies (7, 8 March); *Independent* 19 April; Newbury *Out and About* summer

1988. *Independent* 19, 20, 21, 30 May; *The News* (Portsmouth) 19 May; *Guardian* + *Daily Telegraph* 20 May 1988.

Finally, someone lost their mummy ... the mummy of Petemenpophis, buried in Thebes about AD 116 and brought to Paris in 1822. Regrettably, Petemenpophis had the misfortune to be buried naked, rather than swathed, and had to be taken off show in 1825 when the Duchess of Berry visited his new home, the National Library. He thereafter languished in a storeroom for more than 150 years. The dear old Duchess must have been easily offended ... considering the way that mummies tend to shrink, it seems like an awful lot of fuss over such a little thing. *International Herald Tribune* 17 December 1987.

Marine Mysteries

Mysteries of the sea are legion ... here are just a few.

LONG DELAYED SIGNAL?

In 1978 the liner *QE2* suddenly received, out of the blue, a radio message from the *Queen Mary* followed by a routine position announcement, a call that must have been broadcast *before* the old ship was pensioned off in 1967.

Alan Holmes, radio officer on the *QE2*, in the Atlantic bound for America, was on watch when he received a morse message: 'GKS GBTT QSX AREA 1A'. Recognizing that it was coded in a procedure no longer in use, Holmes deciphered it as a routine position check from the old liner *Queen Mary* to the Portishead Radio, at Burnham, Somerset. There is a double curiosity here – not only the coincidence that the *QE2* had inherited the GKS call sign from *Queen Mary* before the code was discontinued, but that the *Queen Mary* was pensioned off over 11 years previously, sold to the City of Long Beach, California, as a floating conference centre.

Later Holmes said: 'It was uncanny ... The radio procedure used was dropped years ago ... it came from another age. I can't believe it was sent by a ghost ... sometimes radio signals bounce off the moon and 'turn up' in Australia. This message could have bounced out into space more

than ten years ago and just zipped around until it found its way back to earth and we picked it up.' If that's true, we are faced with the staggering coincidence that after ten-plus years the long delayed signal is picked up by a different ship using the original call code! *Reveille* 2 June 1978.

PUZZLING OCEAN THEFT

A heavy cable 165 feet long has disappeared from the ocean floor in 4500 feet of water west of Oregon.

The cable was used as a scale for a camera observing activity in volcanic vents, and disappeared on 7 or 8 June 1988, between two automatic exposures taken 30 hours apart. It would be almost impossible to recover it from a surface vessel, and most submarines cannot operate at anything like the depths involved, so oceanographers are speculating that the cable was melted by an unobserved spurt of superheated water from the vents before traces of the event were obliterated by cold water rushing in to replace the volcanic liquid. *New York Times* 15 November 1988, citing the U.S. journal *Eos* 1 November.

TRIANGLE OF THE DAMNED

On 9 June 1984 the motor fishing boat *Carmela Madre* left Torre del Greco, near Naples for Vibo Valentia in southern Italy. As she passed between Capri and Iscia in the Bay of Naples, the crew swapped news with another fishing boat. The weather was fine and the sea calm. Suddenly, the man in the *Carmela* cut in: 'Christ, I can't say any more!' he exclaimed. 'There's a big light.' Then silence. About a week later three of the crew were found drowned. No wreckage was found.

The Tyrrhenian Sea between Sardinia, Rome and Sicily where the boat went down is supposedly known by fishermen and pilots as 'Triangle of the Damned'. In 1980 an Alitalia DC9 entered the area and the controls went haywire, radio contact was lost and there was an explosion. The 81 passengers died. Shortly before that a Cessna plane had vanished.

Over the last few years, dozens of small ships have been lost, the bodies of their crews picked from the sea weeks later. Empty fishing boats have been found drifting, and captains have reported strange objects in the waters. *Sunday Express* 21 October 1984.

DOGGY PADDLES

● Robert Williamson, 38, and his sons were sailing in the treacherous currents between the north and south islands of New Zealand when their rottweiler Trudi fell overboard. Only a week before, 18-month-old Trudi had given birth to eight pups, and must have rolled off the deck, still weak from the delivery. They sailed in circles for hours in a vain search.

Two weeks later, Trudi was spotted by some fishermen on a tiny deserted island eight miles from where she had disappeared. 'The animal's fatty tissues around the mammary glands, enlarged after giving birth, probably helped to keep her afloat and to keep warm,' said a vet. The Williamsons believe that dolphins might have led her to land. *Sunday Express* 27 May 1990.

● The crew of the Welsh yacht *Crynogwyn* rescued a dog they found swimming two miles out to sea off St David's Head. *Sun* 25 May 1989.

SWIMMING RACEHORSE

The £3000 Irish mare 'Russell's Touch' had unseated its trainer, David Kiely, while training on the shore at Dungarvan, Co. Waterford, before dashing into the foam and heading out to sea. Kiely spent the next two hours finding a phone and trying to raise a rescue boat. Eventually the horse was spotted by a returning trawler. A rope was passed through the horse's stirrups and the noble but daft beast ignominiously towed ashore. It recovered in a few days. *Daily Express*, sometime in February 1984.

This giant 30-ton screw was washed up on a beach at Port Talbot, West Glamorgan. No owner was traced.

COBWEB CLOUD

During the night of 28 October 1988, a trawler off the coast of Dorset reported to the area coastguard that their boat had been engulfed by a giant cloud of sticky 'candyfloss', seemingly composed of clinging white cobweb-like strands. The cloud was thought to be drifting northwards. Consequently, police and emergency services were put on alert. The cloud measured 30 square miles; did this phantom vanish with the morning light? Giant sheets of webs lifted and transported by winds are rare but not unknown. *Daily Mirror* 29 October 1988.

Lightning

We know that lightning never strikes twice in the same place. Don't we?

LUCK RUNS OUT FOR HUMAN LIGHTNING ROD

Roy Cleveland Sullivan, retired forest ranger of Waynesboro, Virginia, is listed in the *Guinness Book of Records* because he survived being struck by lightning *seven* times. At 3:00 am, on 28 September 1983, aged 71, he succeeded by his own hand where Jupiter's bolts had failed. He shot himself, and was finally earthed.

During his 36 years as a ranger he became a celebrity for, but never understood, his singular affinity for the electrical fluid. In 1942 he lost a big toenail to lightning. In 1969 his eyebrows were blown off. His left shoulder was seared in 1970; and his hair set on fire in 1972, after which he always carried a few gallons of water in a can in his car. On 7 August 1973 he was out driving when 'a bolt came out of a small, low-lying cloud, hit him on the head through his hat, set his hair on fire again, knocked him ten feet out of his car, went through both legs and knocked his left shoe off.' He once made the remarkable statement that he could see the lightning travelling towards him. PA/ *Standard* 30 September; *Daily Express* 1 October; AP/Houston *Chronicle* 4 October 1983.

FATAL BOLTS

● Laura McDowell, 22, eight months pregnant, was talking on the phone about 5:00 pm on 21 May 1988 in Montezuma, New York, as a heavy band of thunderstorms moved through the central New York region. A lightning bolt came through the phone, killing her and her foetus, throwing her from her chair and knocking things off the wall. The phone was blackened by the charge, estimated at 10,000 to 50,000 volts. About 50 volts can jog the human heart. *St Louis Post–Dispatch* 23 May; *Star* (Malaysia) 24 May 1988.

● **A bolt vaporized electrical wiring on its way to a fridge, killing a young housewife in Knoxville, Iowa, even though she was standing on a rubber-backed carpet. The baby Vietnamese orphan she was holding at the time miraculously remained unharmed.** *Daily Mail* **11 September 1975.**

● **Zimbabwe suffered the worst electrical storm season on record. By the beginning of February 1985, the season's death toll was 116. The country holds the record for the most people ever killed by a single bolt – 21.** *Daily Express* **8 February 1985.**

LUCKY ESCAPES

● Heidi Madsen, 14, on her six-year-old horse Zita, had finished her round in a riding competition in Gedsted, near Hobro in Denmark, on 29 May 1988, and was on her way out of the ring when lightning struck from a cloudless sky. The horse was killed instantly, the girl had heart failure, and several spectators were knocked down. The buttons on Heidi's riding clothes glowed. She recovered in hospital, but suf-

fered serious burns on her chest and stomach. The hair on her neck was scorched off, and her necklace was charred, leaving a burn on her neck. *Morgenavisen Jyllands Posten* (Denmark) 1 July 1988.

● On 1 July 1988, a woman in Karlskrona, Sweden, who was very much afraid of thunder, got so alarmed during a heavy thunderstorm that she ran out of her house to seek refuge with her nearest neighbour. Lightning struck the top of her umbrella, knocked her down, and knocked all the fillings out of her teeth. She was unhurt, and after she had recovered from fright she called on a dentist to get new fillings.

Professor Stig Lundquist, known as 'the professor of thunder', said that this is the first accident of its kind that he has ever heard of. Lightning may literally strip a person naked if it hits his/her clothes. It may also focus on metal objects. The professor recalled one case when it burned away a gold necklace, leaving only a black mark. *Sydsvenska Dagbladet* (Sweden) 6 July 1988.

LIGHTNING STARTS TRACTOR

● **On 22 June 1988 lightning set fire to a shed in a rural district in southern Finland. Half of the shed was destroyed. The heat started a diesel tractor, which drove itself through the door.** *Helsingin Sanomat* **30 June 1988.**

● **A bolt the year before set off three small rockets, designed to study thunderstorms, from a U.S. space base in Virginia. They fell harmlessly into the sea.** *Daily Mirror* **12 June 1987.**

SAINT PATRICK'S PURGATORY

William Corliss' *Science Horizons* newsletter drew attention to the remarkable case of a family in Maryland who were persecuted by lightning. To have two members of the same family have close encounters with lightning in the same night is remarkable enough, but in this case it was three members in separate incidents.

On St Patrick's Day, G. Patterson of Phoenix, north of Baltimore, was in bed sick during a hard rainstorm, when the bulb in her bedside lamp exploded. Lightning had struck her house. She got out of bed and rushed over to her daughter's house nearby to find a red ball of fire on a skirting board outlet socket. Her daughter's house had also been struck by lightning which also ruined her television and video recorder.

Later on the same day, Patterson's daughter in Bel Air, northeast of Baltimore, called to say that lightning had struck the chimney of her house, scattering fireplace bricks all over the floor. Baltimore *Sun* 9 April 1990.

BALL LIGHTNING ATTACK

● **On 15 May 1976 Freda Bell, of High Green Farm, Middleton, Cumbria, had just tucked her kids in bed and begun her ironing as a storm began. 'A flash of lightning ripped down the iron, bounced across to the iron fireplace guard, then hit me,' she said. 'I was hurled across the room and found that the lightning had torn through my overall, ripped off my trousers and burned off my tights to below the knee, blistering my legs.** *Sunday People* **16 May 1976.**

Meteorological Curiosities

'The Weather' is everybody's favourite topic. Everyone knows that it's unpredictable. But sometimes what happens in the sky is downright weird . . .

CLOUD OF UNKNOWING

Not since the 1908 Tunguska blast and the south Atlantic atmospheric flash of 1979 has there been an explosive event as stubbornly enigmatic as the mushroom cloud off Japan in 1984.

The 1979 flash was recorded by American Defence Department Vela satellites, whose sensors pick up many flashes from lightning bolts and meteors, most of which are very brief. The south Atlantic flash was more like the prolonged sequence from a nuclear blast; but there was no evidence of fallout or atmospheric pressure waves, and a White House 'panel of experts' concluded that the most plausible explanation was that a small meteoroid had knocked debris off the satellite which then reflected sunlight back to the sensors.

The 1984 mushroom cloud appeared 200 miles east of Japan, shortly before midnight on 9 April. It was reported independently by four crews of commercial airliners flying above a 14,000-foot cloud deck, who saw the mushroom erupt, expand to a diameter of 200 miles, well up to above 65,000 feet at an estimated 500 m.p.h., thin out and disappear. No radioactivity was found on the planes, or in dust samples collected from the area afterwards; no flash or other effects of a nuclear blast were seen; and there was no disruption of aircraft electronics.

Dr Daniel A. Walker of the Hawaii Institute of Geophysics operates an array of hydrophones near Wake Island in the western Pacific used to monitor nuclear tests and seismic events. These recorded a swarm of underwater earthquakes commencing in March somewhere west of Wake Island, and peaking on 8 and 9 April. Although several candidates for the site of disturbance emerged from his analysis (*Science* vol. 227, p. 607), the 'best buy' was the subterranean volcano Kaitoku Seamount, located at 26-0°N, 140-8°E, 80 miles north of Iwo Jima. But how could this cause a cloud 900 miles north-east at 38.5°N, 146.0°E? Wind charts showed that the wind was in the wrong direction. The two events were 'purely coincidental'.

Another theory was put forward by André C. Chang and James A. Burnetti in *Nature* (vol. 314, p. 676): that a meteor may have encountered the cloud deck just as it shattered, producing heat which warmed the cloud layer over a large area. Convection would then have produced a cloud plume. Walker maintains that this hypothesis doesn't explain the mushroom shape, nor the energy needed to force a cloud upwards at 500 m.p.h. N.A.S.A. spokesman Arlin Krueger was also sceptical, stating that a meteor would probably burn out at a higher altitude. In May 1985 Walker was assessing such admittedly far-out proposals as an explosion of a tanker laden with liquid hydrogen, which might not produce a bright flash, and so would not be seen through the cloud cover. There is no maritime record of such an explosion.

Tom Bearden, a retired army lieutenant colonel who worked on high-energy lasers and surface-to-air missiles for the American Defence Department, believes the cloud is evidence for a Russian psychotronic beam weapon. The scientific establishment agrees with Dr Kosta Tsipis, MIT arms specialist, that 'Bearden is off the deep end'. However, according to the *New York Times*, the Soviet Union had warned of impending weapons tests before April 1984, but far to the north of the mushroom. Boston *Sunday Globe* 13 January; *New Scientist* 25 April, 9 May; Beaumont *Enterprize* 5 May; Chicago *Tribune* + Milwaukee *Journal* 12 May; *New York Times* 21 May; Greensboro *News & Record* 26 May; London *Times* late June 1985.

WIND BLASTS SHED

One of the strangest railway accidents on record took place on Friday, 30 October 1863. At about 3:30 pm, the engine shed of the London, Brighton and South Coast Railway at New Cross in South London was struck by a blast of wind. The doors were open at the time, and the wind, unable to escape from the confined space, lifted the roof bodily, and blasted open the walls. The roof then fell back upon the debris. The adjacent running line was blocked with debris, and the engine of a passing train was slightly damaged.

The building was 145 feet long by 42 feet wide. It was strongly built of brick work 14 inches thick, strengthened by 23-inch buttresses every 21 feet, yet the sudden blast of wind reduced it to a pile of smashed bricks. The seven locomotives stabled in the shed were covered with rubble. One, number 111, was derailed and severely damaged, being overturned into the ash pit between the rails. The driver and fireman escaped by scrambling into the pit beneath the engine as the roof came in, but a cleaner was crushed to death between the wrecked locomotive and the rubble.

The survivors were dug out of the debris, having been completely trapped. Details of the accident can be found in *Historic Locomotives and Moving Accidents by Steam and Rail*, written by Alfred Rosling Bennett, 1906.

There was a similar accident in about 1956 at Gunnersbury Station in South London, which was totally wrecked by a whirlwind.

JUMPING CLOUD

An active mystery cloud appeared over Motutaiko Island, New Zealand, on 4 June 1978, according to a story in the *Taupo Times* of 8 June. Mrs Christine Dudley, her husband and family watched its antics for an hour as the black cloud swooped around Lake Taupo. She said it moved at speed, continually changing shape, and sometimes dipped down to touch the water surface before shooting up again. The cloud was still visible some time after sunset. 'It was a little frightening,' said Mrs Dudley.

STRANGE CLOUDS

● A spate of nosebleeds and sore throats plaguing the villagers of Culham, in Oxfordshire, has been blamed on a thick cloud that descended on the village on 3 May 1989.

INSTANT HEAT WAVE

On the morning of 7 July 1987 temperatures in Greensburg, Kansas, rose 20 degrees in just ten minutes. At 7:30 am it was 75 degrees, and at about 7:40 it was 95 degrees. It felt as if an oven door had been opened, said Bill Ellis, a volunteer observer for the National Weather Service. Just south in Sun City, the rise was 17 degrees in 15 minutes, and in Pratt to the east it was 10 degrees up in the same period. The temperature in Greensburg gradually began falling until at 10:30 am it was down to 77 degrees.

John May, National Weather Service meteorologist at Topeka, had never heard of such a phenomenon, but speculated that the normal layer of cool air that develops overnight close to the ground simply switched places with much warmer air thousands of feet up: 'We're not sure why this happens,' he said. *UPI newswire* 7 July 1987.

God photographed in the clouds? Only the blindly faithful would discount atmospheric visual tricks or the possibility of psychokinetically imposed images.

Snipers

Some people seem to be bombarded by mysterious assailants . . .

FLYING FOOD ATTACKS

● In March 1989, elderly people in Hayes, Middlesex, were being harassed by eggs hitting their windows or aimed at them in the street. A policewoman thought that groups of local youths were responsible. *Ruislip, Pinner & Rickmansworth Recorder* 2 March 1989.

● A veritable bombardment of flying food had begun. Three days later the same scene was played out in Stepney, east London. Mrs Angela Hall, 58, was left unconscious with a broken cheekbone after she had been hit by a flying egg. She later found she had lost the sight of her right eye. The four men in a car found more victims as they sped through the area but managed to avoid being caught. Ann Raja, Terry Stone and Patrick Lynch all suffered facial injuries. 'Police fear the attacks are spreading,' wrote George Hollingbery in the *Sun* (22 April 1989). 'Even city yuppies have been seen with trays of eggs on their passenger seats, ready to pelt unsuspecting passers-by.'

● On 19 April in nearby Leytonstone, Alan Jones, a 54-year-old jogger, suffered stomach injuries from a cabbage hurled from a car. *Daily Telegraph* 27 July 1989.

● The following month, Laura Williams, 9, was badly injured by a giant Double Gloucester cheese which was being rolled down Cooper's Hill, Brockworth, Gloucestershire, in a traditional race. *Daily Telegraph* 30 May 1989.

● Finally, the wave of food hurling claimed its first fatality. On 14 July 1989, Leslie Merry, 56, was out shopping with his wife in Fillebrook Road, Leytonstone, (near the scene of the April cabbage incident), when he was struck on the back by a flying turnip, which knocked him to the ground. Police couldn't find the turnip, although Mr Merry had seen it rolling away. The blow punctured a lung, and ruptured his spleen, and he died in Whipps Cross Hospital on 23 July. *Daily Telegraph + Sun + Independent.*

At the inquest held at Walthamstow on 16 October, which recorded an open verdict, Det. Supt Graham Howard said there had been more than 23 incidents in east London since February, in which melons, potatoes and cabbages had been used. In most cases a glimpse of one or more people in a car and a part of a number plate was the only description that the police had. *Independent* 17 October 1989.

MYSTERY SHOTS IN THE HEAD

Miner Tom Coxon was driving with his wife and two daughters in the car, on 8 October 1975, near the aptly named No-Man's Heath, Ashby-de-la-Zouche, in Leicestershire. Suddenly he cried out, and blood began to spurt from a hole in his head. He managed to drive to a service station, where someone took him to hospital. He was then transferred to the neuro-surgical unit of North Staffs General Hospital, where he now lies paralysed down one half of his body, with *three* pieces of metal lodged near his brain. *Daily Express* 9 October 1975.

Two days later the police hunted down and arrested two brothers who were driving a van that was passing at the time Tom got 'hit' – their assumption is that they fired an airgun at Tom. If so, they must be the most remarkable marksmen ever, to hit a man through a car window (it is not said whether it was open or not!) three times as the two cars pass, and to get all three pellets into the same hole in the man's head. (The three pieces of metal must have arrived simultaneously, on the same trajectory, because Tom cried out once and put his hand up to his head, which then would have been hit by numbers two and three.) And would an airgun have the power to penetrate a skull? As the hunt began for the passing van, Superintendant Thomas Bush did not sound too convinced: 'We are completely snookered. This is one of the most baffling mysteries I have ever known.'

MYSTERY SNIPER BAFFLES POLICE

A 'mystery sniper' attacked a Riviera villa for almost a week despite the vigilance of three French police forces. Jean Oliveros is an Antibes joiner 'with no known enemies'. He and his wife Olga have adopted two Vietnamese, Isabelle (20) and Jean-Jaques (18). Their villa, at 59 Avenue des Cannes, Juan-les-Pins, near Cannes, lies on the RN7 motorway, separated from the sea by a 100-yard-wide stretch of wasteland from which most of the shots were directed. The prime target was the long picture-window on the villa's veranda.

6 August: fire breaks out in garden shed belonging to M. & Mme Juan Cortez, at one end of the Olivero property.

8 August: bush fire at night in front of the Olivero villa.

9 August: small fire on wasteland shortly before midnight.

10 August: Mme Olivero's Fiat 500 fired in front of villa.

21 August: ground-level fire in villa workshop. Water pipe vandalized and cut through, requiring immediate attention.

22 August: fire in front of villa. Police find bottle of pure alcohol on the property. That evening, external wooden stairs leading to verandah are doused in fuel and fired. Another fire beside villa in

Rhode Island National Guard search for a sniper after 11 shootings in January 1987.

late afternoon, followed by 'shower of stones'. Source is not specific, but presume they were believed thrown or catapulted rather than falling from sky.

29 August: flaming rag around stone thrown through window into wardrobe, starting fire. Shots fired in evening, shattering parts of picture windows. Villa's hedge and verandah awning set on fire.

30 August: Shots continue at 12:30 am despite police presence. Two tendons and artery in paw of family dog severed by broken glass from shattered window.

31 August/1 September: midday fusillade aimed at first floor; shots continue spasmodically for 11 hours. Fruitless police search.

1 September: firing aimed at Jean-Jaques as he shuts the glazed workshop door, and at policeman on same floor. Both unhurt.

2 September: most of local police force on duty at the house; joined by CRS units and GIPM from Nice. Morning fusillade shatters window overlooking RN7, then switched to favourite target, picture windows facing sea (late morning to 3:00 pm). At 6:00 pm, stone wrapped in burning paper 'flies through the window' of Isabelle's bedroom (one source

says Jean-Jaques' room) setting fire to bedding. Police deny it could have got past the policeman outside and through the half-open window. Father and son taken for lengthy – but 'routine' – questioning at local police station.

3 September: all family friends and sightseers evacuated from the area, leaving only the Oliveros. Police report 'all quiet'.

c. 5 September: Police declare that they had been fooled by Jean-Jaques, and pull out. Topic vanishes from local press.

Aside from the problem of just how the sniper eluded massive and repeated police searches, perhaps the most mysterious aspect was the failure to find projectiles, except for the 'shower of stones' on 22 August. On one occasion a window was shattered as journalists stood talking to the family nearby. A reporter from *Nice-Matin* described hearing 'the short dry sound of breaking glass, and nothing else ...' i.e. no gunshot. Whatever it was that was being fired or catapulted, it was breaking 8 mm-thick anti-burglary glass fitted in the picture windows, leaving large holes – indicating a low velocity. No missiles could be found in the house, baffling the CRS chief.

VEGETABLE WEAPON

Ernest Coveley, 36, a drug addict from east London, was tried for 14 building society robberies which netted £12,418. His weapon was a cucumber wrapped in a plastic bin liner. Peter Feinberg, defending, said: 'It is rare indeed that one has a case where a man uses a cucumber to try to gain money.' *Daily Telegraph* 7 October 1989.

Sleep

Perhaps the greatest mystery of all is sleep, when our rational minds stop functioning and fantasy takes over.

DREAM TOPPING

Colin Kemp woke up one night in August 1985 and saw his wife lying dead beside him. He couldn't believe it. 'I slapped her face and tried to wake her up,' he told police. 'There was no pulse and I went barmy.'

Shortly after going to bed the previous evening Kemp dreamed that he was being chased through a jungle by two Japanese soldiers who were trying to kill him. One soldier was armed with a gun; the other had a knife. Kemp kept running but they cornered him. He grappled desperately with the man with the knife, trying to throttle him; then the other soldier raised his gun and fired. Kemp woke up.

For Ellen Kemp, 33, it was more than a dream. She had been strangled by her husband while he was in the grip of a 'night terror' – an arousal from sleep accompanied by intense anxiety. Night terrors last from one to three minutes and generally occur in the first third of the night's sleep. They are not nightmares, which are experienced during periods of light sleep and 'rapid eye movement'; night terrors occur during arousal from heavy, dreamless slumber. They are rare, afflicting only three per cent of children under 15 and fewer adults, and tend to be caused by waking tension. And they are 'almost never fatal'.

Although Colin Kemp's experience does sound more like a nightmare proper – recall of the events of a night terror is unusual – his defence of 'automatism' was accepted and the jury acquitted him of his wife's murder at an April 1986 trial. *Guardian + Daily Mirror + Daily Express* 3 May 1986.

On 18 January 1985, 18-year-old Adrian Lilienfield of Twickenham repeatedly stabbed his best friend, Michael Cummings, and beat him with a mallet, whilst in the grip of a night terror. Cummings was left paralysed from the neck down. Lilienfield was cleared of attempted murder and claimed that he dreamed he was being attacked by four men in a windowless room. 'One of his attackers had been lying down and he just hit him,' the court was told. 'Then he had the sensation of falling backwards down a dark tunnel moments before waking up.' Lilienfield said he had taken a knife to bed with him as a joke. *Guardian* 15 October; *Richmond & Twickenham Comet + Twickenham & Hampton Gazette* 17 October; *Richmond & Twickenham Informer* 24 October 1985.

SLEEP-DRIVER

In an incident curiously reminiscent of the classic cases of somnambulism investigated by pioneering French psychologists towards the end of the last century, a 15-year-old Hampshire boy drove a car miles in his sleep.

The unnamed boy woke up at 3:30 am on 6 December last year, in his father's car, in the middle of Southampton, 27 miles from his home in Portsmouth. The father, who thought the boy was in bed, was woken by a phone call from the lad, who found himself in the car wearing pyjamas and dressing gown, unable to get home. The father called the police, who said the boy was 'very confused' and waiting by the car. Even more curious than the fact that the boy had driven the car so far without any mishap is his protestation, confirmed by his father, that he didn't know how to drive and had never driven before! A Dr Jacob Empson, of Hull University's Psychology Department, said the incident was 'quite extraordinary. I have never heard of anything like this. People who sleepwalk usually do things they would normally do.' Portsmouth *News + Sun + Daily Express + Daily Star + Daily Telegraph* 7 December 1983.

MARK SLEEPWALKS ON THE ROOF

Schoolboy Mark Henderson yawned and woke up to the biggest audience of his life yesterday. He woke up to find himself perched 40 feet up on the roof of his home in Accrington Road, Burnley. Dressed in his pyjamas and fast asleep, Mark, 14, had climbed out of his attic bedroom through a tiny window. Still asleep, he walked ten feet down wet, slippery slates to the edge of the roof above their backyard. Neighbours spotted him and called the emergency services. He was rescued by firemen and returned to bed, shaken but no worse for his 'night out'. *Daily Mail* 18 September 1973.

WHY DOCTORS ARE UP IN THE AIR OVER HENRI

Henri Rochatain was so tired that he slept on a clothesline – probably the only man who has ever done it. Now doctors are trying to fathom out how he managed to snooze without falling off. You might think M. Rochatain is a nut – once he walked 4000 miles around France on a pair of stilts – but his exploits fascinate doctors because they push human endurance beyond limits previously thought possible.

He has just come down from a tightrope, 82 feet up above a car-park in Saint Etienne, France. He lived for six months on the rope, fitted with a covered toilet and a board bed – but these were simply balanced along the line, there was nothing holding them there. 'It is fantastic that he managed to sleep at all,' said Dr Paul Monet, whose team had Rochatain wired up with electrodes to monitor reactions. 'He slept well even in thunderstorms and high winds. It is quite astonishing that he could rest, knowing that if he turned over in the night he would plunge off the rope.'

He spent most days walking up and down, and occasionally doing stunts, like standing on his head or pretending to fall off. His menu was sparse – seaweed soup, biscuits and tea. A local supermarket presented him with a fat fee for using the tightrope attraction as an advertisement. *Daily Mail* 4 October 1973.

Phantom Hitch-hikers

You know the story . . . a driver picks up a hitch-hiker, often a strange conversation ensues, the driver stops to let the hitch-hiker out . . . and finds no-one there.

'TWAS THE NIGHT BEFORE CHRISTMAS

Sebi Breci was a disc jockey from 9:00 pm to midnight in the Armed Forces Radio Service station in Fairbanks, Alaska. About 35 minutes into his phone-in on the evening of 24 December 1951, he received a call that had nothing to do with music. A woman's voice said she needed help; that her car had stalled some 30 miles southeast of Fairbanks on the Alcan (now the Alaska) Highway and she couldn't get it started. She said she had two children with her. She pleaded that he send a tow-truck before she and her children froze to death. She hung up before he could ask her why she had called the station rather than a garage.

Breci called a garage in Fairbanks, and the owner promised to go and help. Shortly after the news, the garage man called up. He had reached the woman just in time, and had taken her and the children to the Y.M.C.A. Where the car had stalled, there was no telephone for miles. He had started to ask her where she had called from, then got busy with her car and forgot to ask her again. The next day, Breci tried to find the woman, but she had apparently left in the night.

The following Christmas, his last in Fairbanks, Breci received a Christmas card posted in some Montana town with no name or address of sender. Its only words were 'Thank you'. He received similar cards for the next five or six years – from Red Bank, New Jersey; Tampa, Florida; Oklahoma City – then the cards stopped.

A psychologist speculated that the woman's fear for her life and those of her children was so great that somehow she was able to contact Breci telepathically. She was probably listening to the station when her car stopped. *Omaha World Herald* 24 December 1978.

RESURRECTION MARY

Every year, on the anniversary of her death, the ghost known as 'Resurrection Mary' appears in Chicago. An 18-year-old girl hitches a lift from a young man, and arranges a date with him. When the unfortunate driver turns up, he's informed that Mary died in the 1930s and is buried near where he picked up, in Resurrection Cemetery: having had an argument with her boyfriend, she decided to hitch a lift home, was hit by a car and killed.

GHOST STOPS BUS

In Taiwan, a bus company in Tainan, two hundred miles south of Taipei, has had to cancel its evening run to a remote village because frightened drivers are refusing to make the trip after dark due to a phantom passenger. It seems that a part of the route passes through a plantation of tall, shadowy sugar cane fields. On one trip a driver picked up a young girl at the spooky spot, only to discover she had vanished from the bus by the time he got to town.

THE GHOST AND THE GUITARIST

Richard Stodholme, lead guitarist with the group 'Chicory Tip' was driving back to London after a night's work and stopped to pick up a girl near the top of Blueberry Hill, four miles north of Maidstone, Kent. 'She asked if I would give her a lift to West Kingsdown. It was on my way so I agreed.' He took the girl's case and put it in the car. 'During the journey she said very little, but asked if I would call at her parents' house at Swanley, further

along the route to London. She gave me their address, and I dropped her off.' The girl's father answered the door, and told the astonished guitarist that their daughter had been killed in an accident two years earlier, at the spot he picked her up. All he could think was that he had been the victim of a cruel hoax. 'It wasn't until some months later that I read in a Kent newspaper of other strange happenings at the spot that I began to believe I had driven a ghost in my car. I touched the girl. I took her bag from her and helped her into the car – there was nothing unusual about it. No particular sensation of coldness, he explained. Apparently, the hiker has been picked up several times at the same spot. *Reveille* 9 May 1975.

DISTRESSED BRIDE

Insurance broker Barry Collings and his friend Stephen Pope were driving up Bluebell Hill, Chatham, in Kent, when they saw a girl standing by the side of the road. She had long blonde hair and wore a white evening-dress, which was in disarray, and carried a handbag. There was a strong wind blowing, yet the girl's hair did not move, and she was perfectly still. At first they thought she was in trouble; then they decided she was a ghost and drove off.

In 1965, a bride-to-be and her three attendants were killed in a crash on the hill, since when there have been at least six accounts of the girl being given a lift. Once in the car, she vanished. *Evening News* 12 September 1977.

GHOST IN THE CAR

This photograph shows a woman who died a week before the picture was taken. Mrs Mabel Chinnery, a 48-year-old Ipswich housewife, says that on 22 March 1954 she went with her husband to the cemetery where her mother, Mrs Ellen Hammell, was buried. She took some photographs of the grave, then used up the remaining film by taking this shot of her husband sitting in the driving seat of their car. But when the negative was developed, it showed her dead mother sitting in the back seat, in the place where she usually sat when out for a drive. Experts are sure that the photograph had not been tampered with and there seems to be no explanation for the 'psychic extra'.

Mass Hysteria

Fort observed that every explanation of 'mass hysteria' left more questions unanswered than answered. Why do people collapse for no apparent reason?

MASS COLLAPSE

Twenty-two pupils from Romney Avenue Junior School at Lockleaze, Bristol, collapsed during a swimming lesson at nearby Lockleaze Comprehensive School, and were ferried in seven ambulances to Southmead Hospital. The headmaster sent a further 31 to hospital for checks. A handful of the children were detained for observation. No fault could be found with the pool, but it was conjectured that the high water temperature had been the cause. *Daily Post* (North Wales) 3 March 1988.

MYSTERY BUGS

Illness of a large group of people without obvious causes are a frequent happening, though the fashion in names has drifted from 'Mass Hysteria' to 'Socially Shared Psychopathology'. But from the phenomenological point of view they are still very real, and never much fun for the victims. One or many are suddenly afflicted – experts are said to be tracking a 'mystery bug' or 'smell' down – there is often a recurrence – experts pronounce themselves baffled – parents complain, victims groan – then perhaps the greatest mystery of all, the whole case drifts out of sight as smoothly as it arrived.

● In Rickmansworth, Hertfordshire, a mystery sickness struck swimmers in a popular lake, and brought on a painful rash. Scientists from the Medical Research Council said there was no cause for alarm, hanging the blame on a microscopic parasite of snails 'which may be responsible'. But this was not confirmed, and if it was a parasite, surely its sudden nonmalevolence should have been an equal cause for wonder? *Daily Mirror* 10 July 1970.

● Seventeen women workers collapsed and were taken to hospital from the Old Hill works of BSR in Warley, Worcestershire. Experts were baffled – oppressive heat, lack of ventilation, a 'mystery virus', and leakages of gas or other fumes were all checked for and discounted. The previous Friday 25 women had collapsed over a two-hour period at the nearby Waterfall Lane premises of the same firm. *Birmingham Evening Mail* 9 July 1974. The next day, the *Daily Mirror* carried an interview with one of the victims, who complained of a strange ether-like smell sweeping through the factory. 'I felt a burning sensation in my chest. All around me people were passing out.' Factory inspectors, health officials and chemists poked around for a second day and still came up with nothing.

● Eighty-four people, most of them teenagers, were attacked by nausea, headaches and dizziness during a feature film in a Gillespie, Illinois, movie-theatre on 28 December. Dr Lee Johnson, a trauma surgeon at St Francis Hospital in nearby Litchfield, where 76 of the victims were taken, said that he didn't rule out the possibility of 'mass hysteria' – whatever he means by that. Sheriff Richard Zarr felt differently: 'It wasn't any kind of follow-the-leader type of thing. Seven or eight people were lying on the sidewalk in front of the show. These people were actually passed out. We were reviving them with oxygen.' Those inside, he added, suddenly and without explanation began to feel ill during the film; they left the theatre and many began to collapse onto the sidewalk. The film showing was *Paper Moon*, hardly a subject likely to give rise to 'mass hysteria'. Authorities were said to be investigating the ventilating system for 'foreign substances', etc. Champaign-Urbana (Illinois) *Courier* 30 December 1973.

● Not long after the previous incident, 54 people, mostly children, collapsed during a Walt Disney film at the Riviera Theatre in nearby Chicago. They were vomiting and complaining of headaches and dizziness. Police were said to have identified the cause – carbon monoxide leaking into the theatre. *San Francisco Examiner* 20 February 1974.

● 'More than 20 guests' at a Birmingham wedding party were taken to hospital after 'collapsing like flies and being sick all over the place'. The reception had been at *The Drake's Drum* pub, with many of the guests praising the chicken meal provided. They returned to the bride's mother's house in the village of Kingstanding, where they started to collapse. Both victims and venue received visits from officials of the Medical Officers' Department, in a bid to find out how the business began. A curious detail comes to light: the first girl to collapse turned out to have appendicitis. Then the bride's grandmother, who was thought to have succumbed to the excitements and the heat in the house. Then the rest. *Birmingham Evening Mail* 18 July 1972.

● The Moore family, including four children, were all taken semi-conscious to Walsall General hospital in the West Midlands, where a doctor declared the 'illness' to be caused by a lack of oxygen or carbon monoxide poisoning. Gas Board officials duly investigated, and found nothing wrong in the Moore house. Later there was a repeat performance – Keith Moore dropped to the kitchen floor. Then daughter Siobhan had convulsions and frothed at the mouth. Mrs Moore managed to stagger to neighbours to call for help. *Sunday Mercury* 16 December 1973.

MASS COLLAPSE AT BAND SHOW

Over 200 children plus some adults collapsed on 13 July 1980 during junior brass band parades at the Hollinwell Show in fields near Kirbky in Ashfield, Nottinghamshire. They were ferried to four area hospitals, with symptoms of fainting, running eyes, sore throats, dizziness and vomiting. No physical cause could be found.

● A 'mystery bug' shut down one of Britain's top private girls' schools for a fortnight. Fifteen girls were laid low by a 'feverish illness', and the medical officer of Wentworth Milton Mount School, Hampshire, decided to take no chances until the 'bug' was identified. Dr Barry Windsor said that until the results of tests were known, he could not definitely say if it was the same illness that had caused a boy's death at Lancing College, Sussex. *Daily Express* 3 October 1973.

Astonishing Recoveries

You'd think somebody with a spear through his head would have had it, wouldn't you?

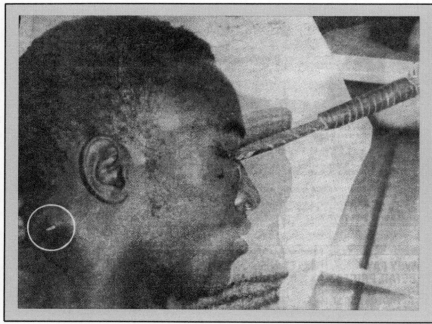

SPEAR THROUGH THE HEAD
This Lupane tribesman of Rhodesia came home to find his wife with a lover. He chased the man into a dark hut and ran right on to the lover's spear. With the spear stuck in his head, he walked 8km to the clinic at St Paul's Mission, wading across the waist-deep Shansani River. After a doctor cut off the main shaft, the man was sent to Mpilo Hospital in Bulawayo, where bolt cutters were used to remove most of the protruding iron spearhead. The rest, including the barbed head, was drawn through the wound. He was released after 35 days in hospital, suffering from 'slight headaches'.

A NAIL ON THE HEAD

Kenneth Blount, 17, was working with other carpenters on the frame of a house in Baton Rouge, Louisiana, on 18 July 1979, when a colleague above him yelled, losing his footing and dropping a pneumatic hammer. It landed on Blount's head; the impact triggered the hammer which punched a nail deep into his head, midway between the crown and right ear.

Blount said later: 'I heard the hiss of air, but . . . I just thought I'd been hit by the hammer. I reached up expecting to feel a bump on my head, but instead . . . I felt the head of the nail. "Oh, God, no," I thought. "That thing is right inside my skull!" Strangely enough there wasn't much pain. I tried to pull the nail out, but it wouldn't come. It was in there pretty tight.'

Blount's workmates panicked when they realized what had happened. 'I had to keep them calm for my own sake,' he said. The nail was eventually removed at Our Lady of the Lake Medical Center, in the city, by neuro-surgeon James Poche, who was astounded by Blount's 'dumb luck'. There was little tissue damage and Blount recovered well after the two-hour operation. He vowed to wear a safety helmet in future. *Sunday Express* 18 November; *National Enquirer* 20 November; *Weekly News* 1 December 1979.

A powered nail-gun also nearly did for Linda Archipolo, of Massapequa, New York. The 18-year-old waitress was working in the local Burger King when a spot on the wall behind some diners exploded with a shower of concrete chips. Linda's boss stormed next door where he discovered some cretin putting up a poster with the gun. After complaining, he returned and asked Linda to clear up the mess. As she bent over the table a second nail ripped through the wall and was driven into her skull.

Linda was rushed to the Nassau County Medical Center with the nail protruding from her head. There was a 'hell of a lot of damage' said neuro-surgeon Robert Degler. She was in a deep coma and not expected to recover – but now, against 'staggering odds' she is making an 'amazing' recovery, moving her eyes, attempting to speak, etc. There is some hope that she will walk and talk again, eventually. *Globe* 14 September 1982.

BRAIN ON A STICK

Carpenter Michael Melnick, 29, of Reseda, California, fell 10 feet through the floor of a house under construction in Malibu, in February 1981. After hitting the ground he tried to lift up his head but couldn't – there was six inches of rough-surfaced steel rod protruding from between his eyes, the other end buried in the concrete floor. The five-eighths-of-an-inch-thick rod, used for reinforcing concrete, had gone through his head from the base of his neck. He remembers lying there trying to figure it out. 'When I finally realized what had happened to me, my heart just dropped. I was sure I was going to die.'

Melnick went into shock when lifeguards from nearby Zuma Beach sawed through the rod at ground level. Melnick says he will never forget the sound echoing

ARROW IN THE CHEST
Muchaki Ayati had a quarrel with his friend, who fired an arrow at him. Unable to dislodge it, Muchaki journeyed for three days, walking over 35 miles and camping in the jungle, before reaching the hospital in Jadgalpur.

and vibrating inside his head. Neuro-surgeon Paul Ironside removed the iron from inside Melnick's skull, rebuilt his shattered nose and repaired tear ducts, nerves, muscles and what tissue damage he could. Doctors, certain there would be permanent brain damage, were baffled to find this not the case. After seven months Melnick's most serious after-effects are psychological: nightmares, insomnia, fear of falling. There have been some unspecified 'physical complications'. AP/Lincoln (Nebraska) *Star* 25 September; *Daily Telegraph* 26 September 1981.

Nowt so Queer

What some people get up to just doesn't bear thinking about . . .

IDENTITY CRISIS

When Elizabeth Howell Boykins, 25, returned to her apartment in Charleston, South Carolina, from a weekend trip, she found another woman living there. The intruder was wearing her clothes. She greeted Ms Boykins, took her luggage and shut the door in her face.

'The woman took all of my paintings off the walls, bought a new lamp and a shower curtain and rug for the bathroom.'

The intruder insisted it was her apartment but gave herself away when she misidentified the owner of the building and said that John Wayne was taking her to dinner. Augusta *Herald* 18 July 1990.

GREAT MEN OF OUR TIME

Jose Luis Astoreka, 34, won the first 'nutcracking with the bottom championships' at the annual fiesta in the Basque village of Kortezubi in July 1990. He crushed 30 walnuts laid out on the ground in two rows between his buttocks in 57 seconds. His brother was second with a time of 80 seconds. The brothers' winning times were attributed to 'a peculiar physical characteristic which runs in the Astoreka family'. *Independent* 24 July 1990.

PLUG IN, TURN ON, DROP DEAD

The *Daily Telegraph* of 18 August 1989 features the story of a pensioner who regularly plugged himself into his electrical supply 'because it turned him on'.

Arthur Sharland, a 77-year-old retired heating engineer from Shepherds Bush, was found slumped dead in an armchair with two crocodile clips attaching bare electric wires to his chest. A post mortem confirmed he had been electrocuted.

At a subsequent inquest, the coroner said Sharland's torso had been covered in a mass of tiny scars, suggesting he had indulged in the practice for much of his life and 'that he enjoyed doing it'.

THAT'S NO WOMAN, THAT'S MY HUSBAND

Rosalinda de Hernandez of Honduras was in shock when doctors told her that her husband was female and six months pregnant. Hernandez said that although their love life was odd, she never thought her husband of nine years was a woman. St Louis *Post-Dispatch* 27 August 1987.

IN NEED OF ATTENTION

A 38-year-old woman thought she had run out of petrol on the Santa Ana Freeway in Los Angeles, so she stood on the bonnet of her beige Plymouth station wagon, pulled her dress over her hips, threw money in the air and whacked oncoming cars with a chrome chain with her keys fastened to the end. Commuters ran in circles chasing the money, neglecting to notice that the notes were torn in half. 'That's just small change!' the woman shouted.

The fact that she hadn't any underwear on helped make a mile-long traffic jam between the Valley View and Carmenita exits in Santa Fe Springs about 11:00am. Someone used their car phone and the police arrived. They found plenty of petrol in the tank when they started her car. Then she said she was a prostitute and needed attention. She was taken to hospital in Norwalk for psychiatric evaluation. Houston (Texas) *Chronicle* 12 April 1989.

JEUX SANS FRONTIERES

● In Tasmania, widow Stella Serth was fined £200 for dancing on her husband's grave singing, 'Who's Sorry Now?' *News of the World* 16 October 1988.

MISS PERSONALITY 1990

In November 1990, a courthouse in Oshkosh, Wisconsin, was the setting for a most bizarre rape trial. The victim – a 27-year-old former waitress identified only as Sarah – was reported to have 18 separate personalities, a number which increased to 46 after the rape. At least one personality seems to have consented to sex, while her dominant personality claims the man took advantage of her mental illness.

The defendant, a 29-year-old married supermarket worker, first met the woman in a park on 9 June, while she was fishing with friends and manifesting a personality called Franny, a maternal figure aged 30. Two days later she went to a restaurant with the defendant, and over coffee introduced him to a number of other personae, including Jennifer, a 'fun-loving 20-year-old'. Afterwards, Jennifer agreed to his suggestion that they have sex in her (some sources say 'his') car, during which the woman became six-year-old Emily, before returning once more to Franny. Franny was horrified to discover the situation and phoned the police as soon as she returned home, claiming she had been raped.

During the pre-trial hearing there were astonishing scenes as the woman changed personalities at the request of District Attorney Joseph Paulus. Judge Robert Hawley said he could not assume knowledge was transferred between personalities; he made each one take the oath as they made their debut before the lawyers introduced themselves anew. Jennifer said that after they had had sex, the defendant specifically asked: 'Can I have Franny back?' Mr Paulus alleged that the defendant knew the woman was mentally ill when he had sex with her. Neighbours had warned him of her illness.

At the pre-trial hearing the defendant pleaded not guilty to second-degree sexual assault on the two personalities, and was released on bail. A Wisconsin criminal law, forbidding sex with the mentally ill, carries a ten-year prison penalty. Official recognition of Multiple Personality Disorder is only a few years old; it was previously thought to be a rare special-condition schizophrenia. Dr Nancy Perry, a clinical psychologist, told the hearing that MPD is frequently caused by early childhood trauma – usually sexual abuse – and is believed to affect one in 10,000.

As the woman prepared to testify, Miss Lori Warchol, her psychiatrist, said 'I know she is not faking,' and listed some of the personalities. Besides Franny, Jennifer and Emily, they included: Sam, who expressed himself only through noises and crouching; John, an angry young man; Ginger, who liked alcohol; Evan, a smoker; Eleanor, eloquent and prim; Leona, who had the role of making internal imagery; Frank, an avid reader; Beth, a personality who emerged after the incident; Kim, who was more 'up-beat' than Beth; and Brian, a muscle-man and protector.

According to Mr Inam Haque, another psychiatrist, Sarah's problems began when she saw her father crushed by a car. Sarah testified she was adopted and remembered little of her early life. 'I know there was abuse,' she said. 'I know it was physical from my father and mental from my mother.' As a child she heard voices in her head, she said.

Four (or six) of Sarah's 'selves' were sworn in separately before giving evidence. She – or they – spent three hours in the witness box. She constantly switched from one personality to another.

Franny said she had told the defendant about the other personalities when he specifically asked for the 'fun-loving' one. 'He asked if he could make love to me,' testified Jennifer in a high-pitched voice. 'I thought that meant that you cared about someone – I thought we were going dancing.' Franny was not conscious of anything more until she returned when the defendant recalled her after he had sex with Jennifer. Other personalities 'witnessed' the incident – including Jamie, Alice (a simple crayon-eating girl), and two males, Sam and John.

The jury decided that the defendant had deliberately taken advantage of the woman's mental disorder. He said he was going to appeal. His defence? 'She was pretty; she excited me; and she was willing.' *Daily Telegraph* 11, 18 August + 8, 10 November; Victoria *Colonist* + New York *Post* + Portsmouth *News* + Middlesbrough *Evening Gazette* 17 August; New Jersey *Record* 8 November; *Independent* 9 November; *Sun* 10 November 1990.

Weird Science

Science is rational, safe, boring – right? Wrong.

SCRABBLED GENES

The 25 September 1986 edition of *Nature* contained an intriguing letter, signed by seven members of the Department of Medical Genetics, at Churchill Hospital, Oxford, who requested help in identifying the mystery object pictured.

'The very tiny object shown, much like a fragmented crossword in appearance, was recently found in one of our routine chromosome preparations for prenatal diagnosis following amniocentesis. But what is it?

'Is it a man-made device? Packing text as binary coded information on the miniature scale (the scale bar is 10 μm) would seem advantageous. Or is it a naturally occurring substance? None of the possibilities we have been able to think of would seem to be appropriate for amniotic fluid ... We are as intrigued as we are ignorant.'

HOT PLANTS

You've heard of hot potatoes, but they aren't naturally hot. However, in the early spring skunk cabbages are and so are some philodendrons during their flowering periods. Some philodendrons burn fat to generate their heat, just like animals, allowing them to reach temperatures of 124°F. In terms of their rates of metabolism, they rival those of the humming birds. Furthermore, philodendrons can regulate their chemical fires, whereas skunk cabbages, which burn only starch, consume all their stored energy like a rocket in one snow-melting crescendo. Why do plants generate heat? Apparently to attract pollinating insects. Blakeslee, Sandra; *New York Times* 9 August 1983, p. C4. *'Are plants really "lower" forms of life?'*

VOLCANIC ACID LAKE

Soviet scientists have begun exploring a volcanic lake which is filled with a mixture of sulphuric, hydrofluoric and hydrochloric acids and not water. This is believed to be the strangest and most dangerous lake on the Kamchatka peninsula and it lies in the crater of the Maly Semyachik volcano. Its stony shores are 200 metres high and the lake can only be reached with the help of a rope.

There is absolutely no vegetation around the crater because of the suffocating gases escaping from it. The scientists have to work in gas masks. They sail on the acid-filled lake in rubber boats which, however, soon become unfit for use. Novosti Information Service Bulletin 14225, 29 August 1973.

THE OKLO PHENOMENON AND EVOLUTION

A decade ago, French scientists discovered the remains of a natural nuclear reactor at Oklo, Gabon, in Africa. Somehow nature had concentrated enough uranium-235 in one place to start a chain reaction, with the attendant production of heat and radiation. Now U-235 is radioactive, and there is now much less around than in past geological eras. This has led some scientists to speculate that many more Oklo phenomena may have flamed momentarily in earlier times, especially Precambrian days. The mutagenic radiation from such natural reactors could have been a major driving force in evolution. *'Natural Reactors Helped Evolution'*, *New Scientist*, 100:737, 1983.

SCORCHED EARTH

The Dorset town of Clavell's Hard, near Kimmeridge, was the scene of some strange effects – smoke rising from cracks in the cliffs, the ground hot to the touch, and evil-smelling gases killing off the grass. Deep down, the ground was actually on fire.

The phenomenon was discovered by Douglas Cole, a young geology research student from Southampton who suggested an explanation. He said: 'There is a three-foot-six-inch layer of oil shale underneath the rock which caught fire. This is an extremely rare occurrence – the last case noted in geological records was in 1826. Immediately under the loose stone the ground is red hot. If you thrust a stick into it, it would burn. I measured temperatures of just over 500°C.' *Daily Mail* 13 December 1973.

WHY DID THE PEAT BOG CROSS THE ROAD?

A 600-yard stretch of the coast road between Ballycastle and the village of Belderg (140 miles west of Dublin) in Ireland's County Mayo was buried between 11:30 and 1:30 one night, by a peat bog, which was moving towards the sea, taking with it a small forest of three-foot pine saplings. The bog was three or four feet deep, right across the road, which was 18 feet wide.

It was discovered by a home-bound motorist, who had to make a detour of ten miles. Mayo had had a wet summer and autumn even by its own soggy standards, and it was thought that this caused the bog to swell up and overflow. Farmer Tom Moran said: 'This is ridiculous. It has been moving down the road for the last two days.' A county engineer farmer said: 'It's moving faster than a man can walk.' Middlesbrough *Evening Gazette* 6 December; *Independent* & [UPI] of 8 December 1986.

Antiquities

*Hidden cities, ancient civilizations, buried treasure . . .
such is the stuff of mystery.*

ARCHAEOLOGICAL FINDS IN CHINA

In south-west China, archaeologists found two white-glazed bowls in a Song dynasty tomb (960–1279 AD). When filled with water, the bowls turn black. When dried, their colour returns to white. No explanations have been offered. *Le Soir* 18 August 1985.

● A 'women-only' script has been discovered in Hunan province, still in use by a few old peasants. The script uses an inverted system of grammar, different syntax from normal Chinese, and has no punctuation. It has been suggested that the script may date back to the Shang dynasty (1600–1100 BC), but locals attribute the script to Hu Xiuying, a concubine of Emperor Qinzhong of the Song dynasty (960–1279 AD). Her writings were brought back to her home town, Jiangyong, where the script came to light in 1982. It was apparently used to record historical events, personal recollections and letters between women, but most of the writings are lost. It was the belief in an after-life which led women to have their favourite books cremated with them so that they would be able to read them again in the next world. *Sunday Express* 18 May; *Guardian* 19 May 1986.

● A tomb in southern Hunan province, dating from 1305 AD, contained the bodies of a man and woman, silk and linen clothes, gold, silver and bronze ware . . . and a dressing box containing two identical printed advertisements for an art materials shop in Changsha. The adverts say: 'A variety of paints and paintbrushes are available. Come try our goods. You can find our store by the eye-catching sign with red characters hanging above the door.' Plattsburgh *Press-Republican* 8 March 1986.

● Lastly, a concrete floor has been unearthed in Dadiwan, Qinan county, Gansu province. It contains cement and similar ingredients to the modern variety, including silicon and aluminium. When the floor is struck with an iron object, it gives out a clear and hollow ring like modern concrete. Radio-carbon dating of the green-black concrete gives an age of 5000 years . . . long before concrete was in use elsewhere. Cleveland *Plain Dealer* 26 January 1986.

LEGENDS OF LOST GOLD

The Lost Dutchman Mine has been hunted by dreamers and fanatics for nearly 100 years in the canyons of Superstition Mountain, Arizona. It was apparently originally located on sacred Apache ground by a Mexican cattle-baron called Miguel Perelta. He sent a force of 400 miners and guards – all massacred by the Apaches for desecration of the land where their Thunder God dwelt. About 30 years later the 'Dutchman', Jake Walz, staggered into Apache Junction, 35 miles east of Phoenix, with a sackful of gold and a tale of a gold-vein 18 inches wide. It's said that an Indian girl had her tongue cut out for leading him there. The Dutchman himself shot several men who tried to follow him into the mountains. He died in 1891, taking his secret about the mine's location with him. Today Apache Junction still plays a humouring host to the steady trickle of gold hunters. But the old-timers suggest there is something 'weird up in the hills' and are content to let the Thunder God keep his well-guarded secret. *Sunday People* 8 August 1976.

Apache gold also figures in another story. The gold, stolen from Mexican and American wagon trains by Geronimo and his fellow chief Victorio, was allegedly buried on a mountain in the San Andres range, in southern New Mexico, now called Victorio Peak. The known details date back 270 years when a French

Jesuit, Father Philippe La Rue, reputedly found a mine full of fabulous riches. The then government in Mexico City sent an army – but La Rue had reburied the mine. He died under torture and never revealed its location. The Lost Padre Mine, as it's sometimes known, was next found in 1937 by an itinerant doctor, Milton E. 'Doc' Noss, who said he stumbled into a narrow shaft to find a room stacked with thousands of gold bars guarded by 27 human skeletons. He dynamited the shaft to widen it – but overdid it and the whole lot caved in. In 1945 the area was closed to the public as the White Sands missile range (where the first atom bomb was about to be exploded) was only 50 miles away. Although he never gave up on his search, his earlier discovery was to be his downfall: in 1949 Doc Noss died; shot by an irate backer after spending a small fortune helping Noss's unsuccessful attempts to relocate the mine.

The *Daily Mail* of 22 June 1976 said the US Army of White Sands, fed up at being continually nagged by treasure-hunters, finally agreed to let a group known as Explorations Unlimited, into the restricted area in July. EU, who specialize in 'electronic searches' and who had been hired by a group of six 'old-timers' all claiming the fortune, estimated in various reports as worth between £500 million and $250 billion, had to postpone their expedition.

On 19 March 1977 the Army again granted permission for a ten-day search. All they found, up to the time of a note in the *Daily Telegraph* 21 March 1977, was a few bloody hand-prints left by Indians. Other sources: Jacksonville, Florida, *Times-Union* 29 January, 19 March 1977.

A DIPROTODON'S PORTRAIT?

Percy Trezise, an acknowledged expert on aboriginal cave art, has claimed to have found a well-preserved image of a diprotodon, a hippo-sized marsupial from the Little Ice Age. He thinks the painted carving is about 10,000 years old, which would make it the oldest example of an indigenous people's art outside Europe, he said. Australian academics, who are said to regard Trezise as a 'maverick', are sceptical of the age of the drawing, and that it depicts a diprotodon; but they acknowledge that it would be a stunning find if he is right. 'It would be [like] watching fossils come to life in front of me,' said a leading paleontologist, who did not want to be named before he could see the painting and judge its authenticity.

Trezise had already left Brisbane to return to the remote northern Queensland site when the story broke. He had said he found the painting six weeks previously on the ceiling of a gallery in the Quinkin Reserve, outside the north-eastern seaboard city of Cairns. The naturalistic silhouette of the animal was clearly defined, and unlike anything found before. It appears to have been repainted at least twice in remote times, he said. The diprotodon was unique to Australia, and is reckoned to have flourished for millions of years before the arrival of the first men around 40,000 years ago. It was thought to have become extinct anywhere between 35,000 and 6000 years ago, making it one of the few prehistoric animals to have co-existed with man for any length of time. Whether or not the image discovered by Percy Trezise was as ancient and authentic as he claimed is still open to debate. Whatever the outcome, the diprotodon's portrait certainly caused a stir. *Daily Telegraph* + St Paul *Press & Dispatch* 11 September 1986, citing the Brisbane *Sun*.

Vampires

Bloodsuckers have an image problem. Once you've developed a taste for it, blood can be very nutritious, even invigorating . . .

BLOOD SISTERS

A blood-sucker, named simply as 'Lilith' (a suggestive name in itself, for in Hebrew myth Lilith was the progenitor of the sexually-vampiric incubae and succubae), told of her encounter with a young man in a cemetery. He tried to kiss her, but she buried her teeth in his neck and held him down with an 'unnatural surge of strength' until she had tasted blood. That was the first of many attacks, though she never thought of herself as vampire in the traditional sense, merely 'a very evil person who liked the taste of blood. I just liked being evil.' However, when one of the coven that she had joined suggested using her own father as a blood sacrifice, she decided to call a halt.

The second vampire, Carl Johnson of Rhode Island, developed a 'thirst for blood' one night. He crept into the bedroom of his sleeping sister, delicately pricked her leg and sucked her blood. He later started a Satanic coven and claimed that when he sucked his victim's blood he could feel himself getting physically stronger. Both vampires are alleged to have been cured, though how this cure was carried out we are not told. *Sunday People* 9 June 1974.

DRACULA BURIED IN PECKHAM?

E very year, scores of people visit a churchyard in Whitby, Yorkshire, searching for the non-existent grave of the fictitious vampire – such is the hold of Dracula on the imagination. *Daily Express* 17 April 1978.

● But perhaps they are looking in the wrong place, for a very solid slab of granite turned up at Peckham, South London, bearing the words 'Count Dracula, 17.12.1847'. Workmen found it buried deep in the earth while carrying out renovations to a house in Peckham Hill Street; but a couple of days after the story appeared in the press a former resident, David Perrin, came forward to say that he had buried the stone as a joke, 13 years previously, when he was 15 years old. Mystery solved, but there are some other curious aspects about the house that have been recorded. Site agent James Davis remarked that he had been to the house at night to watch for vandals, and found the place extremely spooky; also that his Dobermann Pinscher, would not go into the garden. London *Evening News* 15 & 17 August 1978.

● Don Blyth runs a Weird Museum in Hollywood, and one of the main attractions is 'Dracula's corpse'. He claims the body of Vlad Tepes – Dracula's historical forerunner – disappeared near the end of World War II, and turned up some years later in a shop in Meza, Arizona. The proprietors wouldn't say how they got it, but Blyth paid $3045 for it, and has statements 'from various experts' as to its authenticity. Vlad Tepes, as far as we know, had a fairly normal physiognomy . . . but as you might expect Blyth's 'Dracula's corpse' has two large, hooked fangs protruding from the upper jaw. Blyth insists the teeth are genuine: a natural outgrowth from the bone, rather than a clever insertion job. And if that is the case, he has some very peculiar remains in his possession. But do two missing ribs really indicate that the body once had a stake thrust into its heart? *National Insider* 17 November 1974.

GERMAN DRACULAS

H ofmann of Nuremberg, Germany, admitted removing the bodies of at least 30 women from their freshly dug graves at 15 cemeteries in Germany to drink their blood. Hofmann was accused of shooting a sleeping couple in a car, in May 1972, and drinking the blood from their head-wounds; also of a number of mortuary break-ins, and the attempted murder of a mortuary attendant whom he shot when disturbed while looking for bodies. He told the police: 'I drank the blood of the women because I wanted to feel it in my body. I need a litre of women's blood every day. I've got used to it now.' Brought to trial in August 1974 he refused to answer questions put to him in deaf-and-dumb language, merely staring blankly ahead and occasionally pointing to the public gallery. He had, it seems, spent 19 of the previous 24 years in prisons and mental institutions. *Daily Mirror + Toronto Sun + Omaha World-Herald* (Nebraska) 6 August 1974.

● In Hamburg, neighbours lived in fear of 24-year-old Walter Locke: they heard eerie sounds at night and had to address him as Grand Master or Count Dracula; he ate raw meat, slept during the day and roamed the streets at night. Of course, burly 30-year-old electrician Helmut Max knew nothing of this when the tall young man dressed in black came up to him in the street and knocked him unconscious with a karate chop. Helmut woke up in a coffin lined with white silk, in a small candlelit room. Locke, who had a 'stabbing, hypnotic look' announced himself as Dracula, and that he lusted for human blood. He then hit Helmut in the face with great force, and collected the blood that flowed in a white enamel bowl. Then he drank it. With seemingly unnatural strength, Locke lifted his victim out of the coffin, and the latter fell at his feet, begging for mercy and swearing to be his slave for life. When Helmut had kissed his feet, Locke accepted his submission,

and together they ran through the deserted streets to a cemetery half a mile away. There, while Locke performed 'obscene rites', his victim escaped and ran to fetch the police. He led them back to the room where they found Locke asleep in his coffin. Doctors did not believe Locke was mad. He was charged with kidnapping and causing grievous bodily harm. *News of the World* 27 October 1974.

BLOOD SUPPERS

Farm labourer Alan Dyche, 20, of Abergele, Denbighshire, was somewhat less than discreet when he became interested in black magic. He told people he was a vampire, and took friends along when he was making blood sacrifices to the devil. He killed six sheep, two lambs, four rabbits and a cat, and drank their blood. *Daily Mirror* 26 November 1971.

Hairy Children

Adult males grow hair on their face, and to a limited extent on their body. But children don't do this, do they?

'HOLY' HAIRY BOY

● In May 1990, pictures of Sher Ali, aged five, from Chittagong in Bangladesh, appeared worldwide. His father had given up his job as a hawker of kitchen utensils so that he could promote the hirsute boy with his four-inch beard as a saint at country fairs, where he earned around £20 a month for his family. People pay to touch him as they believe he has healing powers.

A local paediatrician said the boy probably suffered from a hormonal imbalance, treatable with oestrogen. This seems unlikely in view of Professor Pembrey's remarks (below). *Daily Star* 11 & 12 May; *Guardian* + *Sun* + *Edinburgh Evening News* + *Portsmouth News* 21 May 1990.

● In discussing hirsute children, Professor Marcus Pembrey stated: 'There is no cure. This is a condition, not a disease, which is no more or less than a chemical error related to the control of hair growth. It is not a throwback to ancient man, or to animals.' The first recorded example of the condition was that of Peter Gonzales, born in the Canary Isles in 1556. Such people were exploited in freak shows until the beginning of this century. *Sunday* 8 March 1987.

HIRSUTE FAMILY OF MEXICO

● Four hirsute children in Mexico featured in various news reports in 1985–87. The extreme hairiness of the children was said to be due to a rare hereditary genetic disorder, untreatable except by very expensive electrolysis. They were taunted as 'Los ninos lobos' – the wolf children. Their mother snipped back their hair every few days.

The four children, Gabriel Ramos Gomez, 10, his brother Victor, 8, their cousin Jesus Manuel Fajardo Aceves, 12, and his sister Marlene, 7, were great-grand-children of Maria Luis Diaz, whose daughters and one son were also hirsute. The children's mothers, Juanita Gomez and Maria Aceves, were normal, and both also had normal-looking children. According to the testimony of a local women called Consuelo Flores, only reported in the *Weekly World News* 10 September 1985, there were 15 hairy children and one hairy adult in Loreto, all descended from Maria Luis Diaz. Omaha *Sunday World-Herald* + *Sunday Journal-Star* 21 July 1985; *National Enquirer* 2 September; *Chat* 1 November; *Malay Sunday Mail* 21 December 1986.

MORE OF THE SAME

Twenty cases of hirsute children have been found in China, and more elsewhere. This is a brief catalogue of known cases:

1. Yu Zhenhuan; Liaoning. Described opposite.

2. An old woman of the same village as Yu Zhenhuan heard, when she was young, old folk saying that a woman not far from there had given birth to a similar black-haired infant. The mother's father-in-law killed it with a blow of a pick-handle.

3. Shandong Province, 40 years ago.

4. Li Pao-Shu: born in the late 1940s near Peking, with a handsome black-and-white mane. Treated as a freak and exhibited in a travelling show.

5. Qi Rong, born 1969, Shachou Country, Jiangsu Province. At ten years of age, he measured 1.25 metres tall.

6. Name unknown: boy, born 1968, Hsincheng County, Hebei.

7. Zhang Xing: born 1950, Hebei Province. He has a sound physique and is 1.76 metres tall. Fond of singing and playing the flute, and a model worker.

8. Jiangsu province: a hair-covered child born to a woman with the same condition. However, the mother shed much

of her hair after her marriage, and though still not smooth-skinned, her condition has improved 'dramatically'.

9. A family in Liaoning Province having hairy persons covering three generations.

10. Zhu Xiulian. Born 10 September 1977 in Guangdong Province. Active and intelligent. Covered in black hair. Her nose is wider, the ditch between nose and lip deeper, her lips are thicker and her ears are bigger than normal. Body and IQ normal. Parents Zhu Shaowen and Li Muqong are members of a people's commune.

11. Other *mao hai* cases reported from the following Chinese provinces: Shanxi, Qinghai, Henan, Sichuan, Anhui and Zhejiang, but no details.

12. Russia, 19th century. A father and son in a peasant family.

13. Burma. A family of hirsute individuals. Date unknown.

14. India. A case where the condition occurred in three successive generations. No further details.

Further examples may be found in Charles Darwin's *The Descent of Man and Selection in Relation to Sex* (1871).

Major sources on Yu Zhenhuan: *China Reconstructs* Vol 28, No 3. March 1979, pp 60–61; Ceylon *Weekend* 31 December 1979: reprinting an article from *Asiaweek + China Pictorial* 1979, No 5 (May 1979) pp 42–3. Minor references: *Rising Nepal & Guardian* 23 October; *News of the World* 29 October 1978; *Daily Star* 17 February; *Daily Telegraph* 24 February; *National Enquirer* 24 April 1979; Belgium *Het Volk* 25 October 1978. And for Zhu Xiulian: Hong Kong *Ta Kung Pao* Weekly (English) edition No 672. (10–12 May 1979) p 12.

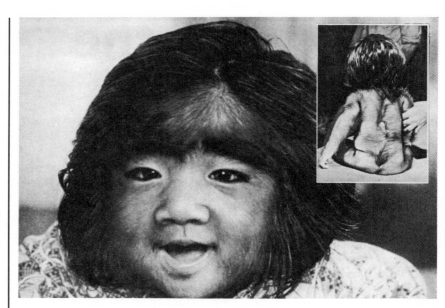

Yu Zhenhuan, the hairy child, at eight months and (inset) the child's hairy back.

THE HAIRY BOY OF CHINA

They called him Zhenhuan, meaning 'shock the universe', and the kid has indeed created something of a stir. Western journalists have handled his story in the usual degrading fashion, calling him 'monkey-boy', 'wolf-boy', freak, mutant . . . but to the Chinese he is simply *mao hai*, a hairy child.

Yu Zhenhuan was born on 30 September 1977 in north-east China. His parents, Yu Wenguang, 27, and Song Baoqin, 25, were horrified to find Zhenhuan covered in jet-black hair at birth: his eyebrows merged with the hair on his forehead, and his entire body except for his lips, palms, soles and the tip of his nose was hirsute . . . the kid even had hairy ears!

Zhenhuan's hair has now turned from black to brown, and varies in length: 7 cm around the shoulder, 4.5 cm on his back, 2.5 cm on his abdomen. Apart from that, he's very much a normal child; all his senses are in good working order,

X-rays and intelligence tests show nothing abnormal. He has a slightly enlarged heart, and at four to five months was taller than an average child. His head and ears are large, and he cut his teeth late, at about one year. He laughs much, cries little and, apart from a little trouble with a boil and eczema, is perfectly healthy. The hair parts at the side of his body and thickens toward the mid-lines of the back and abdomen, forming whorls at various places.

The average Chinese is perhaps the least hairy individual on the planet, which makes the *mao hai* phenomenon all the more unusual. All human foetuses are covered with fine down after five to six months' development, but this hair is usually shed before birth. The cause of the 'mao hai' atavism apparently remains mysterious, but it has been determined that the trait is inheritable. And the hirsute individual keeps his pelt throughout his lifetime . . .

In the Post

Delays will happen . . .

LONG-DISTANCE INFORMATION

Sarah Julian, 12, released a balloon from Heanor in Derbyshire in the summer of 1987. The following May it was discovered in Illinois. *Guinness Book of Records* officials believe it could have travelled via Russia – 20,000 miles – setting a new record.

Paul Vallance, 10, threw a bottle with a message into the sea at Totnes in Devon in 1986. In March 1989 he had a letter from a man who had found it on a beach in New South Wales. The bottle apparently floated 17,000 miles at 15 miles per day. Dr Steve Mascle of Exeter University found it hard to believe. 'I suppose the bottle could have been picked up by someone in a ship and thrown into the sea again,' he said. *Daily Mirror + Sun* 9 March; Daily Mail 13 March 1989.

● An even faster bottle was picked up on the beach at Weymouth in Dorset, although the journey was shorter. The plastic bottle with a self-addressed envelope and a dollar bill had been thrown into the sea off New York 30 days earlier – a speed of 100 miles a day. *Daily Express* 14 January 1988.

POST BAGS DUMPED IN ATTICS

● A duffel bag containing 235 letters written on the single-sheet, fold-into-an-envelope stationery provided free to American servicemen in the war was dumped in a North Carolina attic by a scared soldier who forgot to mail them. They had been written in May 1944 aboard the *U.S.S. Caleb Strong.* While at work in the attic, a pest exterminator discovered the letters in June 1986, and the Veterans Administration set about delivering the mail – 42 years late. By the end of July, 16 of the letters had been delivered. *Columbus Dispatch* 31 July; *Houston Chronicle* 26 August 1986.

● A post bag containing 600 letters and cards posted in June 1971, all for the Saltdean area of Brighton, was taken home by a postman and dumped in the attic of his council house, where it was discovered almost nine years later by workmen repairing the roof. The postman was suspended. *Evening News* 10 April; *Daily Telegraph* 11 April 1980.

● Another attic yielded 100 letters, posted 27 years earlier. *Daily Telegraph* 14 June 1988

CHRISTMAS CARDS

● Of course, it doesn't need a strike to slow down the mail. A Christmas card posted 12 miles away finally arrived at Little Bromley, Essex, on 22 March – 102 days late. *Daily Mirror* 23 March 1989. This, however, is high speed compared with the Christmas card to Bert and Alberta Stocker of Blaina, Gwent, which took 30 years to travel ten yards. Bert and Alberta had been dead 10 years by the time it arrived. *News of the World* 20 December 1987.

● Perhaps the slowest Christmas card in world history arrived at the house of Elsa Johansson near Jonaker in Sweden, 82 years after it was posted on 23 December 1903. *Sun* 7 January 1985.

● Alan Bailey posted Christmas cards to his three children in Great Budworth, Cheshire, on 27 November 1974, from Warrington, 12 miles away. They took eight years to arrive. *Daily Mirror* 11 December 1982.

● The Gleeson family of Cambridge got a Christmas card from some old friends who lived in Gunpowder Road, Hampstead, Baltimore, U.S.A. The card arrived on 11 December 1979, and the postmark was also 11 December. 'By Jove,' chorused the Gleesons as one, 'that was a quick delivery.' They looked again. It was 11 December 1976. *Cambridge Evening News* 14 December 1979.

● Sometimes, although much more rarely, we hear of phenomenally *fast* mail. Frank Rust, 77, of Ilford in Essex, got a Christmas card posted in New Zealand 39 hours earlier – and it wasn't even marked airmail. *Sunday People* 5 October 1980.

POSTAL SHORTCUT

One morning in 1984 I posted 42 letters in the postbox at Terminal One, Heathrow. One of the letters was addressed to my friend Mr Hamish Macaulay who lives in Montreal. As I turned away from the postbox I heard a voice say 'Excuse me, Sir, you've just dropped a letter ... and it's addressed to me.' I turned around to find Hamish holding this letter! He will confirm that this happened. W. J. Hopper Hampstead.

THE POSTCARD FROM POLPERRO

The stout, crinkly-edged card had been creased in two places, and a tiny piece of one corner was missing. It was a 'National Series' card of Polperro in Cornwall. The pencilled message read: 'Dear Glad, Bill and family. Having a nice time here, the weather is very good, hope you are well, will see you soon, all the best. Harry and Ada.' The red George VI penny postage stamp had been franked only once, and bore no date.

The card dropped through the letterbox of Gladys and Bill Smith, now in their mid seventies, in

Outram Road, Southsea, Portsmouth, on 7 January 1989. Harry and Ada were their neighbours when they lived in Leyton, East London, between 1940 and 1956, but had been dead for many years. Gladys thought the card could have been sent just after the war, in 1945, when she believes her neighbours started taking holidays; but a post office spokesman said the last date a penny

stamp could have been used for a postcard was 1 May 1940, when the rate went up. It therefore appears that the card took almost 50 years to travel 71 miles. A cycle tyre appears to have been wheeled over the reverse side, and the address has been updated three times: to their Isle of Wight home, to Fratton, and to Outram Road. *The News* (Portsmouth) 10 January 1989.

Bill and Gladys with the postcard which took almost 50 years to arrive.

Bird Abductions

Giant birds carrying off children abound in legend. But sometimes, it seems, it really happens . . .

EAGLE KIDNAP

An Iranian family, on a holiday outing on 21 March 1990, was having a picnic near Isfahan, when an eagle suddenly swooped down and snatched a two-year-old child. It 'took hold of the kid's clothing in its talons and disappeared into the wilderness before the bewildered eyes of the parents,' according to the Islamic Republic News Agency report. The original story, omitting such details as the sex of the child, appeared in the Farsi language daily *Kayhan*. An intensive search failed to find either the child or the eagle's nest. Atlanta *Constitution* + *Sunday Express* + *Sunday Mirror* + *People* 8 April; Deluth *News-Tribune* 17 April 1990.

THE ILLINOIS BIG BIRD 1977

Late July 1977 saw a Big Bird flap in Illinois, U.S.A., that lasted into August. It burst upon the world about 8:30 pm on Monday evening, 25 July, when two giant birds swooped down on ten-year-old Marlin Lowe, playing in the yard of his home in Lawndale, Logan County, Illinois. One gripped the 65-lb boy by his shirt and carried him 25–30 feet about three feet in the air. When it

released the screaming, struggling boy, he ran indoors. His parents and two neighbours, working in the yard, all looked up at the screams and saw the birds clearly. They described them at first 'like overgrown vultures', dark and with white rings around their long necks, curled beaks and a wingspan of around eight feet. Mrs Ruth Lowe, the mother, thought they might have been condors, but when Logan County game warden, A. A. Mervar, showed her pictures of large birds, neither she nor the other witnesses could identify any with the pair they had seen.

The official responses were as dire as usual. Firstly, based on the description, they pronounced the birds to be 'immature turkey vultures'. Then, after advice from 'experts', State Conservation knowalls said 'there is no known bird on earth that could lift Marlon's weight.' (They sound pretty confident, don't they!) This statement, by people who weren't there, virtually accuses the witnesses of lying or misapprehension . . . it also brought in the nasty crank calls. A disillusioned Mrs Lowe said later: 'I know what I saw and I'm not exaggerating – all four of us stood and saw it. I tried to be a good citizen and report it, but I'll never do it again. It brings only heartache and misery.'

Mervar, in a longer interview, still claimed that the adults only *thought* they saw the boy in the air, when he must have been running with the bird on his back. Discrediting the witnesses is the only way officials can cling to their theories. Apparently unaware of exactly what he is saying, Mervar, sticking to his turkey vulture belief, added: 'We have turkey and king vultures here, but they are considerably smaller than the birds described by Mrs Lowe.'

And there the mystery lay, deadlocked by intractable witnesses and pig-headed experts, until the end of the week when Stan and Doris Thompson and some friends saw a giant bird – a six-foot body with a nine-to-ten-foot wingspan – flying over their farm at Lincoln, Illinois, heading for Bloomington. They swear it looked like a condor. The next day, another witness in Lincoln, Mrs Norma Knollenberg, said a giant bird had landed in their yard 'a week ago', which puts it just before the attempted snatch of Marlin Lowe. Mrs Knollenberg described it as 'the size of a turkey with a four-foot wingspan, long neck and small beak. It made a loud trumpeting sound.' The paper said it looked like an African crowned crane! It's quite possible that the witnesses really are describing different birds, lumped together as one kind by the media.

Dr William Beecher, Chicago Academy of Science, insists that it can't be a condor because they are a type of vulture and quite ill equipped for swooping and lifting. 'There has never been in the history of the world, living or extinct, a bird big enough to lift a person.' He thinks it might be an immature bald eagle and that someone might shoot it. He likens the rash of reports to UFO sightings and urges people not to take the threat of skyward abduction seriously. Meanwhile, young Marlin and his mother have to drug themselves to sleep without nightmares.

On Saturday, 30 July, a six-foot wingspanned bird is seen on a telephone pole at Downs at 2 am. That same morning 'Texas John' Huffer, an experienced fisherman and naturalist writer sees two birds while fishing at Lake Shelbyville, and manages to shoot some blurred film. He describes the larger of the two as about 260 lb with a 12-foot wingspan. Experts could not identify the bird from the film but it certainly wasn't a turkey vulture. Also that same afternoon a Waynesville resident saw an eight-foot wingspanned black bird hovering, at 2 pm. At 4 pm the next day, Sunday, 31 July, Mrs Albert Dunham saw a giant bird for 30 minutes and also managed to film it, outside her home in Bloomington.

On 7 August a garbled version of the story appeared in the *Sunday Express* in England. The boy was said to be 'Rodney Galton', playing in a field near Tuscola, and actually fought the bird, forcing it to release him as it clacked like a Hollywood pterodactyl.

PAST BIRD SNATCHES

'In the Valais (French Alps) in 1838, a little girl, five years old, called Marie Delex, was playing with one of her companions on a mossy slope of the mountain, when all at once an eagle swooped down upon her and carried her away ... Some peasants, hearing screams, hastened to the spot but sought in vain for the child, for they found nothing but one of her shoes on the edge of a precipice. The child was not carried to the eagle's nest, where only two eaglets were seen, surrounded by heaps of goat and sheep bones. It was not until two months later that a shepherd discovered the corpse of Marie Delex, frightfully mutilated, and lying upon a rock half a league from where she had been borne off.' *The Universe*, F. A. Pouchet.

Levitation

Gravity, scientists now tell us, isn't quite as straightforward as they thought. But levitation is, of course, quite impossible.

THE FLYING NUN

The *Sunday People* 15 May 1977 reported the story of invisible assailants, phantom persecutors and demonic doings surrounding the tormented nun, identified only as 'Sister Rosa'. In her presence objects in the room rise up and fly around her – at other times it is she herself who is levitated. This, it is claimed, happened at least once, witnessed by her terrified sisters, who saw her float slowly towards the ceiling and then *pass through it*! The Auxiliary Bishop of Rome said: 'It's amazing but true. The Sisters are highly educated and not the sort to imagine things. They told me about Sister Rosa floating through the ceiling. They found her standing on the floor above.'

Once, on hearing screams from Sister Rosa's cell, they rushed in to find her tearing at her cowl. When they removed it they found thorns from a cactus plant in their garden firmly embedded in her scalp. They resisted all attempts to remove them until they were washed with Holy water, we are told. An iron bar, from the back of the door detached itself and travelled through walls to materialize in Sister Rosa's cell, and began beating her while she slept.

THE AERIAL FAKIR

P. T. Plunkett, who had seen the feat twice before, was invited by a friend, Pat Dove, to attend a performance of levitation on the friend's plantation, and to bring his camera to make a record. Plunkett writes: 'The time was about 12:30 pm and the sun directly above us so that shadows played no part in the performance. The compound was about 80 feet square in the middle of which four poles had been stuck into the ground to support a skeleton roof of branches . . . Standing quietly by was Subbayah Pullavar, the performer, with long hair, a drooping moustache and a wild look in his eye. He salaamed to us and stood chatting for a while. He told us he came from Tinnivelly and had been practising this particular branch of yoga for nearly 20 years (as had past generations of his family). We asked permission to take photographs of the performance and he gave it willingly, thus dispelling any doubt as to whether the whole thing was merely a hypnotic illusion . . . With several gentlemen from a neighbouring village (and the coolies) we mustered about 150 witnesses.

'Everything was now ready. Subbayah Pullavar marked out a circle close around the tent, under which he was going to levitate, by pouring water onto the floor of the hot and dusty compound, and instructed that nobody with leather-soled shoes was to go inside it. When Subbayah's assistant told us it was time for the tent to be removed we took up our positions (on opposite sides) just outside the ring and photographed every position from every angle.' Plunkett even prodded the space around the aerial fakir and had to conclude that the man had 'no support whatsoever except for resting one hand lightly on top of the cloth-wrapped stick. (There seems to be something traditional about the cloth and hide-wrapped accessory.)

The fakir remained horizontal in the air for about four minutes. The tent was put back and the sides let down. 'Pat and I could see through the thin wall Subbayah still suspended in the air. After about a minute he appeared to sway and then very slowly began to descend *still in a horizontal position*. He took about five minutes to move from the top of the stick to the ground, a distance of three feet.'

Pullavar in levitation. He stayed aloft for four minutes.

Subsidences

Sometimes the earth gapes open, and the firm foundations we based ourselves on turn out not to be so firm after all . . .

RASH OF SUBSIDENCES

In the summer of 1977, there was a sudden outbreak of holes in the ground:

● Toledo, Ohio: 1976. A letter to *The Blade* (Toledo) 28 September 1976, from an anonymous woman, complains of a hole in her backyard which had been growing deeper for almost a year. A city inspector surmised the cause as being a spring, an underground branch of the Delaware Creek or an ancient home-made sewer, although the city charts apparently contain no evidence of anything. It was on private property, so it wasn't his problem.

● **Welwyn Garden City, Herts: 4 April 1977.** The London *Evening News* (same date) reports a hole big enough to swallow a car appearing in a road on a housing estate. The hole, 20 feet deep and said to be caused by underground streams, stretched nearly the whole width of the road.

● Birmingham: 2 May 1977. Thirty-year-old housewife Vivian Flynn was hanging out her washing when the ground gave way beneath her and she fell into a 12-foot-deep hole. She managed to cling to the edge until a neighbour pulled her clear, and she was taken to hospital with cuts, bruises and shock. The hole was caused by council engineers building a sewer tunnel under the garden. *Daily Mirror* 3 May 1977.

● **Munich, Germany: 1 July 1977. Rain water getting into a drilling for a subway was blamed for a subsidence in the road beneath a parked car. The car had to be winched out of the hole by firemen.** *Daily Telegraph* **2 July 1977.**

● **Pontardulais, West Glamorgan: 25 July 1977. A section of the M4 motorway began to subside 12 weeks after the road opened. Cause: underground working on a new coal seam. Effect: the subsidence was expected to spread over a 300-yard stretch in the following two months. One wonders if motorway planners check anything before they start work . . .** *Daily Telegraph* **26 July 1977.**

● **Dudley Zoo, West Midlands: 16 November 1977. A 20-foot-wide, 50-foot-deep hole appeared in the zoo. We suspect that the animals were tunnelling out, but there are no records of any escapes!** *Daily Telegraph* **17 November 1977.**

● **Tividale, West Midlands: 21 November 1977. John Stone was driving his van along the New Birmingham Road when the road began to give way beneath him. He managed to accelerate clear, and the hole grew to be 30 feet wide and 450 feet deep. Council officials believe it to be the airshaft of an old mine.** *Sun* **22 November 1977.**

● Grays, Essex: 24 July 1977. A large hole appeared in the back garden of Mr David Brightman's house in Lodge Lane. It started being six feet wide and 20 feet deep, but then grew in the following couple of days to, by some accounts, 12 feet wide and 30–40 feet deep, and a horizontal tunnel appeared at the bottom. The area is known as the Daneholes (i.e. deneholes) because of a series of tunnels and holes cut in the chalk, believed to be ancient mine-workings . . . and there have been earlier subsidences in the area. A council official said the subsidence had been caused by the washing away of a chalk underlayer by heavy rain. *Daily Mirror + Sun + Evening News* 25 July; *Daily Telegraph* 26 July 1977.

David Brightman, his wife Margaret and their two children keep at a safe distance from the cavernous hole in their back lawn, the worst incidence of subsidence in the Daneholes area.

Psychic Powers

Is 'mind over matter' possible? These stories certainly suggest that it is . . .

A REAL FRIEND

A letter from Jo Atkins of New York, discussed in George Gamester's column in the *Toronto Star* (16 June 1989), recollects a peculiar incident involving her youngest daughter, Elizabeth, who, as many children do, had an imaginary playmate. Elizabeth would hold a tea party every afternoon, conducting polite, one-sided conversation with her unseen 'Betty Louty'. The family knew no-one of that name and wondered what prompted the girl to invent it; Elizabeth herself could only offer the information that Betty Louty lived 'a long way away'.

Several years later, the family went on holiday to Jamaica, and during a visit to the famous straw market in Kingston, Elizabeth and her older sister each wanted one of the traditional handmade dolls. 'Our older girl chose one from the first stall in the market,' wrote Jo. 'But not Elizabeth. She moved from stall to stall, until she finally spotted one she *had* to have . . . in the farthest corner of the top row. "Take one from the bottom row," I said. "They're all the same." '

'But Elizabeth was insistent. And the woman running the stall assured us they were *not* all the same. "Each is signed by the person who made it," she said. "This one has been waiting here just for you, darlin',' she told Elizabeth. "This lady is not making dolls any more." "I *know* she's special," said Elizabeth. "I'll take good care of her." '

'She certainly did. She slept, ate and walked with that doll, never letting it out of her sight. Some time later, I remembered what the old lady in the market had said, so I looked for the maker's name. There, on the inside of the apron, was a signature: 'Betty Louty'.

PLANE CRASHES

P erhaps the most remarkable story of the last couple of years is that of Lee Fried, an 18-year-old student at Duke University, North Carolina. On 20 March 1977 he wrote some predictions on a card, put it in a wax-sealed envelope, and had it locked in the office of university president Terry Sandford. On the 28th, with live television coverage, the envelope was opened. Here's how Lee shaped up:

Boeing 747s crash, 583 dead. (On 27 March, 2 Boeings crashed at Tenerife. Our clippings say Lee was wrong by six deaths . . . but the *Guinness Book of Records* gives the figure of 582.) North Carolina University would lose the last basketball match of the season to Marquette, 68-58 (they lost 67-59). A television hostess would wear a lavender outfit with cream blouse and silver earrings (she did), and the Supreme Court would hear four cases on capital punishment (right again). *Daily Mail* 1 April; *Sunday Express* 3 April; *Weekly News* 16 April 1977.

THE NEW YORK CITY BLACKOUT

O ne Tuesday, a small man with white hair and twinkling eyes turned up at the offices of the Seattle *Post-Intelligencer*. He offered to predict Thursday's headline, an offer no newspaper editor could surely resist. He gave his name only as Rogé (pronounced Ro-jay), 52 years old, an ex-newsman come from Salinas, California, to attend a magicians' conference. He sealed his prediction in five envelopes. When Editor Stephen Green opened the envelopes on the Thursday morning, in Rogé's presence, he found written 'Massive Power Blackout hits New York City Area'. Incredibly, this was exactly the same as the headline which appeared on the front page of Thursday's newspaper. How Rogé knew this was anybody's guess. *Time* 25 July 1977.

Housewife Margaret Woellner was busy preparing dinner in the kitchen of her new home when she was alarmed by her ten-year-old son Joachim bursting in. He stood terrified in the doorway as he said: 'Mummy, get out of the kitchen quickly . . . Something terrible is going to happen.'

Mrs Woellner only had to look at Joachim's ashen face to realize he wasn't joking. She scooped up her three-year-old daughter Ulrike and dashed out of the house in Witzhelden, West Germany. Seconds later an explosion – caused by a faulty gas main connection – wrecked the three-bedroomed house.

After the event Mrs Woellner asked her son how he knew the accident was going to happen. Joachim replied: 'I honestly don't know. I just had this strange idea that something was about to happen. It was as if there was a voice saying "Go and fetch your mother and sister otherwise it will be too late."' His mother said later: 'It was a marvel. I still don't understand it.'

Professor Hans Bender, head of the para-psychology department at Freiburg University at South Baden, explained the case differently. He said: 'There are people who have a sixth sense. For years we here at the university have been investigating similar cases where people have known that something tragic was about to happen. Mostly such cases take the form of dreams and visions. In children, this so-called sixth sense is often pronounced.' *Sunday Express* 2 April 1972.

DREAMS

● Shop-girl Mary Redding, 24, of Stirchley, Birmingham, dreamed she was going to win the football pools. All popular dream interpretations agree that to dream of winning at gambling is a contrary dream indicating loss and lack of success. Not for Mary . . . five days later she picked up a cheque for £132,631 from Vernon's Pools. *Daily Mirror* 17 July 1975.

● Mrs Gwen Bridgland's dream predictions were investigated by psychologist Dr John Beloff. On 2 September 1970 she dreamed of seeing a man jump in front of a train with fatal results. In the dream she said to her husband, 'It's probably for the best anyway, Geoff, because the man was wanted for a sex murder.' On the 5th, she sent the dream to Beloff. On the 16th, a girl was sexually assaulted and murdered in Hertfordshire. On the 19th, the suspected killer died under a train.

Mrs Bridgland also claims to have dreamed of being on a train which stopped, and men unloaded vast amounts of paper money; a few days later came the Great Train Robbery. *Reveille* 4 October 1974.

MENTAL METAL-BENDERS

After cutlery-bending Yuri Geller's first British broadcast on 23 November 1973, children began to discover their own paranormal powers. Seemingly just by thinking hard, some children were able to bend knives, forks and spoons, twist door keys, nails and paperclips, snap metal bars, rotate objects enclosed in bell jars and advance the hands on a watch.

Electric People

When we say that someone has an 'electric effect' we mean it metaphorically. But perhaps we should mean it literally?

SHOCKING STORIES

● The new Triumph Dolomite car of a man in Stewarton, Lincolnshire, became so charged that, apart from heavy shocks, he saw sparks flying between key and lock. It had never happened to him before with other cars. *Sunday Post* 27 April 1975.

● Thousands of users of a multistorey car-park in St Helens, Lancashire, get electric shocks in their arms as they take tickets from the barrier machine. Despite £1000 worth of investigation, and statements from the manufacturer, council and Electricity Board officials that the machine is, as far as they can discover, technically safe and sound, the shocks continue. *Liverpool Daily Post* 23 September 1976.

● On 15 January 1977 a lady leading her young husky dog along a snow-covered pavement in Harlem, New York, stepped onto a section that was strangely wet and free of snow. Her dog howled, its hair stood on end and it collapsed and died. A vet said later that death was caused by cardiac arrest and respiratory failure indicating electrocution. Other dogs were known to have yelped and run from that section. The sidewalk was found to be warm, and a

test bulb glowed on contact. It was leaking between 20 and 40 volts; hardly enough to kill a dog, they said. To be safe, current was isolated from the cable in the vicinity. St Louis (Mo) *Post-Dispatch* 20 January; *Atlanta (Ga) Constitution* 21 January 1977.

ELECTRIC PEOPLE

Vyvyan Jones, 12, of Henbury, Bristol, has been shocking people, making lights flicker, watches stop and the television crackle, since he broke his arm! For two days afterwards his hair stood on end, he gave people huge jolts, and once had to be hauled quickly out of the bath because he was 'tingling'. Someone at Southmead Hospital, Bristol, where he was treated, said it was 'a natural phenomenon' but not unique, adding casually: 'We've even had cases of people being able to lift iron bars because they are so magnetic.' *Sunday People* 15 February 1976.

● Bizarre though these reports may be, the case of Mrs Grace Charlesworth is even less straightforward. After living in a detached house in Congleton, Cheshire, for a trouble-free 38 years, Mrs Charlesworth's trouble began in 1968. In the garden and the house

electric shocks torment her day and night: 'Sometimes they have swung me round bodily and in the night my head has started to shake as though I was using a pneumatic drill. One day sparks ran up the walls. Our lights flicker from time to time and nearly go out. The electric wiring has been tested and nothing could be found wrong.' She discounts the possibility that she is the main focus: 'The shocks occur only in this house and garden. I do not get them when away on holiday, staying with my sister, or even in the house next door.' Psychological explanations could be offered for this, but some apparently incidental information adds other dimensions to the story.

Mr Charlesworth remembers that about the time the trouble started, they and other local residents had petitioned the council over 'weird humming and whizzing noises' from a nearby factory. At first we connected the trouble with the factory (although) I heard the humming (but) never felt any shocks ... The noise lessened. Now we hear it only occasionally.' Chief health inspector, Ronald Whiston, said: 'When we received the petition from 46 residents, I traced the noise to a compressor on the first floor of the factory. The firm moved the motor to the ground floor and it could not then be heard. But we were told that Mrs Charlesworth's experiences continued. I could find nothing to go on. It was like looking for something that didn't exist. It is a complete mystery.' Cryptically, Mrs Charlesworth herself adds: 'Our phone has been hit by lightning five times in the last few years. Whether it is the house or me that attracts electricity I don't know.' *Sunday Express* 19 March 1967.

LIVE-WIRE GIRLS

Jacqueline Priestman, of Sale near Manchester, was 22 when it started. Since then she has gone through 30 vacuum cleaners, five irons and two washing machines. When she passes her television, it changes channels; when she plugs in the kettle, sparks fly from the socket; her electric cooker cuts out when she tries to use it. All these appliances work perfectly for her husband Paul, an electrical technician.

After fruitless checks on the items themselves, Mrs Priestman came to the conclusion that she was the problem. She delivered herself into the hands of Dr Michael Shallis of Oxford University, who told the *Sunday Express* 20 January 1985 that Jacqueline had more than ten times the usual amount of static electricity in her body.

'I know of only six similar cases in this country and this is probably the most extreme,' he said. 'I have been researching such cases for two years and have discovered that women seem to be the worst sufferers. It's not certain what causes this severe build-up of static. Such people seem to be able to transmit miniature bolts of

lightning that break down the insulation of some electrical appliances.'

FORCE FIELDS?

● Mrs Dilys Cant is emphatic – an unseen barrier resisted her car as she tried to park in a bay in a new multi-storey park in the centre of Durham. 'It was as if I had come up against a kerb . . . but there was nothing there. It was uncanny. She tried three times, revving her engine to force the car past, and failed. She returned later with her daughter-in-law and they watched another motorist having the same problem in that spot. Then, whatever it was resisting incursion into that space, left. Council officials tried and succeded in parking there – and Mrs Cant, demonstrating for a television film crew, was herself surprised when she backed straight into the space. She adds: 'But I know what happened before was real. It's the truth – even if it does make me look rather foolish.' *Sunday Express* 14 December; *Newcastle Journal* 8 December 1975.

SHOCK-PROOF ELECTRICIAN

Georgi Ivanov, an 80-year-old Bulgarian electrician with a natural immunity to electricity, has been found by Dr Georgi Tomasov. Ivanov never bothered to switch off the mains when doing domestic electrical repairs; it meant too much walking to and fro from the fuse box. He had never had a shock, only a tingling sensation. Household voltage of between 200 and 240 can be enough to kill an ordinary human. Dr Tomasov took Ivanov to a Sofia hospital where specialists ran a series of tests. They found he could take up to 380 volts without feeling any real shock.

The results were published in the *Bulgarian Medical Journal*. (Ivanov's body appears to be eight times as resistant to electricity as that of a normal person.) According to the International Electro-Technical Commission in Geneva, just 50 volts have the capacity to give dangerous shocks, and in cases of high humidity can be fatal. *Sunday Express* 20 May 1984.

Rat Kings

Rat Kings are groups of rats with their tails knotted together. Despite numerous instances on record, how rat kings are formed remains a complete mystery.

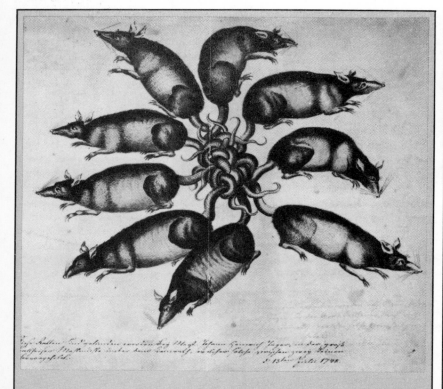

EARLY RAT KING

This engraving is of a rat king found at Johann Heinrich Jager's flour-grinding mill at Gross Ballheiser, Holland, on 13 July 1748. The rats were hidden under the cogwheels and fell out from between two stones. According to Martin Hart's definitive book *Rats* (London, 1982), 57 incidents of rat kings were recorded between 1564 and 1963, mostly in Germany, and all among black rats. Most kings consist of five to twelve animals, which are often of the same age—seemingly not yet adult. They are generally found alive, discovered because of their loud squeals, and in the sort of places where black rats make their nests (behind walls, in lofts, cellars, barns).

UNIQUE DISCOVERY

The rat king above was found in the winter of 1963 by a Dutch farmer in Rucphen, North Brabant, who heard loud squeals coming from a pile of bean sticks in a barn. Upon further investigation, he discovered a rat king consisting of seven adult black rats, five females and two males, all of similar age. The X-ray of the knot opposite showed some fractures, with signs of callus formations, and there were also fractures in some vertebrae. This suggests that the tails had been knotted together for some time, perhaps originally becoming entangled when the animals had crowded together in a nest, and that the rats had tried desperately to free themselves.

Mississauga Blob

OK, so its a trivial story. Nobody got hurt, and it was only a small thing anyway. But what was it? And where did it come from?

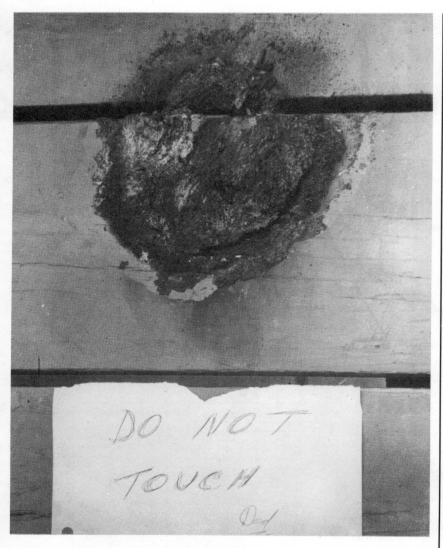

The mystery blob of the Matchetts.

MYSTERY BLOBS FROM THE SKY

In the late afternoon of 16 June 1979, a hot sunny Saturday in Mississauga, Ontario, real estate broker Traven Matchett, 49, was painting lines on his ping-pong table in the backyard of his Melton Drive home. His 19-year-old daughter Donna was skimming their swimming pool 40 feet away. Behind her stood a green picnic table which something suddenly struck with a thud. Thinking the family dog had merely thumped its tail against some cedar decking, she continued undistracted. Seconds later came a cracking sound. She turned.

The next sound was Donna's scream. A cylindrical column of flame was shooting up from a molten green mass upon the centre of the table. Thinking quickly Donna picked up a garden hose and doused the fire as her father ran up.

'It was a picture I'll never forget as long as I live,' says Matchett.

'The flame was like a blow torch, magnified, shooting up through the table,' Matchett later said. He described it as a very intense light, reddish-orange with yellow streaks, perfectly cylindrical, about 18 inches high by eight inches wide. 'A lot of people were puzzled when we said the top of the flame was flat,' he says. 'But it was. Whatever was burning was driving the flame up 18 inches—and stopped flat.'

The burning substance was three or four inches high when Donna turned the hose on it. 'The fire was out as fast as I hit it with the water,' she says. 'There was no smoke, just a little vapour.'

The extinguished mass shrank and solidified to a small, flat, dark-green mass with a fibrous, pock-marked texture, weighing about four ounces.

On the advice of one of his next-door neighbours, a pilot, Matchett phoned the control tower of the Toronto International Airport to learn if the flaming mass might have fallen from an airplane. It hadn't. 'They told me that if anything had fallen that hot out of a plane, the plane had to be on fire,' he says.

Matchett phoned *The Toronto Sun*, which immediately sent a reporter. 'Then I called N.A.S.A. and couldn't get through because it was Saturday.'

But when the story broke in the next day's *Sunday Sun*, bedlam struck. 'This place was like Grand Central Station,' says Matchett, 'and it was like that for a whole week. The story just zoomed across the country.'

An inspector from the Ontario Ministry of the Environment came and took a sample of the green blob for analysis. Their conclusion: it was merely polypropylene, a widely used chemical plastic in such items as plates, ashtrays and toys. The Matchetts had nothing plastic on the table. But polypropylene, the Ministry told them, is also used in frisbees. If the burning mass of plastic had fallen from the sky, possibly an incendiary set a frisbee on fire and

tossed it into Matchett's backyard. The Flaming Frisbee Theory, however, starts Matchett burning. The Ministry's inspector 'walked into my yard with a pencil', he says incredulously. 'He lifted the blob up with his pencil and said, "It looks like a frisbee." I politely invited him to leave. He wasn't interested in listening to what it had looked like, what had happened, the heat of it, he really had no interest at all.'

Matchett decided to conduct his own tests. He bought two $5 frisbees and set them on fire, the first with a blow torch. 'It took about four or five minutes to ignite it and then it just burned like an old, wet rag,' he says. 'It melted and simmered, but didn't explode into any kind of intense fire the way the blob did.' On the second frisbee he poured gasoline, stepped back, and tossed a lit match. 'We watched it burn for a while and there was a lot of smoke,' but when the blob burned, 'there was no smoke at all'. There was, he recalls, after the blob was extinguished, 'a strong acidic odour, a vinegary smell' which lingered about the yard till Monday morning. He says he was too excited, though, to pay much attention to it.

'The police came here and hammered questions left, right and centre,' says Matchett. 'I told them everything I could possibly tell them. In the end I said, "Look, if you want, my daughter and I will take a lie detector test if you think there's anything we're trying to hedge or cover up. We're telling you exactly as it was." ' As he told one reporter, 'I'm not going to ruin my picnic table for fun.' The Matchetts weren't asked to take a lie detector test.

MORE MYSTERY BLOBS

When the Mississauga blob story hit the news, Mrs Dorothy Smith of Sherobee Drive – about a mile from Matchett's residence – came to him with a curious story. About a month before, she said, she found a solid, circular blob of plastic-like material in her own backyard. But unlike Matchett's green blob, hers was black. Matchett then showed her where his blob had melted between two planks of the picnic table onto his concrete patio blocks. There she saw a hardened, shiny, jet-black residue identical, she told him, to her blob.

Chuck Le Ber of nearby Brampton told much the same story. He had found a dark-coloured blob of what appeared to be hardened plastic in his backyard the previous April.

Both blobs, however, met a fate hardly worthy of deadly invaders from space. They were thrown in the trash.

A third blob – a whopper – was given to Matchett by another Bramptonian, a well-to-do elderly gentleman. To describe it in a word: grotesque. Measuring roughly 18 inches long, ten inches wide and one inch thick, it weighs about eight pounds. Its design resembles a huge pancake which someone has squeezed out of a gigantic toothpaste tube, or an enormous brain that's been flattened by a steamroller. Its surface resembles that of china, smooth and shiny. Its colour is pale green, but when Matchett snapped off a couple of fragments, the blob's interior was found to be entirely white. Possibly it's just a mass of industrial caulking. Like its Mississauga cousins, the Big Brampton Blob was allegedly discovered in someone's backyard.

Alien Abductions

The idea that we may be taken off by alien beings seems one that is strongly rooted in our culture. Perhaps these stories that follow are examples of wish-fulfilment?

IN SCOTLAND

On Friday morning, 9 November 1979, Bob Taylor, a 60-year-old forestry foreman generally regarded as a 'sensible, straightforward man', was at work on Dechmont Hill, Livingston, West Lothian, near the M8 Glasgow–Edinburgh motorway, when he encountered a silver-coloured, domed spacecraft in a clearing. Suddenly, two objects shaped like sea-mines, each with six spikes, peeled off from the craft and approached him slowly. They grabbed him by the sides of his trousers and tore them, leaving scratch marks on his thighs. He fainted, but remembers the sensation of being dragged towards the craft. Trailmarks as of dragging feet were later found. He also recalls a foul chemical smell and his red setter barking furiously.

The creatures and craft were gone when he came round, but there were a dozen or so deep triangular marks in the ground, two parallel tracks and flattened grass. *Sunday Express + Scottish Sunday Express* 11 November 1979; *Sun* 12 November 1979; *Northern UFO News* 67; *Scotsman* 10 November 1979; *Glasgow Herald* 12 November 1979; Aberdeen *Press & Journal* 13 November 1979.

Bob Taylor with his drawing of the UFO and one of the 'creatures'.

RIDDLE OF THE VANISHING WOODSMAN

Most papers around 10–11 November 1975 carried the story that forestry worker Travis Walton and five workmates were driving back from trimming trees in the Sitgreave-Apache National Forest, near Snowflake, Arizona, when the crew-boss, Mike Rogers, braked the truck. Hovering 15 feet above the trees there was reported to be a flying saucer. Despite shouted warnings, Walton inexplicably jumped out and ran towards it. Suddenly there was a brilliant blue and white flash and Walton crumpled to the ground. The others panicked and drove off – when they returned for Walton, both he and the object were gone. This happened on the night of 5 November, and in the following five days a massive hunt scoured the countryside for any sign of him. On the fifth day, Travis Walton turned up, gaunt, hungry, 10 lb lighter and talking of capture by an alien race. *Daily Express* 15 November 1975.

The *Daily Express* item contains several interesting statements: the description of the zapping of Walton by Mike Rogers, who says the flash was greenish-blue and had affected their eyes when they later stopped quarter of a mile away to look back; the statement from Marlin Gillespie, the Navajo County Sheriff, who says Walton's workmates all made apparently true statements under his lie-detector. But most interesting of all is a lengthy interview with Walton himself, which is condensed here:

'We all saw the saucer that night. I knew what it was right away. When Duane [his brother] was a kid he was followed by a saucer and we promised each other that if it happened again I would not be afraid ... I just jumped out and ran towards the glow. I felt no fear. I got close and something hit me ... like an electric blow to my jaw ... I fell backwards and everything went black ... When I woke there was a strong light ... I had problems focussing and pains in my chest and head ... I was on a table ... I saw three weird figures ... not human ... they looked like well-developed foetuses, about five feet tall, in tan-brown robes, tight-fitting. Their skins were mushroom-white, with no clear features. They made no sound. They had no hair, their foreheads were domed and their eyes very large ... I panicked ... jumped up, knocking over a plastic tray ... I wanted to attack them but they scampered away ... a man appeared a few feet away ... human, in helmet and tight-fitting blue uniform ... he smiled at me and led me through a corridor into another big, bright room ... a planetarium. Outside it was dark but I recognized some galaxies ... the man in blue reappeared ... led me down a ramp, suddenly I was in bright sunlight ... some kind of hangar. I saw some small space saucers nearby. Then I saw three other people (in helmets). They were human, one a women, all dressed in blue ... They took me to a table and eased me on it. They put a mack on my face ... then things went black again ... When I woke up I was shaky ... on the highway. The trees were lit up because their saucer was just a few feet away. I saw nobody ... I ran until I came to a phone booth. I recognized I was in Heber (a few miles from Snowflake) ... I phoned my sister, and they came to get me.'

FIVE DAYS' BEARD IN 15 MINUTES

A Chilean army corporal on patrol duty vanished in front of his men, and reappeared in their midst 15 minutes later, disorientated and incoherent. The patrol noticed two bright lights descending on them in the sky and saw one drop behind some foothills, its glow remaining visible. The other came down within 500 yards of their camp, putting out a violet light with two points of intense red. Corporal Armando Valdes ordered his men to pick up their weapons, then advanced towards the light a little way, and disappeared.

Witnesses said they had called out for the corporal for several minutes, then suddenly, 15 minutes later at 4:30 pm, he was among them as mysteriously as he had disappeared. He gasped 'Muchachos' and fainted. His comrades noticed that he had about five days' growth of beard, and that the date on his calendar watch had advanced five days. The watch itself stopped about the time he reappeared. As he regained consciousness Valdes said: 'You do not know who we are, nor where we come from. But I tell you that we will soon return.' Valdes apparently, has no recollection of his abduction or utterances. *Age* (Australia) 19 May 1977; *AP* reports in 23 May 1977 newspapers; *Sunday Express* 29 May 1977.

Minds of Their Own

Sometimes 'inanimate' objects switch themselves on or off and generally behave as if they're conscious beings just like us.

DRIVERLESS CARS ETC

● The *Cornish & Devon Post* has quite an interest in runaway vehicles in its reminiscence columns. In the 12 October 1974 edition, it said that on 10 October 1914 a car in Holsworthy had started up on its own, driven into town and smashed into a lampstandard. In the edition for 27 November 1976, a curious coincidence occurs. They remember that on 21 November 1936 a car in Bude ran away with itself, crashing later. A separate, modern incident, involving a cake delivery lorry happened on 22 November 1976, also in Bude (one day over 40 years apart). It careened off a van and went through railings, coming to rest in gardens. It was braked and left in gear and police said they still could not account for it.

● **The end of 1976 and early 1977 saw a nice little run of runaways. A taxi, owned by a man in Grimethorpe, near Barnsley, Yorkshire, burst into life, gave its driver a run for his money, then burst into flames.** *Daily Mirror* **3 December 1976.**

● **A digger on the back of a transporter, negotiating a low railway bridge, began to chug forward, falling off the lorry and tipping nearly 1 cwt of rubble into the High Street at Staines. Slough** *Evening Mail* **7 January 1977.**

● **And an amusing story from Palfrey, near Walsall, Staffordshire: it seems that a car moving slowly down a street without a driver was stopped by a milkman who stepped in front of it, dug his heals in and shoved. His name ... Steve Austin! True!** *News of the World* **(letters) 13 March;** *Weekly News* **26 March 1977.**

A GHOST TRAIN RATTLES LONDON

At 6:34 on the morning of Friday, 29 March, a train pulled out of Caterham, Surrey. Nothing unusual about that, you might say, except that this train had no passengers and no driver. For nine miles it headed for central London on what would be in about half an hour one of the busiest commuter lines, at speeds of up to 40 m.p.h. Urgent calls to signal boxes halted or diverted oncoming trains, as the runaway hurtled through seven stations before it was directed into a buffered siding at Norwood Junction. Had the train not been halted in the nick of time, as it fortunately was, the consequences would have been unthinkable.

The train had been readied for its commuter duty, complete with a pre-run test – then the driver and the guard went for a quick cup of tea. None of the four main drive motors had been switched on – and nearly all of the nine miles is on a downward gradient (in fact it

was 1-in-90 just outside the station where the train was parked). But neither of these facts account for the train starting – somehow both the airbrake *and* the 'Dead Man's Handle' had been circumvented or otherwise rendered ineffective. Curiously, both driver and guard were due for retirement within the week.

A report in the press a week later said that no public inquiry will be held – and even the results of the private investigation by British Rail may not be published. The reason behind the runaway train is destined to remain a mystery. London *Evening News* 29 March; *Daily Mirror + Daily Express* 30 March; *Daily Mail* 30 March & 5 April.

JINXED LOCO

Loco D326 was built by English Electric in 1960, one of the first main line diesels to replace express steam traction. On a freezing and foggy evening two years later, she was hauling the London-bound Mid-Day Scot which crashed into the rear of a stationary Liverpool-Birmingham train north of Crewe, killing 18 people and injuring 33.

The loco was repaired and put back to work on the west coast main line. Within months her picture was flashed across the front pages again: she was waylaid by the Great Train Robbers in August 1963. Her driver received severe head injuries as the gang stole what was then a record £2.6 million from the Post Office train she was hauling through Bucks. towards London.

In 1964 a railman on the roof was electrocuted by overhead wires; and in 1965 her brakes failed outside Birmingham, and she sped out of control towards New Street station at over 40 m.p.h. An alert signalman diverted the 100-ton engine onto a goods line, where it hit a freight train and injured the guard. Later, BR issued computerized numbers to its rolling stock, and in her new identity No. 40126 behaved immaculately. In 1984 she was based in Carlisle, and was spending her last days on freight and general duties. *Daily Telegraph* 3 January 1984.

The River Boy

A strange story, this. Was the boy really human, or was he something else?

The village of Baragdava stands on the small river Kuano in the Basti district of Uttar Pradesh. One afternoon in February 1973 the local priest caught sight of a naked boy who seemed to walk on the water. At one point he dived in, caught a large fish and ate it. Then he lay in the water and was carried downstream. The priest told the villagers of his sighting, and when he described the lad and estimated that he was about 15, an old woman called Somni said he was her son Ramchandra who had been carried away by the river when he was a year old.

Another villager saw him a few days later, and for a while there was considerable local interest, and people flocked to the river. But he was not to be found.

Then in May 1979 Somni spotted him lying in a field. She crept up on him and recognized a birth mark on his back. He awoke and fled. A strict watch was mounted, he was caught and taken to the village. He was virtually hairless and his ebony-black skin had a greenish tinge. He managed to escape, but his experience of human society made him less reclusive, and he would come and eat bowls of spinach in water put out by the villagers.

Hundreds of people have seen him walk, run or recline on the surface of the water, and stay below the surface for longer than ordinary humans. His insteps and toes are as hard as rock. His favourite foods are raw meat, fish, frogs, marine creatures and leafy vegetables, gourds and red chillies.

In summer months, when the river dries, he is ill at ease; but when the river rises, he is gleeful. The main puzzle is how he protects himself against the many crocodiles ... and his alleged ability to walk on water.

Somni had a strange tale of how Ramchandra was conceived. On a stormy evening she was returning from mending a fence around the family field, as her husband was laid low with fever. She was 40 years old, a mother of three. Her way was blocked by an enormous being who seemed more like a spirit than a man. He threw her to the ground and raped her in the pouring rain. As suddenly as he appeared he vanished.

It is believed locally that a long time ago a holy man dug a well in the area. He climbed down to invoke the goddess of water, but was drowned as the well quickly filled. Some of the villagers believe that it was the spirit of this man which possessed Somni and then took the child into his watery care.

In the summer of 1980, I read the shortened account of *Probe India*'s story of the 'Kuano Amphibian Boy'. I was at once aware of the connection with Sir Alister Hardy's theories of man's evolutionary ascent from water, rather than 'descent from the trees' (see Elaine Morgan: *The Descent of Woman* 1974 and *The Aquatic Ape* 1982). I assumed, quite mistakenly, that experts would be competing to investigate this extraordinary record of a small baby who had learnt to survive, and by all accounts to dwell for long periods, in an element normally regarded as inhospitable if not dangerous.

When I went to India in 1985, I wrote to *Probe* in Allahabad to find out what had happened since 1979. To my surprise they knew nothing more and had lost contact with the journalist Nazir Malik who had sent them the article. They did, however, express interest, and encouraged by this and equipped with a large-scale local map I began investigations in Gorakhpur, Uttar Pradesh, 50 miles from the Nepalese border.

I was disappointed to discover that the water-boy Ramchandra died in 1982 in tragic circumstances. The final part of my journey, to Ramchandra's home village of Baragdava on the Kuano river in the Basti district, was made by jeep, together with the editor of the *Kalilabad Times* and his special correspondent. My questions to dignatories, officials and villagers all along my route left me in no doubt that water-boy existed as described – virtually hairless, an ebony-black skin with a distinct greenish tinge, a clumsy loping gait, unable to speak (or hear, according to some), with little or nothing of humanity in his expression, and no marked tendency to gesture – though the strange habit of holding one hand to his forehead even while walking was often observed.

The early reports speak of his ability to walk on water, and I think I can see why. At Ghanghata Bazar, in the vicinity of Ramchandra's haunts, a dam straddles the river to hold back the swift currents of the Kuano in flood. I observed that from a position on the relatively modern, arched concrete bridge where he was sometimes seen swimming, the curve of the river and head of the dam created the illusion of a straight line of water some quarter of a mile downstream. The 'miracle' was quite likely compounded by uncritical observers seeing the lad walk the top of the dam at this point.

Eventually we arrived at the home of Somni, Ramchandra's mother: at least, no-one disputes the relationship, and indeed the father and brother have the same bullet-shaped head so noticeable in the photographs of the boy, but otherwise displayed normality in all respects.

The story of water-boy's death was told me by the head-man of the small village, with the help of my interpreter. The head-man was alert and intelligent, somewhat taller than the other villagers. It

seems that two policemen arrived at the village and with the head-man's help caught Ramchandra and dragged him to Morudehadea, the town that stands by the aforementioned bridge. Waiting there were 'some people from outside with a car', but at this point the boy struggled free, ran for the bridge and jumped into the fast-flowing Kuano. He made off in the direction of Sanrigar, some 12 miles away and standing some 300 yards from the river. Night had fallen. Ramchandra left the river and walked up a road to one of the tea shops. What precisely provoked the attack is unclear – sheer fright at water-boy's appearance would be enough – but a woman there threw boiling water over the mysterious visitor. Dazed and in pain, he ran back to the river, never to emerge again. His body, badly blistered and mutilated by fish bites, was found later in the water by townsfolk from Sanrigar.

The police considered bringing charges against the woman, but these were later dropped.

The question remains, why did the two policemen turn up in the first place? After three or four years of allowing the boy to come and go freely, the arrival of the 'law' must have been by invitation, and implies that the village as a whole had decided that the situation was unacceptable. I certainly discount the stories of rape, told to me in Kalilabad; but it is highly likely that, at his age of about 24, Ramchandra felt strange, incomprehensible urges that drew him to the village women and – like Victor of Averyon – he made clumsy attempts at embrace. The effect needs little imagination. Extract from letter by Hubert Adamson, Hampstead, London.

'The Fish-boy', from a 17th-century bill.

Religious Curiosities

Religion can be a funny thing. Sometimes very funny indeed . . .

WIN FOR NUDE WORSHIPPERS

The annual procession of about 200 nude men and women to the temple of the goddess Renuka Devi on the banks of the river Varda in Bangalore, India, was disrupted by a social reform group and fist fights started. Police tried to restore peace, but were attacked and stripped by the devotees, according to Reuters, who said the police were still looking for their uniforms the next day. A different slant is given by a Madras newspaper, *The Hindu*, quoted by Associated Press: 'The handful of police, finding themselves clearly outnumbered and utterly helpless, joined the demonstrators and appealed for the continuance of nude worship.' Duluth *News-Tribune* + *Herald* + *Emirates News* (Abu Dhabi) + *Daily Telegraph* + *Sun* 22 March 1986.

WILL THE REAL JESUS PLEASE STAND UP?

A newly translated Gnostic gospel, entitled *The Secret Book of Judas of Kerioth*, promises to blow more fuses than *Holy Blood, Holy Grail* and *The Last Temptation of Christ* put together. According to this seemingly authentic early Cainite-Ophite text, translated from the Coptic by Mohammed al-Murtada and Francis Bendik, Jesus had an active bisexual love life, including relations with John, Lazarus and Mary Magdelene, served an LSD-like psychedelic at the Last Supper, faked his own crucifixion in collaboration with Judas and Joseph of Arimathea [as in the Koranic account] and died a natural death in India many years after the alleged Resurrection. Worse: the Old Testament god, as described by Jesus, appears as an evil demiurge who perverted the creation begun by the true Creator. This very interesting text was found in 1986 near the Nag Hammadi library, and has an introduction and annotations by Dr Maxwell Selander of Briggs-Melton Theological Seminary.

STRANGE CULTS

● A weird new cult has come to light in New Mexico. According to shocked police, called in by social workers, the chief ritual involved spraying paint onto babies and young children. Members got high by sniffing the paint as the kids were passed around. I wouldn't be surprised to read, tomorrow, about a sock-eating society in Surinam! Anyway, the police rescued two children, aged eight months and 13 months. *Sun* 11 February 1983.

● How about a cult which has shunned food? That's right – there is one in California, called the Breatharian Institute. You'd be right about it not having many members too, but for a different reason. It seems that most of the leadership resigned following an outrage by Wiley Brooks, the 47-year-old leader who claims not to have eaten in 19 years, and who teaches them how to live on fresh air. He was caught sneaking into a hotel and ordering a chicken pie. *Daily Mirror* 7 March 1983.

BVM SHC!

A shrine with a madonna was set up in the home of Eddie Matthijs, 33, in Haalert, Belgium. The madonna spontaneously combusted, according to the *Daily Express* 3 February 1986, and the following morning Matthijs woke to find all his pain gone.

When his wife Elizabeth and son David examined the scorched wall they say they saw images of Christ crowned with thorns, a dove and two devils. The left foot of the statue had escaped the flames.

Pictured above is Eliana Barbosa during her three-day self-crucifixion.

BRAZILIAN GIRL CRUCIFIES HERSELF

Eliana Maciel Barbosa, a 16-year-old Roman Catholic girl living in Rosario Do Sui, Brazil, for six months had been tormented with nightmares and 'evil visions'. Medical tests proved negative so she concluded that her soul had been possessed by demons and evil forces. Finally, she had a dream in which a kindly old man 'who looked like God' appeared to her, and told her how to drive out the demons. Yes, you guessed it: he told her to crucify herself. So on Friday, 9 February 1978, she dragged a 44-lb wooden cross, 9½ feet tall, up the 450-foot-high Picucho Hill, in an arid, unpopulated part of the state of Rio Grande do Sul, was duly strapped to it, and hung there until the following Monday night. This self-torture was carried out with the full knowledge and assistance of her family. Indeed, her father was arrested afterwards for slashing her wrists and feet with a razor; and that was after the police had refused him permission to actually nail her to the cross.

The whole thing was like a circus, it seems: 20 chartered buses ran in 5000 people, many of them maimed and crippled, dabbing themselves in the girl's blood and praying for a miracle; to the accompaniment of crying beer and hot-dog vendors, preying on the faithful. Whether Eliana was actually cured, we know not ... but by the time she descended from the cross, she was being proclaimed a saint throughout Brazil.

Clonehenge

The New World's answer to Stonehenge – easier to erect and dismantle, and much funnier.

MONUMENT TO OUR TIMES

Clonehenge was assembled in June 1987 by James Reinders, 61, a retired engineering consultant now living in Houston. It stands on farm property left him by his father, just off Highway 385, about two miles outside the town of Alliance in Nebraska (population 9900). The circle of gas-guzzlers, painted battleship grey and planted trunk (or boot)-first into the prairie, have brought fame and controversy to Alliance.

There are 22 cars, from the 1960s and 1970s, all but two of them American, six of them perched to form arches, arranged in the same positions as the megaliths on Salisbury Plain. Reinders visited Stonehenge in the late 1970s, and spent $16,000 of his own money in building his own version to realize a fantasy and bring 30 of his far-flung family together for a two-week reunion under the guise of helping him.

With the advice of Christopher Chippendale, assistant curator of the University Museum of Archaeology and Anthropology in Cambridge, the cars were correctly positioned for the latitude with respect to sunrise at the Summer Solstice. Reinders used cars because no large stones were available in western Nebraska. His only other influence was 'Cadillac Ranch', near Amarillo, Texas, where there are 12 Cadillacs, tail fins up, at the same angle as the Egyptian pyramids.

Lawrence Mannlein, an art consultant to the Nebraska Department of Education, calls Carhenge an example of 'monumental conceptualism', but Reinders said 'I don't think it's art, I don't even think it's an art form. I make no claim to be an artist. It makes a circle; no more . . . My mother was a fine artist, but all I can draw is flies.' He was asked whether he thought of his work as a serious salute to Stonehenge or an elaborate spoof. 'I'm afraid I'm unclear myself,' he said. 'Spoof is closer, but that's not accurate either.'

'What Carhenge needs is a companion piece,' said Reinders. In keeping with the automotive theme, he said he would like someone to erect what he calls 'a leaning tyre of Pisa', a high, off-centre tower of old tractor tyres. At its centre would be a spiral staircase leading to a vantage point at the top for enjoying the scenic wonders of the panhandle prairie, its sandhills, downtown Alliance and Carhenge.

Many locals regard Carhenge as an eyesore; many others are pleased that it has brought extra trade to the town. It is estimated

that between 5000 and 6000 people a month visit during the summer months. A traffic counter was installed on 2 September 1990. In a two-week period, 891 cars entered the parking area. Out-of-state visitors are often enthusiastic. One from Omaha said in a note found in the comment box on site: 'Carhenge is beautiful, the perfect artistic statement for the last years of this century.'

Others are not so appreciative: windows have been broken and shots fired at the cars. The word 'Crips', a Los Angeles street gang, was sprayed on one car. Reinders expects this. It is all part of the perishability of the work, he said. 'One hundred years from now, all that may be left are little shards of aluminium and plastic.'

Reinders 'says he will return and complete the inner circle of trilithons. He has a 1962 Cadillac (it is really big) and Friends of Carhenge will soon place it as the Slaughter Stone. At some future date he may place a Heel Stone and the Four Corner Stones using old cars.' Chicago *Tribune* 6 February; *Times-Herald* August; Omaha *World-Herald* 13 October, 4 November, 29 November, 14 December 1989; *Washington Post* 17 January; Lincoln *Journal* 27 January 1990.

Foafs

'Friend-of-a-friend stories', or 'urban legends', are ones that keep cropping up in slightly different forms and have that curious quality of improbability.

SPIDER PLANTS

Mrs Suzanne Zingler of Cologne bought a potted palm for the living room. During the first week the plant made squeaking and hissing noises when she watered it. She thought it was simply the air escaping from the dried earth in the pot. Six days later, when she watered it again, it not only squeaked but the earth around the roots began to heave. She called the florist where she had bought the palm and demanded that he come and take it back. The florist arrived, took one look and called the police, who called the local zoo. Experts arrived and took the tree away. At the zoo, staff removed a large female tarantula spider, and her nest of 50 young, from among the roots. They said the spider must have been in the pot when the plant was imported from southern Europe. *Sunday Express* 24 March 1985.

A similar story went around about a spider-infested yucca plant from Marks and Spencer's, which was taken to Kew Gardens. In the plant department of Marks and Spencer's in Oxford Circus, the manager Tony Kelly said: 'It's getting beyond a joke. Now we've got an official complaint from the Irish Ministry of Agriculture because someone in Dublin claims one of our people offered a woman £100 to keep it quiet!' Marks and Spencer's stores around the country have been bombarded with complaints and demands for action, says the *Guardian* 19 April 1985. M&S head office claim that the story is 'virtually impossible' since the yuccas are imported from Africa via Holland where they are replanted and potted.

Jim Kessing, the plant inspector in Kew Gardens, said: 'One of our gardeners said it had happened to a friend of his son's. He asked me if it was possible. I told him it was – but a bit unlikely.' Our correspondent Brian Hain heard the story from different informants in the Bristol area.

HEAVING QUILT

● A lady in Winterswijk, Holland, bought a down quilt and at once put it on the bed. A few hours later she found it on the floor. This was repeated several times. She took it back to the shop, where it was found that an immense quantity of maggots was feeding on skin adhering to the down feathers. *Provinciale Zeeuwse Courant* 9 January 1986.

PET HORROR

● John and Valerie Collins, American tourists in Mexico, picked up a stray chihuahua they named Pepsi and took it back to their Acapulco hotel room. Next morning, Pepsi was foaming at the mouth, so they took him to a vet, who told them Pepsi was actually a gutter rat suffering from rabies. *Sunday Express* 2 March 1986.

ROSY'S LAST RIDE

Rosy Sutton went through life with a laugh and a smile, said her friends when she died, aged 72. But the biggest laugh of all, and the one everyone in her home town of Doncaster, Yorkshire, will remember, is her funeral. For as the procession of cars made its way to the municipal crematorium, the streets were lined with thousands of people cheering and waving flags, saluting police and flashing cameras. The crowds mistook the cortege of Rolls-Royces for the cars of Prince Charles and Princess Diana, who were visiting the city that day. Son Richard said: 'Mum always liked a laugh and she had a right royal funeral. People keep saying what a good send-off she had.' Who says there isn't any good news anymore? *Sun* 26 March 1984.

IN THE ROAD

● Ambulance men sped through the night, down the main road from Sutherland to Golspie, in Scotland. They had been called out by a motorist who saw two bodies and a fallen motorbike on the side of the road. He was on urgent business, he said, and couldn't stop to help them, so he decided to get help from the nearest town. When the ambulance men investigated the scene of the supposed accident they could hardly believe their eyes. The partially clad motorcyclist (still wearing his helmet!) and (presumably) his girlfriend were in the middle of making passionate love. Before quickly resuming their journey, the man explained to his unexpected – and somewhat embarrassed – audience that they were overtaken by irresitible urges and simply stopped the bike and let impulse have its way. *Sun* 22 March 1984.

● The only comparable item is a tantalizingly brief note in the *Daily Mirror* 8 November 1983: following a complaint from a startled motorist, who stumbled upon the scene while crossing Dartmoor, police were trying to trace a nude couple making love in the road urged on by a group of men and women, near Hexworthy, Devon.

NASTY SURPRISES

● Distraught relatives were about to attend a funeral in Valencia when the hearse containing the body was driven off at speed. The driver, a young drug addict, was arrested at a road block. *Daily Telegraph* 30 January 1985.

● Robert McQuade, 30, of Salisbury, South Australia, put his five-month-old stepson in a microwave oven and turned it on. The child had to have three toes amputated, then McQuade was charged with assault. *Standard* 30 January, *Sun* 31 January 1985.

● A group of elderly people were holding a séance in a darkened town hall meeting room in Wadebridge, north Cornwall, when they heard moans and groans – but they were not coming from beyond the grave. Two teenagers were making love in a corridor outside, watched by a group of cheering friends. They fled on discovery. *Sun* + *Daily Mirror* 15 February 1985.

THE BODY IN THE BACK

● A thief who stole an estate car from outside a Social Security office in Warrington, Lancashire, abandoned it just half a mile away, when he discovered to his surprise, shock and horror a body in a coffin in the back. The car was being used by a local undertaker. *Daily Telegraph* 30 September 1983.

Hoaxes

Not really incredible or mysterious, but certainly enjoyable . . .

MESSAGE FROM OUTER SPACE

Several thousands of television watchers in southern England were startled at 5:06 pm, just as the news was being read on Saturday evening, 26 November 1977, when a deep voice, accompanied by an eerie booming sound likened to a 'hollow drumming', drowned out the newscaster's voice and delivered a short message: 'This is the voice of Asteron. I am an authorized representative of the Intergalactic Mission, and I have a message for the planet Earth. We are beginning to enter the period of Aquarius and there are many corrections which have to be made by Earth people. All your weapons of evil must be destroyed. You only have short time to learn to live together in peace. You must live in peace . . . or leave the galaxy.'

Somehow the originators of the message had jammed the sound-signals from Southern television's transmitter at Hannington, Wiltshire, so viewers from Newbury and Reading to Winchester and Andover heard the weird voice superimposed over the ITN news bulletin. It caused sufficient panic for Southern television to put out half-hourly announcements insisting that it had been a hoax and

that the planet was not being invaded.

Predictably the IBA and Post Office took a rigid humourless stand vowing prosecution of the culprits. Whoever did the deed knew their stuff, for the 'android' (as one PO representative persited in calling the mystery voice) needed sophisticated equipment or techniques to break into and dominate a television transmission. One perceptive letter in *The Times* pointed out that if this was the first time this had ever happened in Britain, as the IBA claimed, then how could they be sure it was a hoax. Indeed! Inexplicably, the *News of the World* and *Daily Mail* called the owner of the voice 'Gillon, of the Ashdown Galactic Command' and reported that he said: 'Unless the weapons of Earth are laid down, destruction from outer space invasion will quickly follow.' The *Sunday Times* claimed to have tracked down a student group who invented a new kind of transmitter (for £80) which can 'hitch a ride' on conventional transmissions . . . but again how can they be sure that this claim isn't also a bandwaggon hoax? The facts behind the unorthodox broadcast are still to be revealed.

YOU CAN FOOL SOME OF THE PEOPLE . . .

A lecture on 'Mathematical Game Theory as Applied to Physical Education' was given by 'Dr Myron L. Fox', said to be an authority on the application of maths to human behaviour. His lecture was pure nonsense – meaningless double-talk – but it fooled the 55 educators, school administrators, psychiatrists, psychologists and social workers listening. After the lecture and a 30-minute question period, the listeners were asked to fill out anonymous questionnaires to evaluate the performance. Forty-two agreed that 1) 'Dr Fox' used enough example to clarify the material; 2) the material was well organized; and 3) the lecture stimulated their thinking. 14 registered a minor criticism – that 'Dr Fox' dwelled upon the obvious; and some expressed interest in learning more about the subject.

Not one guessed it was a hoax, and that 'Dr Fox' was an actor hired by three medical educators to prove a point, though one did say the lecture was 'too intellectual a presentation'. The hypothesis of Dr D. H. Naftulin, F. A. Donnelly (both of University of Southern California Medical

School) and John E. Ware Jr (of Southern Illinois University School of Medicine) was that: 'Given a sufficiently impressive lecture paradigm, an experienced group of educators participating in a new learning situation can feel satisfied that they have learned, despite irrelevant, conflicting and meaningless content conveyed by the lecturer.' Their purpose, say the two protagonists, was to demonstrate the importance of the personality factor in teaching. Houston (Texas) *Chronicle* 8 May 1974.

TEXAS WORM TURNS

For about an hour in the afternoon of Friday 13 July 1984, a 20-foot-long, 2-foot-high bulge stretched the surface of a street in Forth Worth, Texas. The bulge 'looked like a giant earthworm that was trying to come up from under the road. It stayed up for a while, and it swayed back and forth. It seemed almost alive', said Charlie McCafferty from the fire department. 'What spooked me was there wasn't even a crack in the road.'

Street crews used jackhammers to break through the street's two inches of asphalt and four inches of concrete. They found silt layers intact, and no evidence of a gas build-up that might have caused the bulge. Firemen who arrived after the bulge had gone thought their colleagues were either drunk or crazy. Schenectady, NY, *Gazette*, 16 July 1984.

Shortly after the above event, a strange disturbance in the ground was spotted on a homestead on the outskirts of Fort Worth. Called to the spot by his three children, Calvin Lang prodded the bulge with a rake, and the spreading mound disappeared. Looking round he noticed buildings had been mysteriously ripped apart, fences torn down and shrubs and trees uprooted. *National Examiner* 12 February 1985.

Later, Jeremy Boiter reported spotting what appeared to be a giant tentacle erupting from the ground about two miles away. 'Suddenly the terrible thing sprang from the ground in a shower of gravel and dirt,' he reported. 'Then it seized a cat and her litter of kittens and devoured them in seconds. I wanted to be sick, to run away. Two snapping and growling dogs then approached the monster. And – and I couldn't believe my eyes – it engulfed the dogs in its slick and dripping mouth and swallowed them whole.' Boiter screamed and ran three miles to the home of his friend Phil Dewar. When they returned to the site, they found scraps of birds, rabbits and other wild animals among the rubble of a destroyed hut.

An advertisement for Parker pens shows someone writing a scientific-looking formula. 'We get letter from scientists and chemists who say they can't figure out the formula. Or that it is meaningless,' said Gary Moss of the J. Walter Thompson ad agency who thought the idea up. In fact it's simple when you know it's for a martini: three and a half shots of gin, plus half a shot of vermouth over four parts of water (taken down to freezing and cubed), then plus three revolutions (stirs) and ... voilá. The ad ran in Newsweek and Time. 'We did get one critical letter ... someone asked, "Who ever heard of a martini without an olive?"' (Wisconsin) Journal 27 May 1974.

If you have enjoyed this book, you will want to subscribe to

Fortean Times

THE JOURNAL OF STRANGE PHENOMENA

'The only magazine in the whole world that I enjoy so
much I read every page' (Robert Anton Wilson)
'A sort of vitamin pill for the incurably sane' *Midweek*
'My favourite magazine in the world, material or
otherwise' (Alan Moore)
'Essential reading' *Blitz*
'Invaluable and invariably ahead of the game'
(Heathcote Williams)
'Britain's most astounding magazine' *Time Out*

Ask for information and subscription details from
Fortean Times, Specialist Knowledge Services, 20
Paul Street, Frome, Somerset BA11 1DX, U.K.
Telephone (0373) 51777

ACKNOWLEDGEMENTS

Eddison Sadd Editions would like to thank the following copyright holders for permission to reproduce pictures on the pages indicated. In some cases it has proved impossible to identify or to trace the copyright owners; Eddison Sadd Editions apologizes to anyone whose copyright may have been infringed as a result.

Richard Adams 47; Amateur Photographer 10; Associated Press 35, 77, 87, 127, 135; David Barritt 58; Bedfordshire Times 67; The Bettmann Archive 6; Brisbane Sun 157; Arun Chacko 151; China Pictorial 85, 161 (×2); The Citizen (Gloucester) 91; Daily Express 111; Empics 63; European Southern Observatory 14; Evening Leader (George Green) 23; Fleet News 69; Florida Times-Union 71; Fortean Picture Library 42, 57 (×2), 61, 93, 110, 117, 123, 141, 165, 171, 183; Friends of Carhenge (Paul E. Phaneuf) 187; Glasgow Herald 178; Guinness Publishing Limited 138; Harrow Observer 68; Martin Hart 174, 175; Inland Publishing Company (Canada) 176; Kentish Gazette 115; Neil Lancashire 149; Lancashire and Cheshire County Newspapers 74; Burr Lewis 49; R. T. Mather 79; MCA 43; Alain Morvan 27; NASA 15; National Enquirer 29; Peter Orme 137; Elaine Partington 191; Phoenix Zoo (Dick George) 129; P. T. Plunkett 167; Portsmouth Publishing 39, 59, 163; Clive Postlethwaite 131; Rex Features 55, 99 (×2); Scotsman Publications 41; Scunthorpe Evening Telegraph 116; Syndication International 102, 147; Taiyo Fisheries 45; Daily Telegraph plc 169; US Bureau of Reclamation (Greg W. Behrens) 113; Henry Willes 155.

Editor   Adam Sisman
Designer   Sarah Howerd
Proofreaders   Michele Doyle
                and Victoria Davenport
Production   Hazel Kirkman
                and Charles James